THE FACULTY GUIDE TO A BALANCED AND HARMONIOUS CAREER

This book provides a yogic framework for college educators to take inventory of areas of imbalance in their professional life and work toward more sustainable and meaningful career alignment.

Drawing from chakra theory at the heart of yoga philosophy, DiPietro takes readers through the seven major chakras, explaining their functions and common patterns of imbalance—with particular attention to patterns reinforced by academia—and offers 130+ tools and strategies for realignment. Readers will learn how to ground themselves in nurturing habits, set and stand by professional boundaries, speak their truth even in charged situations, and build a legacy they can be proud of.

Written to be a helpful, trusted guidebook, this text features prompts for reflection, call-out boxes for each chakra, and downloadable worksheets to synthesize thoughts and ideas into an action plan.

Michele DiPietro is Executive Director for Faculty Development, Recognition, and the Center for Excellence in Teaching and Learning, and Professor in the School of Data Science and Analytics at Kennesaw State University, USA.

"*The Faculty Guide to a Balanced and Harmonious Career* weaves together faculty narratives about joy, difficulty, perspective, and community with mindfulness lessons from yoga philosophy and practice. Facilitating alignment of the body, mind, and spirit, this book offers anchors for transformative discussions in faculty learning communities about burnout and renewal."

Katie Kearns, *Professional Development Hub (pd\hub), University of Massachusetts Chan Medical School, USA*

"*The Faculty Guide to a Balanced and Harmonious Career* is the book you didn't know you needed. In the noisy world of work–life balance research, Dr. DiPietro provides a challenging and refreshing perspective on how to attain and sustain a balanced and harmonious career. He deftly balances conventional evidence-based principles with the chakra system, inviting readers to consider the relationship between the body and the mind and, more importantly – and systematically – how a system of seven energy centers provides a pathway to professional fulfillment. This Guide is firmly rooted in the reality of faculty life and the myriad of identities, goals, and tensions associated with it. Dr. DiPietro weaves an elegant tapestry of experiences – their own and others' – to demonstrate the vulnerability and power of agency. Critical practices like engaging in creative recovery, cultivating trustworthiness, stating one's path, amplifying other voices, and challenging injustices are brought to life differently, here. This is not a 'how to' book, but a 'how to become' companion. It is that rare treatise that invites, encourages, and empowers faculty and faculty developers to know themselves and thrive in the ever-changing landscape of higher education."

Brian Smentkowski, *Vice President and Chief Academic Officer, University of Alaska, USA*

"*The Faculty Guide to a Balanced and Harmonious Career* brings a much-needed formula for wholeness to the world of academia. With DiPietro's keen eye and open heart, engrossing stories are carefully combined with erudite scholarship on the chakra system, to highlight the inner world of those who work in academia and provide the backbone of learning for our society. The insights in these pages will unite a world that is fueled by passion but plagued with discontent. Not only does the book highlight the areas of difficulties that are so common in university life, it gives you concrete tools to survive and transcend those problems, opening the way to changing them for the better. I hope everyone in and out of academia takes time to read this important work."

Anodea Judith, *Author of* Eastern Body-Western Mind, Wheels of Life, Chakra Yoga

THE FACULTY GUIDE TO A BALANCED AND HARMONIOUS CAREER

Yogic Strategies for Self-Growth and Fulfillment

Michele DiPietro

Designed cover image: Getty Images

First published 2026
by Routledge
605 Third Avenue, New York, NY 10158

and by Routledge
4 Park Square, Milton Park, Abingdon, Oxon, OX14 4RN

Routledge is an imprint of the Taylor & Francis Group, an informa business

© 2026 Michele DiPietro

The right of Michele DiPietro to be identified as author of this work has been asserted in accordance with sections 77 and 78 of the Copyright, Designs and Patents Act 1988.

All rights reserved. The purchase of this copyright material confers the right on the purchasing institution to photocopy or download pages which bear a copyright line at the bottom of the page. No other parts of this book may be reprinted or reproduced or utilised in any form or by any electronic, mechanical, or other means, now known or hereafter invented, including photocopying and recording, or in any information storage or retrieval system, without permission in writing from the publishers.

Trademark notice: Product or corporate names may be trademarks or registered trademarks, and are used only for identification and explanation without intent to infringe.

ISBN: 978-1-032-78322-2 (hbk)
ISBN: 978-1-032-75782-7 (pbk)
ISBN: 978-1-003-48737-1 (ebk)

DOI: 10.4324/9781003487371

Access the Support Material: http://www.routledge.com/9781032757827

Typeset in Times New Roman
by Newgen Publishing UK

CONTENTS

Foreword		*viii*
Preface		*xiii*
Acknowledgments		*xx*
	Introduction	1
1	How do we lay a strong foundation? The ground chakra	12
2	How do we nurture our passions? The desire chakra	47
3	How do we grow our agency? The power chakra	74
4	What is the role of love in the academy? The heart chakra	103
5	How do we cultivate our voice? The throat chakra	129
6	How do we build a fulfilling vision? The third-eye chakra	154
7	What kind of consciousness will best guide us? The crown chakra	182
	Conclusion	211
Index		*217*

FOREWORD

We wonder, with heaviness in our hearts, how many faculty may read the title of Michele DiPietro's fantastic book, *The Faculty Guide to a Balanced and Harmonious Career,* and smirk with disbelief, thinking to themselves, Oh, if only it were possible; this is far too lofty an ambition! Yet like Dr. DiPietro, we have dedicated our careers to supporting faculty, and this has long been our sincere wish for each of them, for each of you: that your careers be balanced and harmonious, even joyful. And while there are no simple solutions, we hope you'll agree that the aspiration is worthwhile and that, like us, you find promise in each tool added to your professional toolkit. At the broadest level, this is what Dr. DiPietro's book represents to us, a set of invaluable tools for a thriving career, along with a blueprint outlining a holistic vision of faculty work – and how to use those tools to build a sustainable, rewarding professional life. This book couldn't have come at a better time.

This is an unusual moment in higher education. Academics in nearly every role and at all kinds of institutions are challenged with questions that many of us have long had the privilege of ignoring – questions about the value of higher education and the work we do each day, questions about safety in speaking our minds and hearts, questions about our job security amidst college closures and enrollment challenges. Certainly, many faculty find themselves at a crossroad. As Dr. DiPietro describes, this is at least in part because the residual effects of the pandemic have not been dealt with, reminding us that an unprecedented number of faculty have left/are leaving higher education.

All the while, a college education continues to be a transformative experience, one that forms students along varied dimensions from social mobility to intellectual and moral development to civic engagement and well-being. So it should go without saying (although far too few leaders seem to be saying this right now!) that our students and institutions *need* faculty. And they need faculty who are thriving. To quote teacher and scholar Eugenia Knight, an associate professor at Simmons University, "For our students to be well, they need us to be well" (in Cavanagh, 2023). But how?

Since the pandemic, the academic press has brimmed with essays and books on faculty and staff burnout. Dr. Rebecca Pope-Ruark's (2022) *Unraveling Faculty Burnout*, perhaps the best of these, offers helpful guidance for individuals and institutions. In a nutshell, Pope-Ruark emphasizes the importance of connecting outward – "to colleagues, to students, and to the mission that you believe in" (p. 84). Yet the aim, as Pope-Ruark explains, is more than simply *not* burning out in your career. We should aspire to flourishing professionally.

In *The Faculty Guide to a Balanced and Harmonious Career*, Dr. DiPietro suggests that faculty balance and harmony can be attained through a holistic approach to well-being, one that both looks outward (as Pope-Ruark and others advise) and looks inward, beyond our teaching schedules, research agendas, and service commitments, to the core of our being.

Specifically, Dr. DiPietro introduces readers to a framework for analysis and reflection that's likely new to many of us: a contemporary form of chakras, or energy centers. Some readers may worry that the chakras system will feel dogmatic or hokey. Our colleague's wise and practical book is neither of those, in part because it draws on extensive research and on in-depth interviews with scores of faculty who work in the professional trenches day after day. Others may wonder about Dr. DiPietro's authority to present these chakras. They have impressive academic credentials including a PhD in statistics and an appointment as professor in a School of Data Science and Analytics, and their publications on learning and teaching have been cited thousands of times and translated into multiple languages, but chakras? Yes, chakras. Dr. DiPietro has studied the chakras for two decades, yet even so, as they explain, the book treats the chakras as neither religion nor magic. We appreciate how this book approaches the system with scholarly rigor and deep respect.

Each chapter skillfully guides readers through a chakra, exploring its meaning and implications for faculty work lives. We can't do justice to the complexity of each here beyond noting that the chakras correspond to our groundedness, our deepest desires, our need for balance and connection, our right to be heard, and even our legacies. This holistic approach to professional and career development is unusual – and liberating. Too often, our own focus—and the focus of programs designed to support and "develop" faculty—is narrow. We dive into a particular pedagogy or professional stepping stone. That is significant, but Dr. DiPietro invites us to raise our eyes and our aspirations to not just doing things better, but to doing better things. What if we sought to be both effective *and* fulfilled professionally?

Dr. DiPietro's expertise in teaching, educational development, and storytelling are reflected in the book's inviting style and skillful guidance, with no trace of judgment or prodding. Throughout, Dr. DiPietro creates the conditions that support our learning, giving us varied, useful, even unexpected tools—including questions and practical exercises far beyond ones we might expect (like "meditate" and "journal").

To illustrate the book's approach and impact, as Isis reflected on her experience reading Dr. DiPietro's manuscript, she found she had learned a great deal, as one might expect. But she was caught off guard by the extent to which the text prompted self-reflection. Reading it felt cathartic, often hard; yet she felt supported the whole time. She wished she had already asked herself Dr. DiPietro's questions and wondered how she proceeded through her professional life somewhat blinded to what the reflections revealed.

The book also honors the voices and lived experiences of faculty, sharing vivid examples from interviews of the struggles and the possibilities of an academic career. Indeed, Dr. DiPietro's close attention to storytelling as a way to "stretch your vision" is particularly inspiring because it prompts us both to critically reflect on our own aspirations and to connect with our colleagues through the process of telling and hearing stories. In higher education, we often work alone, which is no surprise in a profession where our success typically is measured based on individual research, teaching, and service. By centering the voices of 51 faculty who were interviewed for the book, Dr. DiPietro invites us into community with colleagues as we read, seeing our experiences reflected in theirs and sometimes witnessing things happening at our institutions from which at least some of us are sheltered. Reading this book reminds us that we have a responsibility not only to ourselves and our students but also to each other.

Indeed, just as our students need us to be well, we need each other to be well. This book will help each of us individually take important steps toward a "balanced and harmonious career," and, as we each progress toward this ideal, we will also be cultivating the more humane academy our students, colleagues, and communities—and we—deserve.

Peter Felten
Executive Director, Center for Engaged Learning, Professor of History, and Assistant Provost for Teaching and Learning, Elon University

Isis Artze-Vega
College Provost and Vice President, Academic Affairs, Valencia College

References

Cavanagh, S. R. (2023, May 2). 'They Need Us to Be Well' The surprising recipe for building students' emotional well-being in the classroom? Rest and joy—for professors. *Chronicle of Higher Education.* Accessed online at www.chronicle.com/article/they-need-us-to-be-well

Pope-Ruark, R. (2022). *Unraveling faculty burnout: Pathways to reckoning and renewal.* Johns Hopkins University Press.

PREFACE

I always wanted to be an educator. Some kids play house. I remember playing school. I was the oldest of my siblings and cousins, and I would round them up and try to teach them long division or whatever I had just learned. Indeed, learning is one of my core values. One could say I was destined to become a university professor. I emigrated from Italy to go to graduate school at Carnegie Mellon and earn my PhD in Statistics. Upon graduation, I stayed on to work at the Eberly Center for Teaching Excellence as an educational developer, with an adjunct appointment in my home department. I then moved to Atlanta to become the Executive Director of the Center for Excellence in Teaching and Learning at Kennesaw State University, earning tenure and promotion to full professor. Through all the forms my academic work has taken, I have always loved the core components of my work, and I still believe it is one of the best jobs in the world.

Indeed, the promises of the academic life are so alluring that many of us were willing to live in near poverty for five to eight years in grad school to get to the good part one day. And the good part is *really* good, as the faculty interviewed in this book attest. We have the honor of being in the classroom with the students, guiding them to knowledge and to the a-ha moments, a trajectory that feeds the soul—ours and theirs—and can also be life-changing in terms of opportunity, upward mobility, and prosperity. We have the privilege of setting our own research agenda driven by our curiosity, be it in the lab, the studio, the archives, an archeological dig, or wherever our thirst for knowledge takes us. We have the opportunity in our service and shared governance to address our institutional challenges using the collective expertise of faculty from virtually every discipline. And we have the mandate to be out in the community, applying our knowledge to solve real problems for real people, meeting the world's grand challenges head on.

But the bad can also be really bad. Internally, the requirements for tenure and promotion keep increasing, creating stress and work–life balance challenges; at the same time, salaries generally do not keep up, creating issues of salary compression and even inversion. Externally, the profession periodically falls under attack, with state legislatures accusing professors of indoctrinating their students, leading to increased surveillance and restrictions on faculty work, and the erosion of shared governance and academic freedom, particularly for faculty who research and teach identity, power, privilege, and oppression. Large swaths of the public stereotype us as moochers who only go to work two days a week and get summers off. The burnout and exhaustion left over from the pandemic have not been dealt with, resulting in psychological and spiritual harm. These and other pressures created the "Great Resignation," an unprecedented number of faculty leaving higher education. For a profession socialized to privilege academia over any other kind of employment, this trend is staggering. It is clear that faculty need support. In my work, I facilitate workshops for faculty on how to prepare themselves for annual reviews and for tenure and promotion, as well as how to apply for awards and other funded opportunities. A lot of that advice boils down to understanding policies and procedures and tailoring the narrative—and the work supporting it—to institutional priorities. That is certainly sound advice. But if the only arrow in our quiver is to teach faculty how to better jump through the institutional hoops, this strategy misses the mark when faculty feel stuck, unfulfilled, or devalued. I always tell the educators I work with that that teaching to the test is at best the start but not the endpoint, and that the students they teach are not just brains to fill with knowledge but whole people with bodies, hearts, souls, histories, aspirations, anxieties—whole lives.

The same is true of faculty, of course. This book is an attempt to recover a holistic approach to professional and career development for faculty. Unfortunately, academia was traditionally built privileging mind and reason, according to the enlightenment principles, with the belief that only impartial objectivity could lead us to the capital T Truth. As a scientist, I deeply appreciate reason. My doctorate is in statistics, so I started my career with a data-driven, evidence-based orientation, and a healthy skepticism for esoteric, touchy-feely approaches that don't include empirical verification. I retain this mindset in my faculty and organizational development work. My workshops include research-based strategies, as does this book. But I also know that I thrive when all parts of my being are attended to.

My attempts to reunite mind and body, or, better, to appreciate that they were never separate in the first place, have led me to yoga, which literally means, yoke, union, between mind and body. Yoga philosophy is the best tool I have found toward my goal of an embodied, mindful approach to career development.

I have experienced the power of yoga in my personal life first. I have been practicing yoga for over 20 years. I found it when I was going through a divorce, and it helped me find ground through the upheaval, build strength, balance, and flexibility, both physical and metaphorical. Seeing the gains from the physical practice, I was encouraged to go beyond. I read yoga philosophy, and even took Sanskrit courses for a deeper experience. I became a certified yoga teacher at the 200 hours level. I brought yoga to my professional life. For years, I ran a Faculty Learning Community on yoga, based on practicing, studying a bit of its philosophy, and applying its principles in the classroom and at work. Participants came back year after year because they appreciated the practice, the insights, and the community. One credited his very survival in academia to the yoga Faculty Learning Community. I have run professional development workshops on applying yoga philosophy to professional development, helping many faculty who felt stuck. I have published scholarly articles to disseminate this approach in my disciplinary societies (DiPietro, 2018) and presented it at various conferences and institutions, applying it to organizational development, professional development, and LGBTQ liberation, including the presidential address I delivered when I served as president of the POD Network in Higher Education, the premiere educational development society in North America.

The specific tool I employ is the chakra system, which the introduction will explain in broad strokes and the rest of the book develop in depth. For now, I will say that the chakras are a system of seven energy centers and that this philosophy maintains that we find (professional) fulfillment when all of these energies are cultivated and expressed in harmony and balance with each other, which fits well with my goal of a holistic, mindful, embodied, approach to professional development. Before delving further into the system, I need to clarify how I approach it. Even though the chakras have deities presiding over each one, I do not treat this system as religion. For instance, I do not believe that Ganesha is an actual blue god in the sky with the body of a man and the face of an elephant. Rather, I see him and other deities as metaphors for specific energies.

I also do not treat this system as magical. For instance, a fulfilling professional vision is the province of the indigo chakra, in the third eye, but it does not mean that if I burn an indigo candle and place an indigo crystal and other charged indigo objects on my altar, the vision will come to me by magic. I might still do an altar, but as a focus point, to remind myself every time I walk by the altar of the thing I am actively working toward and to redirect my energies in that direction when I lose focus. Others treat the system as science, for instance, highlighting that each chakra corresponds to an endocrine gland or that nerve ganglia come out of the spine in loose correspondence with chakra locations in the body. As a scientist, I do not find those arguments convincing, or even scientific, because this correspondence exists by design as the simple consequence of placing the chakras at major organs. In principle, we could apply the scientific method to this theory, because it generates hypotheses that are empirically testable, and we could gather evidence in favor or against the theory. For instance, can we measure excesses and deficiencies in chakras accurately? Can we prove that certain strategies work to rebalance them? Can we predict behaviors based on chakra configurations? Unfortunately, I have not seen this approach employed, and therefore the only evidence I can offer is from my own life and from the faculty I worked with and those I interviewed for this book. Joseph Campbell, of the hero's journey fame, locates the chakras in the category of Myth, universal metaphors that can help us understand our reality (2011). I treat the chakras as a language to describe the main energies in my life and their interdependence, and as a tool to help myself take inventory of which energies are not flowing well and need to be brought into balance with the others.

Even though I have wanted to write a book on the chakras for a long time, I was finally able to envision a format that made sense to me during the pandemic. Seeing so many of my friends and colleagues struggle—over COVID and related health challenges (such as long COVID), the pressures to move online, the isolation, the attendant epidemics of systemic racism, police brutality, misinformation—some collapsing from burnout, made this book urgent. If this philosophy has anything good to offer to the world, now is the time. I conceptualized this project as half inquiry, investigating whether the chakras were a workable interpretive frame for the faculty experience, and half professional development, providing research-based strategies for a fulfilling and productive career. I reached out to 61 faculty members in a variety of disciplines, institutional types, and geographic locations in the United States. I asked them for an hour of their time over video to discuss the following issues: Finding their ground/building their foundation, nurturing their professional desires, growing their power, centering the heart in academia and cultivating balance, finding their voice/speaking their truth, generating a fulfilling vision, and building their legacy. Most of those faculty responded and tried to schedule an interview within the data collection timeframe. Some interviews never happened because of scheduling difficulties, but I was able to conduct 51 complete interviews, an amazing yield. This sample was comprised of faculty on and off the tenure track, including part-time faculty, with an intentional slight overrepresentation of Black, Indigenous, and People of Color (BIPOC) and Lesbian, Gay, Bisexual, Transgender, and Queer (LGBTQ) faculty.

Priya Parker, the author of *The Art of Gathering* (2018), titled one of her chapters "Keep Your Best Self Out of My Gathering!" What she means is she wants the people at her events to be real and not to perform perfection. I also wanted to uncover the real, lived issues of faculty, and not an idealized ivory tower persona. To that end, I turned to storytelling. As a storyteller myself, I am fascinated by faculty stories, so, after the administrative preamble about consent and confidentiality, I opened the interview asking them to tell me a story that stands out when they look back over their professional life. This did the trick. The floodgates invariably opened. As Zora Neale Hurston writes in *Dust Tracks on a Road*, "There is no agony like bearing an untold story inside you" (1991). And the stories poured forth—stories about "the moment they knew," the joy that teaching or research brought them; stories about "the terrible awful," indignities suffered, bullying, racism, sexual harassment, injustices in the tenure and promotion process, and much more, which soured their whole experience; crucible stories, events that forced them to dig deep within and come through to the other side stronger. Using these stories as the jumping-off point, we then dove into the chakras. Most of the interviews lasted longer than the allotted hour, and most people stayed longer. Some who had to run off to teach asked to schedule a second appointment to keep exploring the issues. "*These* are the questions that matter," a common refrain declared, followed by "and yet nobody ever invites these conversations!" Some shared that the interview felt cathartic, just telling their story and having it listened to and cared for. Some cried. Some said that talking through some of the issues helped them see new angles and feel less stuck. At the end of the interview, a few asked me how much they owed me. This felt like therapy, they confided, and should be compensated at the same rate. To be clear, it is I who owe them a great debt for their generosity, sincerity, and vulnerability, and I hope that I do their stories justice. One faculty close to retirement said:

> Gosh, Michele, I wish I had known you at the beginning of my career because this theory frames what I believe. And having that early on would have helped connect the dots of all the pieces I was fumbling for. I believe that with all my heart.

The doubts I had about offering this "touchy-feely" metaphorical/mythological framework to evidence-based academics dissipated. The evidence was right in front of me.

Before we delve fully into the chakras, I wish to touch on cultural appropriation. I have been influenced in my thinking by the work of Layla Saad in *Me and White Supremacy* (2020). Two ideas stand out to me. The first is that when we borrow concepts from other cultures, we should be transparent about that process. Initially, my idea was to represent the chakras as close as possible to the ancient philosophical texts, which is why I started studying Sanskrit. I quickly realized that is not possible. Not only did I encounter several chakra systems, based on five, six, seven, nine, twelve, to several thousand chakras, but I also realized one needs to be steeped in a certain worldview and spirituality to receive them in the way they were originally intended. The version of the chakras that is prevalent in the West is a reinterpretation of the traditional philosophy through modern psychology. Carl Jung started that process in *The*

Psychology of Kundalini Yoga, the seminar cycle he delivered in 1932, reprinted in 1996. My understanding of this system is based on the work of Anodea Judith and her coauthors, who have developed it in a systematic way (Judith, 1987, 2004, 2006, 2015, 2018; Judith & Vega, 1993; Judith & Goodman, 2012). Some, like the late yoga teacher Michael Stone, might emphasize that it is important to reinterpret yoga, a pre-modern philosophy, to make it meaningful to the post-modern moment we live in (2011).

Purists differentiate between the classic philosophy and the modern blend by referring to the latter as "chakra" (pronounced with a sh- sound, like chandelier) and reserving the original Sanskrit "*cakra*" (चक्र, pronounced with a ch- sound, like Charlie) for the former. They do however consider the modern system a legitimate form in and of itself. This is the form that I have encountered, practiced, studied, and reaped benefits from, and this is the form I can offer with confidence. The second idea from Saad's work is that this book would not be possible without the generations of thinkers and artists and their intellectual and creative labor, which created the original philosophy. And yet, even for the modest financial returns of academic books, I am the only one who stands to profit from that effort. My ethicality compels me to reinvest some of that financial gain into the culture that created the system. For that reason, I pledge half of the post-taxes royalties from this book to the India Literacy project, to which I have already donated an advance. After researching various charities, I chose this nonprofit because its focus on literacy matters to me as an educator. As of 2024, India has a 75% literacy rate, so there is lots of work to do. On the operational side, this organization has a four-star rating on Charity Navigator and a platinum rating on Guidestar, speaking to its operational transparency.

Finally, the opinions and values expressed in this book are mine only. I do not speak on behalf of any institution.

References

Campbell, J. (2011) *The power of myth*. Anchor Books.
DiPietro, M. (2018) The chakra system as a framework for holistic educational development. *To Improve the Academy, 37(1),* 88–99.
Hurston, Z. N. (1991). *Dust tracks on a road: An autobiography*. HarperPerennial.
Judith, A. (1987) *Wheels of life: A user's guide to the chakra system*. Llewellyn Publications.
Judith, A. (2004) *Eastern body, western mind: Psychology and the chakra system as a path to the self* (rev. ed.). Clarkston Potter/Ten Speed.
Judith, A. (2006) *Chakra balancing*. Sounds True Publications.
Judith, A. (2015) *Anodea Judith's chakra yoga*. Llewellyn Publications.
Judith, A. (2018) *Charge and the energy body: The vital key to healing your life, your chakras, and your relationships*. Hay House.

Judith, A., and Goodman, L. (2012) *Creating on purpose: The spiritual technology of manifesting through the chakras*. Sounds True Publications.

Judith, A., and Vega, S. (1993) *The sevenfold journey: Reclaiming mind, body, and spirit through the chakras*. Crossing Press.

Jung, C. (1996) *The psychology of kundalini yoga: Notes of the seminar given in 1932 by C.G. Jung*. Princeton University Press.

Parker, P. (2018) *The art of gathering: How we meet and why it matters*. Riverhead Books.

Saad, L. (2020) *Me and white supremacy: How to recognize your privilege, combat racism, and change the world.* Sourcebooks.

Stone, M. (2011) *Awake in the world: Teachings from yoga and Buddhism for living an engaged life*. Shambala.

ACKNOWLEDGMENTS

This book has been years in the making and would not have happened without all the people who helped me traverse the rainbow bridge. I want the whole world to know their names! Gratitude is both located in the heart chakra and also diffused through the system, which makes the chakras a great framework even for acknowledgments—would you believe that?

I begin at the ground chakra, with gratitude to all my yoga teachers who introduced me to this philosophy and established a foundation of loving kindness and self-compassion: Anne Marie Johnsen, Nat Kendall, Becky Mingo, Danni Pomplun, Janet Stone, and Joanne Valicenti VandenHengel. I am an excitable person, with the good and the bad that comes from it, and I am thankful to my dearest ones, who ground me with their steadfast, loving presence: Cory Albertson, Jeffrey Helms, and Jerry Nash.

When I was in graduate school, I would see other graduate students working at a coffee shop, and I was always so envious. I craved to be as cool as them, but I needed the computers in the department of statistics to run all the data analyses and simulations for my thesis. I could finally make my wish come true while writing this book. So, for the desire chakra, I wish to thank Varuni Napoli in Atlanta and Philz Coffee in the Castro, San Francisco. I would camp myself in their stores and write, delighted by their pizza and cannoli and espresso and negroni and chai and kouign amann and cinnamon rolls.

I have always struggled with the power chakra. Harnessing my will to be productive and stay on schedule and avoiding procrastination does not come easy to me. Thank Ganesha for my coach Traci Stromie, who has provided constant loving accountability, and helped me find ways to clear obstacles or get back on track when I lost my way. Thank you, Anodea Judith, for developing this powerful framework, and especially for giving me the most impactful and terrifying gift of all. Anodea forced me to set a deadline for holding a copy of my book in my hand. The manuscript only started making real progress after that. And thank you, Kathy Newman, for showing me your "Hope Machine," which inspired my own "Yes I Can Machine." Finally, though we have never met, I wish to thank Andrew Flieller, known on the internet as the "kid in the orange jacket." Lady Gaga pulled them onstage at one of her concerts in 2012, and I have watched that clip every day in the doldrums of the power chakra to get motivated, repeating to myself: "If they can get onstage with Gaga, I can finish this book!" I did not list this as a strategy, but literally do whatever you need to do to activate the solar plexus!

The heart chakra is so daunting to write about. How can I thank all the people who sustained me in this process with their love and appreciation? If you offered love to me, please know I have received it and tried to return it and pay it forward. I do want to single out two groups. One is a group of colleagues who has attended my workshops on the chakras and has helped me refine their applications to the faculty context. Tyra Burton, Este Jordan, Jennifer Purcell, Mona Singh, and Linda Stewart stand out in that already amazing group. The other collective is the Faerie Writing Group. Every Tuesday night we have gathered together to write, share, and support each other, on any kind of writing—books for sure, but also blog posts, journal articles, grant applications, screenplays, and even poetry, diaries, letters, haiku, music, Dungeons and Dragons campaigns. I have looked forward to my Tuesday nights with these amazing humans: Cator, Chapter, Decibull, DJ, Eveready, Hro, Icarus, Legacy, Luis, Lyte, Nick, Raz, Theodora, Zephyr, and all the other luminous beings who have passed through that group.

I used to say I had a love/hate relationship with writing, except the hate came first. That is no longer the case, but it took many people to help me hone and amplify my voice. So, for the throat chakra, I am particularly grateful to my editor, Jim Berg; Sumitha and the production team at Newgen; my advance readers, Katie Kearns and Brian Smentkowski; my foreword writers, Peter Felten and Isis Artze-Vega; Helen Sword for her insights on writing and for having me as a guest on her WriteSPACE event "Writing the Chakras." What a lovely audience to start disseminating these ideas prior to publication! In addition, I wish to thank the Camp Camp writing group, which I have been attending since 2013. Dozens of people have floated in and out of it over the years, but I am particularly grateful to Forrest Cliff, Michael George, Shoshana Goss, Shawn Nelson Jordan, David Puterbaugh, Kim Sergent, Douglas Smith, Jay Louis VanLandingham, and Robin White. I was shaking with anxiety and fear of rejection the first time I read my words to that group, but they absolutely embraced me and encouraged me to write more. Out of the many, many insights on writing I gained from that group, one stands taller than the others. While leading a session, Elaine

Beale said: "Everybody writes. But a writer is somebody who has the audacity to believe they have something worth saying." I am a writer.

The third eye chakra conjures those who have helped me shape my vision for this project so that it could reach its audience better. I am thankful to the folks at Routledge, especially Alexandria Andrews and Kyanna Nusom, as well as the anonymous peer reviewers who combed through my proposal and offered helpful suggestions, particularly about burnout. I listened, and the book is better for it.

The crown chakra brings in the idea of purpose and transcendence. In the beginning of this project I simply felt words screaming to get out, without a clear purpose, then I had a purpose but I didn't think it was good enough, or interesting enough, or original enough, then I thought I could not do my purpose justice, or actually help anybody. It took months working with my coach Susan Hrach (you read that right, it took two coaches to birth this book!) to believe and claim and own my purpose! Thank you, Susan! And finally, this book absolutely would not exist without the faculty who agreed to be interviewed and shared their challenges and triumphs with such generosity and vulnerability. They are how I tap into something greater than myself for this project, and I am honored to have witnessed their journeys.

INTRODUCTION

Trapped in the princess problem

I worked as a journalist in a previous life, so I was already a published writer when I went back to graduate school. I wasn't necessarily looking to become a traditional academic, but I wanted a solid theoretical grounding in sociology for my writing. I got through my coursework and assembled the committee for my master's thesis. My advisor, who inspired me to be a sociologist, was of course the committee chair, and my teaching mentor was on it, in addition to the department chair who was included as an expert on the theory I was using. The chair was a classic patriarchal figure, who wielded his power in problematic ways.

When the committee gave me feedback on my draft, many of their comments were about making my writing style more academic. I see myself as a public scholar rather than a traditional academic, so I complained to a fellow graduate student that I didn't care for those comments. That must have gotten back to the department chair, because a few days later, he accosted me when we ran into each other in the hallway. He started yelling at me that I was insubordinate and disrespectful and poking his finger into my chest. I was actually scared of this physical confrontation. It marked the first time I realized I could be hurt in the academy.

Up until then, I had held sociology on a higher bar than other disciplines because of its ability to shed light on the ugly face of group behaviors—the patriarchy, homophobia, bullying, violence. We study those things but we are not actually those people. To realize that we sociologists can be just like everybody else was completely disillusioning. On top of that, I was in a complete panic, and worried I would have to leave the department because I angered the chair. My second career was about to end before it even started. I was so upset I had to take a semester off. I couldn't even be in the department.

I came back, and finished not only my master's but also my PhD. I stayed on in a visiting lecturer position. I loved teaching and connecting with the students, and I was good at it! I had even won a teaching award as a graduate student. My plan was to get a book deal based on my dissertation, then go on the market in earnest. That year, my department posted a full-time permanent lecturer position. The call was for a person in my specialty area, and multiple colleagues, including my advisor, invited me to apply saying this was perfect for me. The prospect of staying near friends and family was enticing. I loved my advisor and was excited to continue working with her and be the version of sociologist that she inspired in me, so I applied. I got an interview, and I nailed it. I both felt it and received confirmation from many who attended my job talk. The grapevine was buzzing. On the day of the department meeting to decide who got the position, I was confident and went to yoga. Afterward, I turned the phone back on to a notification from my advisor—a stark "I'm sorry."

Apparently, multiple faculty had issues hiring a former graduate student, including people I trusted, such as my teaching mentor. She said she could never view me as anything other than a graduate student. I realized she trained me in her image, and I would always be a mini-me to her. They also demeaned the fact that I was a public scholar. None of the reasons given were about my performance on the interview or the teaching demonstration. Once again, I was hurt by sociologists who branded themselves as queer and feminists but did not exhibit feminist principles in action, such as an ethics of care or a breaking down of hierarchical gatekeeping. To be rejected like that after being encouraged to apply by so many colleagues was almost unbearable, but I resolved to show them what they had missed in not hiring me.

The next year, I ended up getting a book deal with a prestigious publisher, and had multiple offers for visiting positions, including one at a prestigious private teaching institution. I had to move to an unfamiliar place, but I grew as a scholar and a teacher. My book was well received in the field, and I loved the students and the colleagues. They loved me back and extended the visiting position for several years. But visiting positions have to end at some point. Fast forward to today. I know the appointment is about to wind down, so I am on the job market, but this time around it's not going well for me. None of my interviews have been successful. I feel like I am running out of options and out of time, but I just got word that my previous institution is hiring a full-time lecturer. I feel weary of even considering the possibility because of the mixed emotions that come up. I would love to go back to my advisor, my friends, and my community, but that place seriously hurt me. The chair has retired, but other colleagues are still active. Beyond that, I am pondering what going back would mean for my development. I did not grow so much in the past years only to slide backward. It feels like a self-fulfilling prophecy, reducing myself to little more than a graduate student. Plus, do I want to open myself up to the possibility of further rejection? But really, can I afford not to? I am trapped in the princess problem.

—Conrad, queer feminist White male lecturer of sociology at a private research institution in the Northeast

What is going on in this story?

This story is a great fit for the introduction because it recapitulates issues from several other faculty interviews. Conrad is not inexperienced, entering academia already with professional accomplishments under his belt. He is passionate about a certain kind of scholarship and discovers teaching as another passion when he tries his hand at it, even winning an award and boosting his power and confidence. Unfortunately, his passions don't fit the mold the chair has for the graduate students, leading to a physical confrontation and a profoundly ungrounding experience, calling into question Conrad's own safety. The disillusionment could have rendered him cynical but he is able to recover a sense of purpose, graduate, and find his voice to write his book on his own terms. The book is well received, growing Conrad's power and ability to secure a position at a prestigious institution. He loves his job, his students, and his colleagues. And they love him back, extending the position several times. But as this chapter comes to an end, the old anxieties resurface, prompted by the unsuccessful job search. The fact that his old institution has a position open is a double-edged sword. Should he apply or pass? If he doesn't apply, what options are on the table? Will this be the end of the academic chapter of his career? If he applies, will it lead to rejection? And if he gets the job, will going back feel fulfilling or ungrounding and disempowering? For reference, the princess problem Conrad mentions is a classic problem in sequential decision theory. A princess evaluating suitors for marriage does so one at a time, and if she passes on them, they move on and she cannot change her mind and call them back. It's very easy to pass on Prince Charming while holding out for someone even better, or to stop the search too soon, and settle for a mediocre candidate. This is a hard problem. From its mathematical formulation, we know that the optimal stopping rule, when the number of options tends to infinity, leads to choosing the best one in only about 27% of the cases. For academic job searches, where the number of options is decidedly small and nowhere close to infinity, attacking this problem can be daunting.

In such situations, it is helpful to take stock of ourselves. How grounded do we feel? After several years away, have we built a strong foundation that depends less on the approval of our colleagues? Is our voice strong? Is our confidence high, or is our inner critic/impostor raging? Do we have a guiding vision and a sense of purpose that can carry us through uncertain times? And if we are running low on some of these energies, are there strategies we can use to build them back up and make them work in synergy? As mentioned in the preface, chakra theory addresses all of these energies and more, so the first step is to understand the energies relating to each chakra and their interdependence. The next section will sketch an introduction to the chakra framework, with subsequent chapters diving deep into each chakra one at a time.

What does chakra theory say?

In order to bring chakra philosophy to bear on Conrad's situation, as well as academic careers in general, we first need to build that machinery. We will do that through each chapter, but here is a brief introduction. Chakras are centers for the reception, assimilation, and expression of life force energy (Judith, 2018). Physics will give us mathematical definitions of energy, such as $E=mc^2$, but at its core, energy is the capacity of an object to exert itself and affect the world around it. Physics also considers several types of energy: Gravitational, the grounding pull the earth exerts on objects and people; kinetic, the ability to move in the world; potential, stored energy, which can be released when the right conditions arise; chemical, such as the energy stored in food that can nourish us; sound, the energy created by vibrations, which we can hear; light, energy created by electromagnetic waves, which we can see; and more. These energies correlate with the energies assigned to various chakras in this theory.

As such, the chakras are not in the physical body. Just like we have layers to the self in Western thought (for instance, body, mind, and spirit), Hindu philosophy has five layers, or *kosha* (कोश), representing the physical, energetic, mental, wisdom, and bliss body. The chakras are located in the energetic, or subtle, body. In this theory, the energetic body is composed of energy channels called *nādī* (नाडी), which carry *prana* (प्रण), the life force, through our body. The most important nadi is called the *sushumna* (सुषुम्ण), meaning "very gracious," which runs up and down the spine. The chakras (meaning wheel of vortex) are energy centers located along the nadis.

The seven major chakras are located up and down the sushumna. Two other important nadis are *Idā* (इडा), meaning comfort, and *Pingālā*, (पिंगला), meaning orange. They start in the gonads, curve around the sushumna, intersecting at the chakras, and reunite up the nostrils by the third eye. Their interweaving symbolizes the dynamic balance of masculine and feminine, active and passive, giving and receiving that should be present in a healthy individual. The image of the energy coursing through the sushumna in a straight line, with the currents of Ida and Pingala weaving around it, is iconic in Hindu culture, and crossed over into Western culture as the caduceus, the staff with two snakes intertwined around it carried by the god Hermes/Mercury.

Each of the seven chakras has a designated function and specific associations built into its interpretation. Each chakra is also associated with a right and a demon. Here, demon does not have a religious connotation. Rather, we can also think of those as tricksters. Chakra demons are the things that trip us up in our journey through the chakras. They show up because they have a lesson to teach us, and they will keep tripping us until we learn that lesson. Chakras can be open, like a blooming lotus flower, and balanced, or they can be blocked or imbalanced when energy is not flowing correctly due to *granthi* (ग्रन्थिः), or blocks. When there are blockages in one chakra, the whole system suffers. The imbalance can be excessive or deficient. Energy might not be able to flow to one area and be pushed into other areas. Or, energy might by syphoned to one area and be trapped in it, unable to escape, thus diminishing our capacity in other chakras. Some patterns are predictable. For instance, because academia is built to privilege the life of the mind, the upper chakras might be more developed, and the energy might not reach the ground. The stereotype of the absent-minded professor captures this dynamic.

Working with the chakras means locating the blocks and clearing them. In chakra mythology, the *Kundalinī* (कुण्डलिनी) serpent goddess, coiled three and a half times, sits at the base of the spine. Our task, like a snake charmer, is to awaken it and make it rise up the sushumna, piercing each chakra open, so that they are all active and express harmoniously with each other.

In this sense, the chakra system is a language, a way for us to name certain currents or energy blockages, take inventory of our life, our professional life in the specific, and invite growth and fulfillment. Let's start with a quick rundown of the seven chakras. In Table 0.1, you can see the functions, layers of identity, rights, and demons associated with each chakra. For instance, the first chakra presides over the function of grounding, and it governs our physical identity and our right to be. It is associated with the demon of fear. As we move up the spine, we encounter the chakras of movement and desire next, then power and transformation, love and balance, voice and truth, vision, and, finally, transcendence and legacy all the way up to the crown of the head.

Starting at the bottom of the spine and making our way up to the crown of the head traces the energetic current termed *moksha* (मोक्ष), or liberation. Other energy currents are present in this framework. The reverse current, from the crown to the ground, is called *bhukti* (भुक्ति), or enjoyment. This is the manifestation current, the path we need to travel to bring ideas from the crown of the head to the ground of their physical embodiment. In addition to these vertical currents, we also have horizontal ones going from each chakra to the external world and vice versa. The reception current is how each chakra gets activated and charged in response to stimuli from our environment. The expression current is how each chakra discharges its energy into the world.

Let's start at the beginning, with Chakra #1, *Mūlādhāra* (मूलाधार), the Root chakra (literally "Root of existence"). As the number implies, it is the chakra of unity and identity. It is the most solid of the chakras, and it is tied to the

TABLE 0.1 Characteristics of the seven chakras

Chakra	Function	Identity	Right	Demon
1. Base of the Spine	Grounding	Physical	To Be	Fear
2. Pelvic Bowl	Movement/Desire	Emotional	To Feel	Guilt
3. Solar Plexus	Power/Transformation	Ego	To Act	Shame
4. Heart	Love/Balance	Social	To Love	Grief
5. Throat	Voice/Truth	Creative	To Speak	Lies
6. Third Eye	Vision	Archetypal	To See	Illusions
7. Crown of the Head	Transcendence/Legacy	Universal	To Know	Attachment

earth. Life is change, but this chakra represents the stability through change, the parts of ourselves that endure. It denotes our roots stretching back, and in general the things that ground us, including our values. It is the most physical of the chakras, and it presides over our physical body, our health, as well as our physical possessions and their health. In that sense, we can think of this chakra as the subroutines running in the background of a computer, such as the antivirus—all the processes that ensure that we keep ourselves in good health, or see a doctor to restore it, as well as take care of our debts and cultivate our financial health, understand the tenure and promotion requirements and keep them in the back of our mind, and so on. Not because that is the meaning of life, but because those are the building blocks, the foundations, the root. Evolutionarily, this chakra is connected to the fight or flight response. If you imagine yourself in the woods and you hear a strange sound, immediately the instinctual physiological response is for the knees to bend a little and the hips to coil in ready to spring, either toward the threat to fight it or away to flee. In that sense it is the chakra that keeps us alive, presiding over our survival. When Conrad's chair poked his finger in Conrad's chest, it threatened Conrad's sense of safety, activating that energy. It set up a hyper vigilance that lasted long after the physical threat had passed, necessitating a semester-long leave. This chakra is associated with the right to exist, to be here, to take up the space that we need, to have our needs met. Its demon, or trickster (in the sense that it comes with a lesson to teach us, and it will keep showing up until we have learned that lesson), is fear. We are afraid when we don't feel safe and our right to be who we are is threatened. As explained above, one can be balanced, excessive, or deficient in the energy of a particular chakra. When the grounding energy is well established, one is in good physical health, feeling safe, secure, and stable. If we are not capable of grounding well, we will experience anxiety, worry, and restlessness. We will have lots of ideas that have a hard time manifesting because we cannot bring them down from the head into a physical reality. Conversely, an excessive first chakra might preoccupy itself with futile resistance to change, or workaholism.

The second chakra, *Svādhiṣṭhāna* (स्वाधिष्ठान) (meaning the dwelling place of the self, or also "to take pleasure"), is located in the pelvic bowl. As the number implies, this is the chakra of duality. In the first chakra we were focused on ourselves. In the second chakra we open our eyes and see the world, and we realize it is something separate from us. Working like magnets, we establish polarities between us and the things in the world. We are drawn to some, and we are repelled by others. Some bring us pleasure, others don't. So, this is the chakra of desire and movement. Fittingly, its element is water. Emotions are awakened in this chakra (the right to feel resides here), but academia has traditionally devalued emotions in favor of reason and objectivity. We need to contain those emotions when they would impede our work, but also express them where appropriate, and find joy, excitement, and surprise in our work. Therefore, the issue of boundaries comes up in this chakra. This is not only true of emotional boundaries but also of boundaries in time and space. The world in its multiplicity continually places demands on us (student papers to grade, emails to reply to, committees to serve on). We need to protect our time in order to meet expectations in all our performance areas. This brings us to the demon of the second chakra, guilt. Many of us feel guilty for pursuing our professional desires, for wanting to protect our time. There are lessons to learn in exploring that guilt. A balanced second chakra will exhibit emotional intelligence and passion reinforced by healthy boundaries. An excessive chakra will be at the mercy of its shifting desires and impulses, have poor professional boundaries, and be overcommitted as a result. Conversely, a deficient chakra will exhibit a lack of excitement, or boredom, as well as very rigid boundaries. Conrad is well aware of and in touch with his passion, writing as a public scholar, addressing a large audience rather than the small circle of academics in his subfield. Unfortunately, his passion is not seen as legitimate by his chair, creating conflict.

The third chakra, *Manipūra* (मणिपूर) (meaning "resplendent jewel"), is located in the solar plexus right below the navel. This is the literal place in the body where matter, through digestion, becomes transformed into energy. Therefore, the function of this chakra is transformation, and, fittingly, the element is fire. Earth sits still, and water flows downwards, but with fire we are starting to ascend toward the higher chakras. In the lower chakras, animated by our values and motivated by our desires, we have generated considerable charge, but up until now this energy is not harnessed. In the third chakra that charge becomes power, when we add the will. We set goals, and a plan of action to achieve them. We want to get promoted, so we understand what it will take to do that, and we start acting in the world in ways that are conducive to our goal. And that's why this chakra embodies the right to act. This is where we build the ego identity, the part of our psyche that mediates our unchecked desires with societal mores and makes us act in ways that are socially acceptable. The demon of this chakra is shame because it paralyzes and prevents us from acting. For instance, even though academics have advanced degrees and long strings of accomplishments, many report feeling like an impostor and waiting to be found out. A balanced third chakra will be confident and able to take risks, while being responsible and reliable. A deficient chakra will lack self-confidence and be passive, while an excessive third chakra might be competitive, controlling, or arrogant. Conrad appears pretty balanced in this chakra, feeling confident in his approach despite his chair's disapproval, and he eventually secures a book contract from a prestigious publisher, without compromising his approach. The external validation he receives when the book comes out reinforces the energies in this chakra. His success in the classroom also builds up his power, to the point that he is recognized with a teaching award.

We are now at the heart chakra, *Anāhata* (अनाहत) (meaning unstruck or unhurt). As the location implies, this is the chakra that presides over love. The element is air, the oxygen in the lungs that oxygenates the blood sent from the heart. This chakra is all about connection, not just the romantic or spousal connection, but any loving connection, with our students, our colleagues, and so on. Therefore, this chakra is related to our social identity. This is a crucial step. The previous (lower) chakras are all about the self, understanding who we are, what we value, what we decide to do, but in this chakra, we finally see ourselves in a web of interdependence. This is Chakra #4, the middle chakra of the seven, and as such it concerns balance. Not just because it happens to be in the middle, but because in order to be in relationship with others we must find our own balance, reconcile and integrate our various parts. For academics, the concept of balance carries other nuances, balance between teaching and research, balance between work and life. Those all need to be reconciled, perhaps in a dynamic balance that shifts over time. But more than that, what does it mean for educators to look for the heart, or the love in academia? The demon of the heart chakra is grief, which weighs the heart down and closes it. A balanced heart chakra will be empathetic and be able to put oneself in somebody else's shoes. We will be able to balance our needs with other people's needs, call for help when needed and lend a hand or sacrifice when the shoe is on the other foot. Predictably, a deficient heart chakra will feel disconnected and isolated. Some might wonder, how can one be excessive in the heart chakra? You can never have too much love. But chakras are energy. If there is too much energy expended without being replenished, the excessive heart chakra will act as if everybody else's needs come before their own, and will feel depleted as a result, like a martyr. Conrad doesn't speak explicitly about love, but we can see how feeling betrayed during the job interview by people he thought were in his corner makes the grief from his rejection particularly hurtful.

The fifth chakra is the throat chakra, *Vishuddha* (विशुद्ध) (meaning "especially pure"), right by the vocal cords, so it presides over the function of communication, under the element sound. This is where we find our voice and learn to express ourselves and speak our truth. Writers, storytellers, singers, all get their energy for their creativity in this chakra. And they can speak with a voice that goes beyond their individual self if they have done the work of the heart chakra. A simple look at our anatomy reveals insights about this chakra. The throat is the nexus between the head and the body. So, pure communication only happens when we speak in alignment between our thoughts in the head and our emotions in the heart and needs in the gut. Those two energy currents meet in the throat and express out into the world as words. This kind of effective communication is especially important in situations of negotiation (for a raise, or for our next Faculty Performance Agreement), or outright conflict. Speaking firmly about our needs but with empathy for other people's needs greatly helps in those situations. Obviously, the right of this chakra is the right to speak and hear truth, and its demon is lies. A balanced throat chakra will speak with a resonant and full voice while at the same time exhibiting good listening. A deficient throat chakra will show up as a fear of speaking up, or difficulty verbalizing concepts and feelings into words, while an excessive throat chakra will present as excessive talk, like gossiping, not keeping confidentiality, or inability to listen. Conrad's voice is already well developed, having worked as a journalist, but it grows even more through the process of incorporating sociological ideas in his book designed for public consumption. On the other hand, he never attempts to talk back when he is under criticism. Speaking up to people with power over us, such as our chair, is never easy, but more oomph in this area would serve Conrad well.

We are now completely in the head. The sixth chakra is *Ājñā* (आज्ञा) (meaning command, or perceive, or beyond wisdom). The third eye is located in the space between the eyebrows, making this the chakra of wisdom ruled by the element of light. What function does a third eye add beyond the two physical eyes? With our eyes we see the world as it appears, but in the third eye we can see through the world for the deeper layers. We claim the intelligence of signs, and we can follow the signifier all the way to the signified. We can read between the lines and see things for what they really are. We can also see things that haven't happened yet, either as insights or vision for a new teaching or research or leadership path. Building on the purifying work of the previous chakras, we are nurturing a new consciousness that can imagine possibilities for a more fulfilling professional life. Naturally, the right of this chakra is the right to see, and the demon is illusions, visions that instead of clarifying reality distort it. There is another layer to this chakra. The further up in the chakras we get, the more we connect to pieces of identity beyond our self. This is where we connect with our archetypal identity, where we understand our individual story as a reenactment of a universal template. A balanced third eye will have intuition, insight, creativity, and imagination in service of a fulfilling guiding vision for life. A deficient chakra will lack those things and therefore will not have the capacity to see alternatives and generate multiple solutions to problems. An excessive chakra will be prey to its spinning mind, with excessive fantasizing and difficulty concentrating, or obsessing. Conrad has a well-developed vision for himself. He wants to be a public scholar and to direct his writing toward a broad, nonacademic audience. This vision is not well received at his first institution, but it is embraced at his current one to the point that they keep extending his appointment just to keep him around. As the visiting position comes to an end, the problem of finding a new place, where his vision won't clash with the powers that be, becomes salient.

The seventh chakra, *Sahasrāra* (सहस्रार) (meaning thousand-petal lotus), is located at the crown of the head. In the traditional formulation, this is where we transcend and become one with the universe. In fact, some represent this chakra as above the crown of the head, to signify it is already beyond our own individual experience. For that reason, it is not ruled by any element, but instead it is beyond the elements. This is where, having done the liberating work in the previous chakras, we finally realize our universal identity, and we see ourselves as part of something greater. Imagine how we would treat our students and colleagues if we had this constant awareness. With this consciousness, we are able to give meaning to our life and work. We realize we are part of a universal flow, and we find fulfillment in contributing to the world. In doing so we build our legacy, the ways in which the world will be different because of us having been in it. The right of this chakra is the right to know (to know the deeper truth of things). The demon of the crown chakra is attachments—status, wealth, and other obsessions that weigh us down. The work of this chakra is to jettison our attachment (for instance, to the way it's always been) so that we can transcend. A balanced crown chakra will be fully present, connected and plugged in to the heart of things. We will be recognized for our wisdom, open-mindedness, and ability to question. A deficient chakra will exhibit apathy, and cynicism, while an excessive chakra will overintellectualize things, causing us to live in our heads. Conrad's disillusionment could have been a path to cynicism, but he kept his focus on his purpose. Now the question comes up again—can he find gainful employment without sacrificing his purpose?

This was a very brief overview of the chakra system. The seven chapters of this book will take us through each of the seven chakras. The book will use stories from a diverse group of faculty to illustrate the concepts and to offer strategies to bring areas of our professional life into balance.

How to read this book

This introductory chapter prefigures the structure of the following ones. Each chapter will open with three stories from the faculty interviews, highlighting different aspects of that chakra. The next section—"What is going on in these stories?"—will unpack the issues each chapter focuses on and set the stage for chakra theory. The following section—"What does chakra theory say?"—builds the machinery to truly delve into the topics from this mindfulness perspective. The first time each Sanskrit word is introduced to explain a concept from the theory, it will be italicized and the corresponding Devanagari script will be provided, as a way of honoring this philosophical tradition (a practice already applied in this introduction). The next section(s), "Faculty insights," will bring in additional perspectives from faculty interviews, corroborated by faculty development scholarship. The next two sections bridge chakra theory with faculty insights, specifically as they pertain to the right and the demon associated with each chakra. "Prompts for reflection" is exactly that—prompts to journal and expand our thinking about the issues related to each chakra. Then, we get to research-based strategies in the section titled "Tools, strategies, and possibilities." Chapters close with worksheets related to each chakra. These activities build on each other so that by the end you will articulate your purpose and your vision for your career, anchored in your values, your passions, and the other related issues.

Reference

Judith, A. (2018) *Charge and the energy body: The vital key to healing your life, your chakras, and your relationships.* Hay House.

1

HOW DO WE LAY A STRONG FOUNDATION?

The ground chakra

Quality and significance

I was at my institution for a number of years and had worked my way up through the ranks. As a tenured associate professor, I was offered an administrative role at the university level. I enjoyed that role very much, and I know I had an impact in making things better for the people I served in my role. But when the institution went through leadership turnover, I did not see eye to eye with the new administration, so I was asked to step down and return to faculty. It is not unusual to see turnover in the administration with a new leader, so I did not take it personally and reframed it as an opportunity. I could pour myself into my scholarship and finally make full professor. I focused on getting all my ducks in a row, revving up my publishing output—peer-reviewed articles, public scholarship, way more than our bylaws required.

After a couple years, I felt ready and applied for promotion to full professor. At my university, it takes almost a full year for a portfolio to wind its way through the system, but I was getting updates at every step. The first review was by the department committee, and the evaluation was positive. The next level was the department chair, which was also positive. The portfolio then headed to the college committee, another positive review, and then to the dean, positive as well. I was flying through the academic levels, so I celebrated with my family over winter break. In the spring, all the portfolios from all the colleges head to academic affairs. These levels are usually pro forma, at least for those who have all positive reviews at the lower levels, and, predictably, the letter from the provost recommending me for promotion to full professor arrived.

I was waiting for the rubberstamp from the president, but when that letter arrived it denied my promotion! Where I work, the president has the final decision power, no matter how many positive reviews one accumulates through the process. His "no" upended the whole process. I could not believe my eyes. I read the terse letter over and over, willing it to say differently, but the steely sentence did not budge. How is this possible? Granted, since my return to faculty, I had been a vocal critic of the administration if I felt some of their decisions were unsound. I used my platform in the faculty senate to speak up, ask to see the evidence justifying particularly dubious decisions, launched petitions to ask the administration to reconsider, but isn't that all part of my role? As a political scientist, I am invested in democratic process and shared governance. I took my duty to represent my department seriously and amplify the voices of those who do not have the security of tenure like I do.

In retrospect, I was naïve to think my advocacy would be inconsequential, but I was being punished for engaging instead of being checked out. And at the end of the day, none of that should matter because I met all the standards! Doesn't the faculty handbook state it's all about the quality and significance of our work? I excelled in both teaching and research, and I have won awards at the college and university levels, as well as at the state level and in my professional association. Speaking of the state level, I commiserated with some of my contacts at the state office, and they said they had no record in the whole state of a president overturning all previous levels before my case. Wow. It felt very destabilizing, like somebody had pulled the rug from under me.

I had to take some time to retreat and lick my wounds, but I came back determined. I took this as a challenge. I will publish more, and my next case will be airtight. I even published a book. I submitted again, and again my portfolio sailed through all the lower levels. But this time, it got overturned by the provost! This felt like such a low blow. The same provost who had previously recommended my portfolio (sans book!) suddenly found fault with it. It felt very suspicious. I seriously wondered if there was a future for me at this university. My professional association was indignant on my behalf and decided to go to bat for me. They were going to call for a boycott of my institution, launch a formal complaint, and suggest to their members that nobody write tenure letters for candidates from my institution since its process is so corrupt. Faced with all this external pressure and potential bad publicity, the president relented and overturned the provost's recommendation. And that's how I became a full professor!

—Colin, White male professor of political science and philosophy at a large research-intensive university in the South

A killer job

I got my PhD in American Studies. Herman Melville and Toni Morrison were my bread and butter in grad school, but early on I got involved in institutional reforms toward student success. That really energized me because it very clearly fit with my personal values and goals—to assist first-generation students, or students who might not be typically prepared for college, help them thrive, break the cycle of not being able to achieve their goals. After doing this work on the side, I found a killer job in a non-degree-granting department with the mission of helping students acclimate to college and start off on the right foot. It was so energizing and so grounding, in fact the most grounding experience I've ever had in academia, to have colleagues who were also similarly committed. I developed a series of skills over time that made me more successful in my job, administrative, pedagogical, scholarly, social skills of bringing people into consensus. I could see the clear benefit to the students in real time, and it was very rewarding.

Then a new president came in, and it was clear he was less interested in this work and more interested in his own career advancement. I was concerned, but the department was nationally recognized, and we had won prestigious awards, so I thought we would be secure. But in a series of precipitating events, my department was dissolved in one go! I felt very unmoored, like I was at sea. It was such a weird feeling to feel so unsupported by my institution because I had just been awarded tenure, right before the department got dissolved. As a tenured professor, they had to find a place for me, and of course the most logical place was in American Studies. It was a disconcerting identity shift, but I decided to remain optimistic. After all, I was merely going back to my original academic home, and I thought I would be able to continue my student success work. Alas, my optimism was misplaced. I was wrong on both counts.

On the disciplinary side, even if I was in the department I was "supposed" to be in, I felt like an impostor because I had not been doing scholarship in American Studies for years. I felt like I had to start over and prove myself again. On the student success side, the work I find interesting necessitates administrative support at the higher level. I can certainly do the work in my own class, but what I found rewarding was working at a scale where I was impacting thousands of students, making those structural changes. Instead, with the university resources dismantled, the discussions about student access were more about giving students band-aids. Here are some resources, go and fix yourself, rather than us having a holistic approach.

This upheaval was not happening in a vacuum. My marriage was in trouble, in the thick of lockdown. It was sad and tragic. Talk about losing ground! Everything was shifting. We have two small children, so I was staring at a long, protracted custody battle. On top of it all, I was in recovery from a liver transplant. Rejection rates are a major concern for liver transplants, so I was trying to navigate my professional dissatisfaction, my crumbling personal life, and my delicate health, when the school ordered us back to campus for in-person instruction—without mask or vaccine mandates. Of course I could not come back, and I requested an exception. My chair was supportive, but the dean and the administration were indifferent to concerns about my health. I had a meeting with HR, where I explained my situation as immunocompromised and asked for an accommodation. Their response? "Oh, we're all a bit immunocompromised." Denied.

I felt betrayed, cast aside, expendable. But in a way, their response allowed me to leapfrog to a solution. This was no longer about professional fulfillment. I was now in a fight for survival. Forget that I no longer found my job fulfilling, or that my ex-wife wanted to move to Boston and take the kids. Staying here would have literally killed me. I had to pivot, somehow. If a fortune teller had told me I would get a tenure track job and earn tenure only to give it up, I would have never believed it. But I did it. And in a way, it was easy to do.

Being at a state institution in a conservative state was so limiting. My tenured job did not allow the academic freedom I thought I would have. Words like "social justice" had to be taken out of syllabi. The dean was blasé about it, "it is what it is, you just have to do it." I realized that this is not what I signed up for, and that I was under no obligation to stay in a job I no longer found rewarding or even manageable. I looked for jobs in the Boston area, and I found one in administration. It didn't come with tenure. But now I can say tenure is overrated. I am back to having the kind of scalable impact that interests me, making a difference with both students and faculty; I am close to my daughters; and I don't have to worry daily about my job killing me.

—Rahul, male Asian tenured associate professor of American Studies transitioning to a university in the greater Boston area

The best representation of my work

I've been a transdisciplinary person in my whole career. I am an engineer, but I am drawn to environmental justice. Traditionally, the two have been at odds, but I wanted to bring the two together. As an assistant professor, I wrote a book titled *Engineering and Social Justice*, a roadmap for engineers to become empowered and engage one another in a process of learning and action for social justice and peace. It was a risky book. Mentors pulled me aside—Wait after tenure, they said. I didn't wait. The book was a joy for me to write, and it was important and needed. Looking back, it was a career defining moment.

Fast forward to 2017. I moved to Purdue to take a position as a school head. The school did a press release on my appointment. A journalist in Texas found it, took objection with my social justice work, and did a hit piece on me. I sent it to the dean so she would be aware. The strategy for this shocking takedown was to quote liberally from my own work. I personally didn't find it particularly damaging; in fact, some colleagues told me it was the best representation of my work. The dean briefed the president of the university and placed my work in context, showing that the principles I was advocating for (bringing into engineering ethical, social, cultural, global, environmental, and public health responsibility, as well as creating collaborative and inclusive working environments) have become mandated by ABET, the engineering accreditation board, and valued by bodies like the National Academy of Engineering, so we are all supposed to incorporate them in our work.

That defense drew further ire. A known White supremacist professor (so notorious that he is tracked and monitored by the Southern Poverty Law Center) published another hit piece on me. The piece was sloppy and contained mistakes. It attributed other people's work to me, specifically the work of Richard Felder on understanding student differences and teaching in a way that honors all of them. I need to make that distinction for transparency, but of course I agree with Felder's ideas. However, that professor found those same ideas anathema and excoriated me. It snowballed from there. The story of my appointment got picked up by "The Michael Savage Show," a conservative podcast. From there, I became a target. His followers started harassing me. It was nonstop calls—and not just me. They harassed the people who reported to me. How can you work for this horrible woman, they demanded to know. They called other engineering department heads. They called the dean. There was more at stake beyond the annoyance and the disruption. Even though I had already started working, the trustees had not formally voted on my appointment. In fact, the harassment began three days before the trustees' vote. It was a relentless, coordinated, strategically timed effort. Thankfully, the trustees approved my appointment anyway, but the harassment continued.

In December I published a feminist critique of rigor. I had given a talk in 2013 on queering the idea of rigor using penis jokes which is something males do all the time and makes engineering hostile for women. So I turned that technique on its head. *Wired* had published an article on slide rules that was full of penis jokes, so I mocked it and used an image from that article with a Kurt Vonnegut quote from *Breakfast of Champions*, about the penis size of the character. I got a standing ovation! Everybody loved the talk, and they asked me to publish it. It took me four years, and it was just my luck that it got published during the controversy. They were ready for it. They distorted my argument and spread it all over twitter. The harassment got so bad that I had to shut down my Twitter account. They targeted my colleagues as well. They made a YouTube video about one of my faculty where she and I are juxtaposed with bridges collapsing. In March 2018, the Florida International University pedestrian bridge over the highway collapsed while under construction, and they blamed me! I'm a chemical engineer! Talk about a bridge too far! But that didn't stop them. They called me a bitch and used other violent language. It was super traumatic, and made it frightening to be at work. By this point, the university was no longer defending me. They were asking *me* if I had solved my problem yet, as if an attack on the academic freedom of one faculty member is not an attack on the whole profession.

There were many days when I felt afraid. I had to summon all my courage. Courage didn't take my fear away but allowed me to move through it. What helped? The people I really felt supported by were my home department, the Lesbian, Gay, Bisexual, Transgender, and Queer (LGBTQ) center on campus, and the women's studies faculty. They were a lifeline. They not only provided emotional support but also connected me to resources I needed for my physical safety. With their encouragement, I turned the whole ordeal into scholarship. It's that community that gives me ground, those friendships. In the end my whole profession came through for me, publicly siding with me and other faculty who came under attack. The harassers eventually moved on to other targets.

—Donna Riley (real name), queer White woman, professor and dean of engineering and computing, currently at University of New Mexico

What's going on with these stories?

These three stories feature faculty at universities with different missions, different disciplinary backgrounds, and at different points in their careers, but they all have one thing in common. They describe struggles to regain ground after a destabilizing experience. Even the images they use (feeling unmoored, at sea; having the rug pulled from under) speak to not feeling grounded. One is related to the tenure and promotion process (by far the number one issue among the faculty I interviewed); one is about harassment, academic freedom, doxing, and, eventually, lack of support from one's own university; and one is a perfect storm of external circumstances (pandemic), personal ones (a divorce, a liver transplant), and institutional ones (the dismantling of one's department and the inflexible enforcing of employment policies).

Sometimes the destabilizing is so pervasive that it calls into question one's professional or literal survival, as with Donna and Rahul, respectively. In these situations, fear becomes a recurring theme in the stories. Thankfully, fear is not the end of the story for these faculty. Their narratives speak to personal values that give them a strong foundation that supports them during challenges (speaking up and hard work for Colin; family and supporting students for Rahul; social justice for Donna). They also speak to attitudes and coping strategies, such as accepting change and reframing challenges as opportunities, that help them regain ground.

All these issues, and more, pertain to the root chakra. As an organizing principle, it can help us explore and connect several issues. What is our foundation? How do we stay solid in the face of change or adversity? How do our values help us embrace change or fight it as appropriate? How do we regain ground during instability? How do we take care of our own survival (academic, medical, financial, and more)? When do our fears help our self-preservation and when do they only cause stagnation? This chapter will explore these themes and more. We begin to build chakra theory in the next section, covering the first chakra. Then we will contextualize these issues to academia through empirical findings and faculty voices, and finally we will delve into opportunities for reflection and strategies.

What does chakra theory say?

We start our journey up the spine on the liberation current with the first chakra, Mūlādhāra, the root chakra (literally the "Root of Existence"). This chakra is represented as a red lotus flower with four petals. Inside the circle of the lotus is inscribed a square. Inside the square, we find the seed mantra, "*lam*" (लं). At the center of the square, there is a triangle with the point facing down, symbolizing the grounding energy. Inside the triangle, we find the *Shiva* (शिव) lingam, with the Kundalini serpent coiled three and a half times around it, waiting to uncoil and start its journey up the sushumna. A number of deities are represented inside each chakra. The root chakra is the seat of *Shakti* (शक्ति), the feminine principle and the immanent aspect of divinity. The journey along the chakras is so that Shakti can reunite with her consort Shiva, the masculine, transcendent principle, already signaling that this process is about establishing alignment between the two principles.

Another deity associated with the root chakra is *Ganesha* (गणेश). Ganesha is the elephant-headed god presiding over beginnings, and it is considered the remover of obstacles. Academia is rife with sedimented, systemic obstacles and barriers to success, and no magic formula can substitute for the hard work of surfacing and clearing them. But Ganesha is here to remind us that we do have the wherewithal to bypass many of the obstacles on our path, and that some of the obstacles are of our own making or are magnified out of proportion by our mind. The journey up the chakras is a journey of removing obstacles and blockages so that all our energies can be expressed in harmony.

As its position in the system implies, the first chakra is the chakra of unity and identity. It is the most solid of the chakras and it is tied to matter and the earth. In yoga philosophy life is impermanence, but this chakra represents the stability through change, the parts of ourselves that endure. It represents our roots stretching back, and in general the things that ground us, including our values. It is the most physical of the chakras, and it represents our physical body and our health, as well as our physical possessions and their health. If we compare prana, the energy coursing through the body, with the electricity flowing in an electric circuit, this chakra is our ground. In a circuit, the ground has the function of absorbing excess voltage and discharging it into the earth to avoid shock hazard. Similarly, if our ground chakra is in good working order, we feel safe and stable; we are not overwhelmed by stressors of the world; and we can engage in behaviors that support health, prosperity, and academic success. Colin, for instance, was not overwhelmed initially by being sent back to faculty and could reframe this significant change as an opportunity to finally make full professor. But sometimes an unexpected influx of energy can short-circuit even well-grounded systems, as in the case of Rahul, and we end up feeling ungrounded. When we are ungrounded, we experience anxiety, restlessness, and worry. We may have lots of ideas that have a hard time concretizing because we can't bring them down from the head into a physical reality. Conversely, an excessive first chakra might preoccupy itself with futile resistance to change or workaholism.

Continuing with analogies, we can think of this chakra as the subroutines running in the background of a computer, like antivirus software. All the habits that ensure that we maintain or restore our health and prosperity, keep an organized and functional office, update our course's gradebook, monitor our progress toward review, tenure, and promotion are facilitated by a healthy ground chakra, not because that is the meaning of life, but because those are the building blocks, the foundations, the root. With an updated gradebook, for instance, we can advise students about their progress, stage interventions for students at academic risk, and generally facilitate student learning and success and make a difference in their lives. When Rahul was relocated to a different department, his well-established subroutines were disrupted, and he felt like he had to start over reestablishing them. The scripts that spelled success in one department (for instance, his established percentage breakdown of teaching, research and service) did not transfer to the other.

Evolutionarily, this chakra is connected to the fight or flight response. If you were in the woods and heard a strange sound, an instinctual physiological response would make your knees bend slightly and your hips coil in, ready to spring toward the threat to fight it or away to flee. In that sense, this is the chakra that keeps us alive, presiding over our survival. Normally, the survival program runs in the background, but when it is activated by an imminent danger, all the energies are directed toward the effort of keeping ourselves alive, as Rahul discovered during the pandemic. Therefore, the ground chakra is associated with the right to exist, to be here, to take up the space that we need, to have our needs met.

The concept and practice of non-violence, or *ahimsa* (अहिंस), is essential to the right to exist. This truism is so rooted in yoga that it is the first principle of its philosophy. Yoga philosophy is structured into eight limbs, or *aṣṭāṅga* (अष्टाङ्ग). The first limb consists of five restraints, the *Yama* (यम), the first of which is non-violence. In our quest for fulfillment, before we get to the poses and the meditation, we need to learn to contain ourselves in several ways, firstly by doing no harm.

When the right to be is upended, for instance, through an attack on her professional expertise, academic freedom, and livelihood in Donna's case, or a physical confrontation in Conrad's, or a threat to Rahul's very life, it can make us afraid. It should be no surprise, then, that this chakra's demon is fear. As we have discussed, the purpose of the demons is to teach us certain lessons. Fear is how our body moves us out of harm's way, but it can also fossilize us in comfortable but stale or dysfunctional situations. We will introduce other Yama as they become relevant in each chakra, but one that is directly relevant now is *asteya* (अस्तेय), non-stealing. One can reasonably argue that Colin's president and provost choosing to withhold the promotion that Colin had rightfully earned were violating asteya. Through the rest of this chapter we will expand on these topics, using both research findings and faculty quotes and stories, and then we will offer strategies to regain balance.

BOX 1.1 GROUND CHAKRA CHART

Sanskrit name: Mūlādhāra
Meaning: Root of Existence
Element: Earth
Function: Survival
Color: Red
Identity: Physical
Right: To be/be safe/take up space/have one's needs met
Demon: Fear

Faculty insights: Grounding and subroutines

It is somewhat of a paradox that we can only ascend the chakras if we are firmly anchored into our roots. The journey is not about leaving things behind, unless they no longer serve us, but about acquiring new tools to take with us on the path. One of the most important tools is learning to ground ourselves. Without the ground beneath us, we would be in freefall. Instead, the earth supports all living beings on it. It is solid but it is permeable, allowing trees to sink their roots deep within it. Through the roots, the earth provides nourishment. Further, deeper roots anchor trees during upheavals such as a landslide, providing stability. Trees ground themselves naturally. But what might grounding mean for humans? Ernest, a White cis married middle-aged gay man, associate professor of history at a large private research institution, whose story we will learn more in depth in the third chakra, describes a lovely grounding moment:

> I had a bad case of writer's block. I was in New York on sabbatical and could not write. I was completely in my head. I started seeing a therapist, and she stressed body work. Her orientation was to help me maximize my brain power by inhabiting my body. She said she would give me homework. The very first task was to go to Central Park and ride the merry-go-round. That's it. That was the whole assignment—that, and journaling about it. I wrote about the feel of the wind on my skin and the feel of the leather bridle in my hands and the smell of the leather on a merry go round horse after 50 years of kids touching it. I wrote about simple sensory things, and that was a new beginning for me. From that experience, my therapist and I developed a set of five practices, which I call my daily sacraments. They include eat well, vigorous physical exercise, play the banjo, keep in touch with people I love, and of course write in my journal. These practices make me feel connected. And if I realize I am feeling disconnected, from my discipline, my colleagues, or if I have writer's block, I take stock and usually realize I've neglected some of my sacraments, and I immediately know what to do.

Ernest's story might feel like a warm fuzzy, and hardly the advice to jumpstart a career. Leaving aside the fact that after his new beginning he was able to finish his book, get it published by a very prestigious academic press, and win multiple awards, paying more attention to our body and our senses is sensible. As I wrote elsewhere,

> the importance of focusing on the body is underscored by Foucault's (1977) observation that the body is the locus of oppression, the principal target of disciplinary power. The most demoralized faculty and graduate students I consulted with over the years wore their failures on their skin—slumped bodies, curved-in shoulders, floorbound gaze, lower back pain, posture problems from sitting at the computer, unwanted weight gains from unhealthy eating habits in the pursuit of maximal productivity. None of them was living the life they wanted.
>
> *(DiPietro, 2018)*

When I get tenured, or promoted, or whatever the next brass ring is, we tell ourselves, then I will slow down and take care of myself. Even though academia's pressures are endless, we are complicit in this deferral. Instead, a balanced career starts in the here and now. In this context, grounding is the practice of deepening our connection with the earth, our energies, and the present moment. When we are well grounded, feel safe and secure, we are engaged in the here and now, not worrying about the future or replaying the past. We don't dwell on the worst-case scenarios and their consequences. We don't obsess replaying an argument in our heads and the perfect comeback that eluded us at the time. Going back to the circuit analogy, an energy surge (such as an entitled student or an aggravating colleague) can be appropriately discharged and doesn't overwhelm the whole system. When we are grounded, we are attuned to the needs of the body, such as food, rest, movement, or boundaries.

It is maybe easier to realize the importance of grounding by noticing the times when we are not grounded. As faculty, almost all of us share a common ungrounding experience, that of being a new faculty member at a new institution. In addition to the excitement for the new job, there is often a destabilizing energy. My center runs new faculty orientation. We want to use that time to have meaningful broad conversations about student learning and success, about the power educators have to make a difference. But many faculty members are so worried by the menial tasks that their minds keep drawing them away—and it is easy to see why. Think back to the upheaval caused by not having an ID, a working email account, a parking permit, direct deposit set up, health insurance (those lucky enough to be provided with it in their contract), and much more. Conrad, who we met in the introduction, speaks to the challenges of adapting to an unfamiliar place when he moved to New England to take that visiting lecturer position:

> I was born and raised in the South, and, for all its challenges, it feels very comfortable there. New England was not my first choice. The job was very appealing, but the location was not. Everything was different. Geography itself was ungrounding. The landscape was different, both the architecture and the natural scenery. The people around me were different. As a queer individual, I have struggled in the South. The people up North had no issue with my sexuality, but they were different in other ways . . . the sheer density of people around me was different. The move from urban to rural was a big shift, the demographics were different. My students were different, the institution was different, the cultural values were different.

The issues are compounded for international faculty, as Petra, a White United Kingdom citizen, professor of biology and administrator at a rural state college, attests:

> I was offered the job on a work visa, but the paperwork kept getting delayed. I kept getting more and more anxious. It got to three days to the start date,

and still no sign of it. I had to call the dean to turn down the job. Graciously, the dean enlisted my husband, a lawyer, and together they wrote to the area congressman on my behalf to rush the visa through. It literally came at the last minute possible. Even with all the paperwork squared out, it was difficult to find ground as a new faculty member because the educational systems are completely different in the UK and the USA. Even outside of academia, I felt like a fish out of water. Many of our faculty are alumni, so they are already locally connected. I had no car, no driver's license, no credit history. It took a good six or seven years until I felt grounded.

Without the university ID, we can't even get in the building to go teach our classes; without an email account, we are cut off from the information flow. The first task, then, is to attend to these material dimensions. Some of these tasks only need to get done once. Once you have your identification card, that issue is taken care of. Others require regular habits. Once you have an email account, you have to check it regularly and dispose of those emails. Establishing these habits is a function of the ground chakra. We've already drawn the analogy to the subroutines of a computer. When things are functioning as they should, we are not even aware of the subroutines. We simply experience smooth functioning. But if the antivirus stops working, that will be immediately clear. We rely on scores of personal and professional habits that, ideally, we don't even think about. Lachlan, a lecturer whose story we will encounter fully in the next chapter, puts it this way:

> I don't like to dwell on chaos. I am a problem solver. That's my foundation. That's the baseline of moving forward. And actually, it's more than fixing problems, it's preventing problems. The fuel light never comes on in my car.

Lachlan's subroutines are well established, but other people struggle in this area. Over the years, faculty have shared a multitude of stories with me: funding applications rejected because they forgot to route the document by their chair for approval first; timely emails discovered in the drafts folder days later because they didn't press the send button; deadlines missed because they never made it into their calendar; electricity cut off in their home because they simply forgot to pay the bill; and yes, even running out of fuel and being stranded on the highway. When the root chakra is not expressing fully, the healthy habits that support baseline tasks are not as easily established. In his book *The Power of Habit*, Charles Duhigg (2014) reviews the evidence on habits and offers principles to establish healthy habits or to disrupt unproductive ones. The science is complex, and the practice lengthy, but they rely on understanding the habit loop, including the cue, the routine, and the reward. For instance, the self-sabotaging habit of waiting until the last minute to fill the gas tank or to procrastinate until the deadline might involve the reward of avoiding an unpleasant task. Or it might involve deriving satisfaction, a basic form of charge in the chakra system, from seeing how close to the end one can get and still make it. Once we have an understanding of the mechanisms at play, we can take action. For instance, we could devise ways of obtaining the rewards in other ways (e.g., put the spouse in charge of getting gas in exchange for some other chore); we could replace those rewards with others (e.g., the satisfaction of completing a task under the wire with the satisfaction of not having to stress about the deadline); we could insert better cues for action (e.g., the fuel light coming on versus the fuel light having been on for two days).

Faculty insights: Values and identities

Establishing basic habits of productivity might make us feel less ungrounded, but it won't take us all the way to that state of being connected to our authentic self and being present to the world in the moment. For that to happen, there needs to be an authentic self so that we can be rooted in our identity and our values and build on a stable foundation. Research has paid considerable attention to values in the last decades. Values are the beliefs and principles at the core of how we move through the world. When we are present to our values, we gain clarity in the face of complex decisions, and we exhibit resilience under challenges. To the point, when our actions are congruent with our values, we feel more aligned to our core self. In building our integrity, we also build our capacity for healthy relationships. In one word, we are more grounded. Science confirms that being in touch with our values fosters well-being and happiness and can reduce stress and anxiety (Fledderus et al., 2013; Veage et al., 2014; Sagiv & Schwartz, 2000; Wersebe et al., 2017). For example, Damian, a White male professor of psychology specializing in clinical work at a large state institution in the South, recalls:

> At my previous institution, I was in a conservative area and a relatively conservative department, so I did not feel I could be fully out. That made me miserable, so when I was on the job market, I decided that I would actively disclose my sexuality at every interview. When I interviewed at my current institution, they asked me: "How do you think that you will add to the department?" And I answered: "I'm not sure how people identify in the department, but I am openly bisexual so that may end up adding to diversity of your faculty in particular because I'm out." If this is not OK, I'd rather not work there at all. Clarifying this stance of living out loud was very grounding, because it upheld several core values of mine—truth, integrity, and not letting my life be ruled by fear.

In Damian's case, a strong sense of his values helped him find a satisfying answer to challenging questions (should I come out on a job interview?) by clarifying his preferences (I'd rather not have a job where I cannot be out). Damian was savvy enough to present himself not as somebody to be tolerated in his department because of his identity, but as a somebody who would add value precisely because of his identity (connecting the dots, the interviewers could likely imagine he would be able to advise LGBTQ+ students in the department in a way other faculty could not).

Devlin, a Latino White immigrant tenured professor of analytics at a private research university, recounts how focusing on his values helped him weather professional and personal setbacks:

> I was denied promotion to full. I won many teaching awards over the years, and my research output actually increased after tenure, but I was denied while others with less impressive portfolios got promoted. Even my chair called me to say it was an outrage. It deflated me. I am also dealing with a divorce so both home and work are a challenge. I've made a sign and placed it on my fridge as a reminder to myself. It says: "My priorities: 1) My daughter 2) My physical and mental health 3) My family and friends 4) Everything else." So work is number 4. Work is something I do to get money so I can live my life. If I can get joy out of it, that is awesome—not the other way around.

Many academics' identities are wrapped up in their profession, but when circumstances are trying, it is helpful to remind ourselves that we are not our job and that our job is, ultimately, only a job. Other times, our jobs highlight tensions between conflicting sets of values. Carly, a White woman professor of communication and administrator at a regional state university in the South, illustrates these tensions:

> My dual role as faculty member and administrator sometimes creates situations where I can't stand fully in my values. I direct a unit on campus. Some of the women who report to me have come forward with allegations of sexual harassment. As a professor of communication, women's disclosures of sexual harassment are a well-studied issue. We know that most of the time, those are not fabricated and incredibly courageous to make. Believing women is definitely a value of mine, especially after the #MeToo movement. But as a manager, I must uphold institutional processes. The burden of proof is on the victims. I must involve HR and other administrative offices. It takes time. It's not an ideal situation, and it breaks my heart when the system does not vindicate people I care about. In the particular case I am thinking of, we put the harasser on a performance improvement plan, and eventually he violated those terms, so we were able to let him go. But some of the women

had already left because they refused to continue to work with him. We failed those women, and it is our loss as a university that we lost their talents and expertise.

Many professionals occasionally experience conflict among competing values, especially if they assume multiple roles in an organization. What is important is if we can see an overall long-term fit between our values and the values of the institutions we work at. Cable and DeRue (2002) show that a strong value alignment between individuals and the organizations predicts engagement and commitment at work. Further, they show that significant misalignment predicts employee turnover more than the demands of the job and the employee's capabilities. Aretha, a former professor of mathematics, demonstrates these research findings in her story:

> In my career, there have been struggles between the leadership and the faculty a number of times. That's expected. I understand that institutions face numerous pressures from internal and external stakeholders, and it is hard to keep everybody happy. As long as my colleagues and I felt we were pulling in the same direction as the institution we could feel grounded. But at some point that changed, and that's when I felt adrift. Without getting into the specifics, faculty and leadership were not pulling in the same direction anymore. We disagreed with the values that informed the leadership's decisions in fundamental ways. I was part of a working group to try to solve the problem, but I came away from that experience realizing the leadership had no interest in maintaining the once-shared values. The situation was so bad that it landed us on the censure list of the American Association of University Professors. I come from a long list of labor-supporting people in my family. I felt the whole situation was disrespectful to the workforce and the humanity of the people in it. That is when I decided to retire.

Aretha's story is both rare and common. As of February 2025, the American Association of University Professors (AAUP) censure list includes only 59 institutions, 1.5% of the nearly 4,000 institutions of higher learning in the United States. At the same time, several other interviewees voiced a disconnect and distrust between faculty and senior leadership.

Another way to deepen our connection to our authentic self is to consciously connect our actions to our identities. Eden, a Chinese-American immigrant, nonbinary queer professor of psychology at a public research university in the Rockies, discusses how her identities inform her actions:

> During the pandemic, there was a significant increase in violence fueled by anti-Asian hate. There are very few Asian-Americans in my tiny college

town, so if I didn't say something chances are nobody would. I gathered resources and sent them to the administration and to colleagues. I attached them to a positive, encouraging email. I know you all care about this, I said, and I assume the administration is putting out a statement, so I took the liberty to compile this list, which you are all welcome to use if it helps. I had never written to the president of my university. I was speaking as an Asian-American, but I was also speaking as a professor of psychology, an expert. The resources I sent are the tools of my discipline.

Bronfenbrenner (1979) uses a concentric circle model to unpack identity. The innermost circle, the Micro level, includes our individual qualities that are stable over time and differentiate us from others (e. g., stubborn, easy-going, and geeky). The second layer, the Meso, represents the parts of our identity that developed in relationship with others, for instance, qualities we have cultivated because we have admired them in a mentor. The next layer, the Exo, refers to outside forces outside of our control that influence our identity; for instance, the pandemic has changed some of us in long-lasting ways. The fourth layer, the Macro, refers to our social identities, identities we take on as members of certain social groups. The final layer, the Chrono, refers to the shifts in our identity as we age and hit certain milestones. As we move from lecturer to principal lecturer to a leadership role over time, the micro layer might be stable but other things shift as we gain experience and expertise. In her testimonial, Eden is honoring two of her social identities, Asian-American and psychologist. Myers & Id-Deen (2023) remark that centering one's racial identity reframes what is normal in academia, helps to find community, particularly for those from underrepresented groups who would otherwise experience isolation, and is ultimately beneficial to our students as well.

Faculty insights: Safety and survival

There is another important element to consider in the ground chakra, and that is safety. As we have already mentioned, survival is the province of the first chakra, through the fight or flight response. Xander, a gay male tenured associate professor of medicine at a private research university, articulates a sentiment that all interviewees in grant-funded positions shared:

> I feel like I am constantly in survival mode. The funding model for many medical school faculty is that they must raise their own salary. My contract states I must raise 65% of my salary, at a minimum. They would like that percentage to go up to 95%. And of course, I have to cover 100% of the cost for my team of graduate students at all times. Publish or perish is a very real predicament.

While Xander is talking about financial and psychological safety, others are worried about their physical safety. Sasha, a former dean who we will also meet more in depth in the heart chakra, recounts how she wrestled with a moral dilemma:

> When my state passed a campus carry law, I had to process what it would mean for me. I came to the conclusion that, in case of a campus shooting, I couldn't in good conscience run away from the shooter. Ethically, I would have to run toward the danger, because, as a dean, I feel responsible for all my students and faculty. And I am not willing to do that. That marked the beginning of my decision to look for a job in a different state.

Academics in the United States are regularly terrified by unending news of campus shootings. As of 2025, 12 states allow or mandate campus carry for public universities. We know the probability that we will be next is low, yet somebody has to be next. Victims in shootings are often random, but sometimes faculty are personally targeted. Vivian, a middle-aged White woman professor of English and administrator at a small private liberal arts college in the South, was deeply affected by a near miss:

> At my previous institution, a former student came to campus to kill me. I know this is true because she asked people in the hall where I was, and she said she was going to kill me. I happened to be off campus at that time. When she couldn't find me, she left and went to look for my then-husband. In a small town, everybody knows everybody else, and he worked for a well-known local business, so she knew where to find him. It just so happened that he was out to lunch, so nothing happened that day, thankfully. When I was notified, I was shocked and scared. This happened three days after the attempted assassination of congresswoman Gabrielle Giffords, and emotions were running high. I had to go to court and provide a victim impact statement. The student left a long meandering message on my voicemail. She said she wanted to kill me because she loved me, but not sexually. She loved me so much she wanted to save me from feminism. She mumbled something about keeping my own name instead of taking my husband's name. That was hard to make sense of. I've read stories of disgruntled students shooting professors over a bad grade, but in her twisted way she wanted to protect me! In my state, the sentence for one death threat (witnesses only heard her say it once) is probation and mandatory counseling, so she was still out and about. I was scared. The student was clearly mentally ill, but my institution did not do much to protect me. They did not have my back, so I felt unmoored.

The feeling of safety clearly happens on a spectrum, but it's hard to overestimate its importance. Developmental psychologists point out that the first big question (an identity crisis indeed) a child has to answer in their first two years is: "Is the world safe for me?" The answer (affirmative, ambivalent, or negative) will have a profound effect on their development (Erikson & Erikson, 1998). This question takes center stage when we enter a new environment. We have to decide rather quickly whether our new university, department, and even classroom is safe for us. Many factors can affect feeling safe at work, and the stories so far have only scratched the surface. Plouffe et al. (2023) have created a psychological safety inventory indexing multiple dimensions.

If this sounds too touchy-feely, consider that research about faculty survival in academia is a proper academic field—they just call it "retention." The COACHE project at Harvard has been studying the factors that overwhelm faculty to the point they leave their position for over two decades, gathering a massive dataset that has supported scores of studies, papers, and books. In their retention study, Ambrose, Huston, and Norman (2005) identified several factors that affect faculty decisions to stay or leave: the sense of collegiality in the department; having mentors and advocates on one's side; the clarity and fairness of the tenure and promotion process; a strong chair; a competitive salary (although its importance is not as high as the other factors); the city or town around the university and how welcoming and inclusive it is; and the way the university evaluates and rewards faculty work, particularly interdisciplinary work. Most of the faculty stories so far echo and illustrate these findings.

Faculty insights: Burnout

Events that trigger the survival instinct should be relatively rare; instead, some have observed that life in academia, or modern life in general (Schoen, 2013), has turned our survival instinct indefinitely on, inundating the whole system with energies that can't readily be discharged or grounded. What happens to our body, our life, and our productivity when we feel under that continued, chronic stress? Often, the result is burnout. Confirming Schoen's analysis, a Chronicle of Higher Education survey of tenure track professors found that when asked what metric they would employ to measure the success of their university in the next 5–10 years, the most common response (62%) was "reducing burnout and improving morale" (Wheeler, 2024).

Honorine, a Black female tenured associate professor of leadership studies at multiple institutions in the South, who we will encounter in more depth in the fifth chakra, describes her burnout as follows:

> The narrative is that our profession is a calling. All the long hours are taken for granted, and sacrificing everything for the students was rated as "meeting expectations". I felt like I had to give and give and give. I am fine with giving, and I do love the students. What I'm not fine with is endless giving, especially

with no reciprocity from the institution. I was simply labor. I was so burned out, that I spent a month in bed after December graduation. I was that depleted. I did make tenure, and when I got the president's letter, I remember I cried in my car reading it. But mine were not tears of joy. Crossing the finish line only reminded me just how difficult the journey had been. A small voice inside told me I needed to get out. That voice would become louder and louder.

The pandemic has placed a renewed focus on faculty burnout. My understanding of this issue is informed mainly by Rebecca Pope-Ruark's book, *Unraveling Faculty Burnout* (2022), an unflinching, vulnerable and compassionate account of her own burnout as well as that of other faculty, framed by empirical research findings. One of the dictionary definitions of burnout is "the reduction of a fuel or substance to nothing through use or combustion" (Google Dictionary Box, n.d.) and that reduction to nothing might really resonate with some of us. But in a more precise sense, the World Health Organization defines it as a syndrome

> resulting from chronic workplace stress that has not been successfully managed. It is characterized by three dimensions: feelings of energy depletion or exhaustion; increased mental distance from one's job, or feelings of negativism or cynicism related to one's job; and reduced professional efficacy.
>
> *(WHO, 2019)*

From a chakra perspective, the physical exhaustion pertains to the ground chakra, the cynicism and sense of futility is an ailment of the crown chakra, and the reduced professional efficacy affects the power chakra. It further adds that burnout is an occupational phenomenon, not a clinical one. It only happens at work, as a consequence of what happens at work. Honorine's story speaks to the depletion and negative feelings about one's job. Accruing expectations on faculty have been identified as a problem in higher education for decades already (Sorcinelli et al., 2005), but this issue has exploded since the pandemic, with record numbers of academics reporting exhaustion, frustration and cynicism, and a sense of futility (Flaherty, 2020). It is important to acknowledge that burnout is not proof of individual professor's inadequacy to function within the academy. Rather, it is a manifestation of the problems with the system itself, with the capitalist takeover of higher education, and the attendant emphasis on productivity over any other concern, including well-being and fair compensation. Burnout and compassion fatigue are more common in service professions, which can tax our empathy and emotional presence capacity (Maslach, Schaufeli, and Leiter, 2001). And yet, perhaps because we don't talk about it enough, it leaves the individuals affected by it with heavy feelings of guilt and shame. These are the demons of the second and third chakras, and we will explore them in the next chapters. Given the number of chakras involved, it is clear that burnout affects the whole person. Therefore, a multipronged approach is necessary, with individual solutions to restore both physical health and a sense of purpose and agency, as well as systemic solutions that create more humane labor conditions. While this book focuses more on individual strategies, Maggie Berg and Barbara Seeber offer us a great start in the latter direction in their book *The Slow Professor: Challenging the Culture of Speed in the Academy* (2016).

In *Unraveling Faculty Burnout,* Pope-Ruark identifies four vectors of burnout recovery: restoring a sense of purpose, cultivating (self-)compassion, building connections, and creating balance. Purpose is the function of the crown chakra, while the other three vectors are associated with the heart chakra; therefore, we will unpack these concepts in more detail in the relevant chapters. But burnout takes a toll on the physical and mental well-being, which means that first we need strategies to heal our body and to ground ourselves in our values. Then we can add on the strategies from the other chakras as we move up the liberating current. Of course, individual paths out of burnout will depend on how our context responds. Honorine's story is sobering:

> When I brought up issues (workload, transparency, fairness, salary) I was routinely dismissed. That told me the university was not interested in retaining me. Could I survive in this environment? I'm sure I could. But I wanted to do more than survive. I want to lead, to excel, to thrive. It was clear I could only do that somewhere else.

Chakra right: To be

Of all the associations chakras have been imbued with over time, one of the most powerful is the connection to rights. Each chakra is associated with a basic right, and the root chakra relates to the right to be. We can articulate it as the right to be here now, the right to be safe, the right to take up space, the right to have our needs met. Beyond the rare cases where our physical survival is threatened, such as Vivian's, this right extends beyond our life, to our livelihood and to our worth. It means that I, you, we all deserve to be here, and we deserve to be here independently from how many students we teach or how many research dollars we bring in. How do we claim this right for ourselves? Aida, a tenure-track associate professor of statistics, whose story we will learn in the third-eye chakra, struggled with it:

> 'I have the right to exist.' I put this sign up on my desk as a reminder. I thought there was something wrong with the way I was put together, and it took me a long time to feel I am an acceptable human being.

Claiming all aspects of our self has to be an intentional act for many, especially in light of the expectations society places on us, as Bridget, an English professor whom we will encounter in depth in the third chakra, explains:

> It is a challenge for me to uphold my right to take up space because of the way I was socialized. Like many other women, it is not easy for me to demand to be given resources, or to ask for what I need. To help with this issue, I try to remember it is not only to my disadvantage, but also to the disadvantage of my students and the people I serve in my multiple roles.

Bridget astutely understands that tracing the downstream effects of an ask can help us present a more powerful case. If the first question is whether we claim each of the chakra rights for ourselves, the second one is whether our institutions support our chakra rights. Rahul did not feel that his right to survive was supported during the pandemic (when his institution imposed a return to work without mask mandates), a sentiment shared by multiple interviewees from states with similar mandates.

Certain categories of faculty also felt their right to exist not supported. Clara, a middle-class first-generation college student who is now an adjunct professor of psychology at a large state university, elaborates:

> As a part-time faculty member, my right to exist is constantly threatened in academia by full-time academics who don't take me seriously and by the time pressures. Sometimes my anti-racism work, something I take very seriously, is a threat when it becomes inconvenient to my institution.

Donna's perspective illuminates a related issue:

> My existence as a female queer is under threat all the time. The threat is that of erasure, and it is real, especially with all the unwanted attention. The message is that in order to be here, I need to blend in. There is a lot of invisibility that happens, so I try to be extra conscious of being visible.

Versions of this statement were shared by other members of the LGBTQ+ community as well as faculty from racially underrepresented groups. Some observant White faculty on the tenure track shared that they felt fine but could see the precariousness of their minoritized colleagues' rights.

What can we do when we feel something as basic as the right to be here is threatened? Honorine looked for pockets where she could cultivate that right:

> I reached out to a colleague I admired. It turns out she had just started a mutual mentoring group for faculty women of color through our institution's

office of diversity. I didn't have to explain myself to that group. They knew, because they were all going through similar things. With those women, I could just be. We all supported each other. It was my lifeline.

Chakra demon: Fear

Each chakra is associated with a demon. This trickster trips us until we learn its lessons. The demon of the first chakra is fear. What lessons could fear teach us? Fear warns us of danger, but undue fear shrinks our life. Conversely, we might need to learn prudence if we are reckless and do not heed fear's messages.

Out of all the chakra demons, fear is the one that came up the most in my interviews. What were these faculty afraid of? A very common fear many faculty had to conquer in their first years on the job is the fear of not knowing, particularly not knowing the answer to student questions, and the resulting embarrassment. Serena, a White, female, recently retired program director of fashion marketing at a two-year college in the Midwest, describes her journey through that fear:

> When I first got started in academia, my implicit model was that faculty are the experts and hold all the knowledge. Not knowing the answer to a student question brought up the fear of being exposed for not knowing everything. How ridiculous is that? Nobody knows everything! Why was I holding myself to that standard? Eventually I was able to reframe my stance as "Yes, I don't know, so let me go off and investigate." At first it was just a reasonable out, to not lose face with the students. But now technology moves so fast, so it's much easier to say, "I didn't know that existed! Come on up and show all of us how that works." That was the real switch, when I learned I don't need to be afraid. Student questions are an opportunity for the whole class, so my approach now is to honor them.

Beyond this common fear, other themes in faculty answers range from fear of not finding their footing again after an ungrounding experience; fear of uncertainty; fear of bullies; fear of taking risks in an unforgiving environment; fear of not belonging; not working hard enough; not being good enough. These are all root chakra issues. Recall that the lesson Donna learned from fear was courage, moving through the fear. Eden learned to reframe perceived threats as challenges to overcome.

Beyond the experiences of my sample, much has been written about threats to faculty. Faculty are afraid and/or suspicious of accruing expectations on their performance, opaque tenure and promotion processes, salary compression and furloughs, erosion of shared governance, political interference in higher education, declining enrollments, and financial instability. This is clearly a time of danger and disruption in academia, and many of these concerns are justified. For instance, according to the Hechinger Report (Barshay 2022), 861 colleges and 9,499 branch campuses have closed down between 2004 and 2022 in the United States. According to the American Association of Colleges and Universities (AAC&U, 2020), 17% of instructional staff in higher education experienced food insecurity, while 33% experienced housing insecurity, including 8% who experienced homelessness in the previous year. Predictably, these statistics relate to adjunct faculty for the most part, and disproportionally affect faculty of color, LGBTQ+ faculty, and younger faculty.

The landscape is shifting rapidly, but as new threats emerge so do new opportunities. New technologies, new generations of students, and renewed calls for accountability might present challenges, but they might also open up possibilities for our teaching or our scholarship. For instance, Gabby, a White female associate professor of English at a small private research university in the mid-Atlantic, recounts:

> As a graduate student, in addition to my coursework and dissertation, I was involved in campus activism, a very collaborative endeavor, working with 60 graduate student leaders where we made tangible gains for all. By contrast, the transition to professorial work at a new place felt isolating and high-pressure, with delayed rewards. I felt overwhelmed as a new professor. I wrote about it and turned my experience into scholarship. It helped me feel less overwhelmed and it also counted as a publication.

Remember that one of the characteristics of imbalance in the root chakra is excessive resistance to change. Therefore, part of the work of this chakra is to grow our capacity to deal with change.

Prompts for reflection

- How do you feel about your body? Are there areas of (chronic) pain? Are there areas of dissatisfaction or difficulty? How do you nourish and care for your body? What have you been meaning to do for your body that you have not gotten to yet?
- What subroutines are working smoothly for you? In what areas would you like to build in more organization and structure? Conversely, in what areas could you invite more freedom?
- When do you feel in survival mode at work? What does it feel or look like? What strategies work for you to get through those times?
- What gives you roots, foundation, and stability? Do you prioritize these things or take them for granted? If the latter, what could you do to center them?

- What parts of your identity are salient to you? How do they inform your decisions and your priorities?
- Recall the three dimensions of burnout: exhaustion, sense of futility/cynicism, and lack of efficacy. Recall also the four vectors of burnout recovery: restoring a sense of purpose, cultivating (self-)compassion, building connections, and creating balance. How do you fare along these coordinates?
- How is your right to be, to take up space, and to have your basic needs met supported in your context? How is it threatened? What can you do to protect it?
- When does fear show up for you? What are you afraid of professionally? What lessons have you gained from this trickster?

Tools, strategies, and possibilities

Several of the stories and quotes so far immediately suggest strategies. This section will compile and expand them. As a general rule we will follow in all the chapters, we will start with general strategies related to the chakra that would be beneficial to most people. Then we will move to strategies specific to academia. But before we get going, I need to share a caveat that arises from a personal story. These strategies are not a panacea. Reflection prompts will not fix all that is wrong in higher education. I started exploring the scholarship on academic bullying at a time when I was being bullied and, ever the academic, hoped to find a solution in the literature. I was severely disappointed. There are no foolproof strategies that force the system to reckon with this problem in every case. In fact, bullies are rarely held accountable. The only strategies that research deemed effective operate at the individual level, not at the systemic level (Clark et al., 2013; Twale and DeLuca, 2008). In other words, these are coping strategies. Bullying is ungrounding because it threatens our sense of self. It makes us wonder if we did the right thing or should have reacted more strongly, but then risk being seen as not a team player. It makes us question our reality. Did it really happen or did I imagine it? Was there malice behind it or was it a miscommunication? Is it my fault for not having been clear in my intentions from the beginning? And so on. The self must be recovered and rebuilt so the work must start at the root chakra.

Whenever that is the case, whether we are talking about bullying or any of the other ungrounding events we have discussed in this chapter, these strategies help reestablish ground. In fact, they work best as regular ongoing practices, rather than when started in dire straits. They get us in touch with our body, nature, and the things that matter to us. They remind us that while pain is an inevitability in life, it too will pass. They help us observe ourselves and our suffering with detachment and equanimity, so we are not ruled by our emotions or our circumstances and we don't turn to unhealthy behaviors to compensate.

They do not magically change the circumstances, but they lay the foundation for us to build our power (see Chapter 3) and focus on our goals, so we are more likely to reach them in spite of the circumstances.

At the same time, we should take Beverly Daniel Tatum's advice in her book *Why Are All the Black Kids Sitting Together in the Cafeteria?* (2017): we should work in our spheres of influence. Along with working on ourselves, we can connect with others, share our problems and our values, organize, strategize, generate possibilities, try things out, advocate–build pockets of fairness, community, and support, then grow those pockets and institutionalize them into processes and policies. The focus of this book is on the personal level—grounding ourselves in our values, cultivating our power, growing our voice, and speaking our truth (see also Chapters 3 and 5), so that it will resonate with like-minded people and build a coalition that can act in the world.

Connect with nature. The earth is our literal ground, but modernity has us disconnected from it, locked away in offices under artificial light. Reconnecting with nature is healing. This can take many forms: from hiking on the weekends to tending a garden, to a regular 15-minute walk in the middle of the day. The proven benefits of being in nature are manifold: it can lower blood pressure and stress hormone levels, reduce sensory overload and anxiety, and improve mood, among others. Keniger et al. (2013) review and categorize the existing literature in psychological, cognitive, physiological, social, spiritual, and tangible benefits. In his book *In Praise of Walking* (2020), the neuroscientist Shane O'Mara reviews the benefits of walking on mood, mental health, brain function, creativity, and, for communal walks, social connections. He summarizes the evidence by saying that walking makes our brains "cognitively mobile." Charlene, a heterosexual Black Haitian woman, professor of French and Francophone studies at a research university in the Northeast, acts on these findings in immediate ways: "I regularly schedule walking meetings. I email the files before, and we discuss them while walking."

Exercise. Keeping our body in good health is one of the tasks of the root chakra, and exercise is one of the things that helps the most. Any form of moderate-to-vigorous physical exercise helps, according to the Centers for Disease Control and Prevention (2023). Whether one prefers a team sport, weightlifting, running, or any other age-appropriate form, exercise can help cognitive functions, strengthen bones and muscles, improve mood, reduce pain, reduce anxiety, reduce the risk of certain diseases, and increase the chances of living longer. Bridget had to navigate challenges but prioritized her physical activity: "I've always been a runner and that could have been a challenge when I had kids. Instead, I got a running stroller and was able to keep that up." Many campuses offer free or reduced exercise options as part of their benefits, and many libraries even let you check out exercise equipment.

Practice yoga. Yoga is a particular form of physical exercise focused on stretching, balance, and flexibility; therefore, it reaps all the benefits of physical exercise. In addition, it is an integrated physical and philosophical system, which claims to offer insight into the human condition. Research into yoga shows that it can improve mindfulness, reduce stress and anxiety, and increase well-being and quality of life (Woodyard, 2001).

Meditate. Meditation is a practice to still the racing mind by focusing on the breath and practicing equanimity and non-judgment. It is often coupled with a physical yoga practice. As such, it is an ideal tool to cultivate being present in the here and now. Research confirms that meditation can reduce anxiety and improve quality of life (Goyal et al., 2014).

Practice healthy eating. While this is not a fitness or nutrition book, and I am not qualified to give nutritional advice, one of the functions of the root chakra is that of elimination. Therefore, issues in this area (such as constipation) point to an imbalance. Our culture enables eating excesses, both in quantity and in quality (i.e., regularly eating lunch at our desk while we work). In addition, many of us are not properly hydrated. Yet the positive effects of healthy eating as well as the negative effects of excesses are clear (Willet & Stampfer, 2013). Reflecting on our eating habits and introducing some changes where needed might pay dividends.

Get enough sleep. In our fast-paced world, slumber is essential to recharge. Sacrificing sleep to meet looming deadlines has cumulative effects on our physical, cognitive, and mental health (Medic et al., 2017). Conversely, sleep quality has positive associations with memory, learning, positive affect and even gratitude, and can decrease burnout (Wickwire, 2021; Padilla & Thompson, 2016).

Go to the doctor regularly. Another way of taking care of our body and ensuring it supports our professional goals is to go to the doctor regularly, if at all affordable. Regular checkups allow for preventative care and can catch dangerous things early on. This advice is listed here because I have met many professors who neglected to do so, feeling they had too much to do to spare a couple hours for a visit. When we think we are too busy to go to the doctor (or exercise, or any of the above practices) it is beneficial to remember we are too busy not to go.

Nurture connections with others. The heart chakra is all about connecting with other people, so we will explore this in detail in Chapter 4. The reason this strategy shows up here is that connecting with others is also grounding. Social connectedness is defined by the Centers for Disease Control and Prevention in terms of the quantity, quality, and diversity of relationships that create a sense of belonging, support, and feeling valued. It is one of Ernest's "sacraments," and research shows that strong social connectedness is associated with positive mental, cognitive, and physical health outcomes (Holt-Lunstad, 2022), including increased capacity to recover from stress and anxiety and improved quality of life.

Invest in a hobby. Whether it is art, music, collecting, playing board games, or anything else, hobbies serve multiple functions. They help us build skills and virtues (patience, self-forgiveness, etc.). They put us in touch with our limits and show us our progress. They demand that we carve out time, time that is not going to overwork us. In fact, they allow us to switch off mentally, which can serve as a reboot. They put us in touch with a community of people with similar interests. Research also shows that participating in leisure activities is associated with increased productivity, psychological and physical well-being, better workplace relationships, an increased capacity to deal with challenges at work, and a decrease in burnout (Pressman et al., 2009; Padilla & Thompson, 2016; Pang, 2016). All of these things add to our grounding.

Journal daily. Each chapter offers journaling prompts related to the chakra under consideration. But journaling does not have to be focused on the chakras only. Julia Cameron, author of *The Artist's Way* (2016), recommends three pages a day of freewriting first thing in the morning. Similar to what we have been discussing, she recommends the morning pages (and a variety of other tools) as an antidote to blockages, specifically to blocked creativity. While, technically, creativity is the province of the fifth chakra, journaling and reflection can help us step back from our anxieties, observe them without judgment, and plan responses that are intentional rather than reactive, bringing us back in touch with our values and our ground. Research confirms that long-term benefits of regular journaling include a reduction in stress, an increase in psychological well-being, improvements in memory, and more (Baikie & Wilhelm, 2005).

Understand expectations. Being blindsided by a deadline or a requirement we were not aware of can be very ungrounding. The easiest way to avoid this is to understand expectations. If your chair does not share essential documents with you, make sure to find them. Find the most recent, approved version of the department bylaws, the tenure and promotion requirements, the faculty handbook and study them. In my workshops on tenure and promotion, I am always amazed at how many participants going up for those reviews are not in possession of the documents detailing the requirements for the milestones they are applying for. Not only do these documents chart a path for us, but they might also provide us with options that feel freeing.

Take the burnout assessment. The full version of the Maslach Burnout Inventory (with tailored variations for educators, medical personnel, students, and more) is proprietary and available on the Mind Garden website, but a free, simplified version is available at www.mindtools.com/auhx7b3/burnout-self-test. While this test has not been validated, it can give a first approximation and spur further reflection and action.

Run a workplace safety analysis. How safe do you feel at work? In this chapter, we have encountered stories of people who were rattled by their work in multiple ways with lasting effects. We all have different triggers and different capacity to cope, so what is relatively safe for one person might feel relatively unsafe for another. Beyond reflecting on what feels safe or unsafe to you, you can also take the Psychological Safety Inventory by Plouffe et al. (2023). See how you score on the continuum from safe to unsafe and if any dimensions are particularly worrisome to you. The inventory is available at www.osiresearch.ca/psi

Decide whether to stay or go. If your environment is toxic, you don't get extra points for surviving it. Colin stayed and fought. Rahul left. Donna stayed for that particular fight but eventually left. I purposefully included stories of people who left their environment. Many of us are socialized in graduate school to view the professoriate as the only worthy career, but our professors comprise a highly biased sample. The world is changing and the percentage of faculty who change institutions or even leave academia has increased since the pandemic (Jaschik & Lederman, 2022). There is no shame in leaving, and we owe it to ourselves and to the world to be in the place that allows us to do our best work.

Consider the Stockdale paradox. For those of us who feel in a situation of crisis but can't leave yet, there might be a lesson in the story of Admiral Jim Stockdale, the highest-ranking prisoner of war during the Vietnam war, as recounted by Jim Collins in his book *Good to Great* (2001). Stockdale recounts that may of his fellow captives tried to hang on in those unbearable situations by pinning their hopes on being rescued. Surely, by Christmas they'll come for us, they would say. Then, when Christmas came and went, they would hope for an Easter rescue, and so on. Those who had to keep moving the goalpost are the ones who didn't make it. The ones who survived are those who realized that it was up to them to keep themselves alive. They worked on growing their capacity to survive under tough conditions until the conditions improved. We might not all have the wherewithal to survive a prison camp, but, as ungrounding or even toxic as our workplaces might be, they are not prison camps. Like Honorine, we can find or build pockets of safety and support while we bide our time.

Establish your subroutines. Boice (2000) studied new faculty, those who rapidly acclimate to the institution's culture, rhythm, and expectations (whom he dubbed QuickStarters), and those who do not. He derived helpful suggestions for new faculty. Part of his advice, both in teaching and research, is to work in short, regular intervals. This strategy has been operationalized by others as 30-minute sessions, sometimes known as the Pomodoro technique (Cirillo, 2018). Boice's advice is not meant to be quite as draconian. Long stretches of uninterrupted time are a luxury in academia, he says, therefore we need to learn to work in these interstitial spaces between one meeting and the next. Building this habit at work will serve us well. Scheduling writing days and protecting our calendar as we best can will also serve us well, but we'll have fewer of the latter than of the former.

Invest in things that are grounding for you. Every job consists of several tasks, some more enjoyable and others less, and the professoriate is no exception. My colleague Este Jordan, an organizational developer, divides jobs into three areas. The top area is comprised of the tasks that build charge, are fun and interesting, may be challenging but are definitely nurturing. The middle area consists of transactional tasks that are not particularly enjoyable but also not particularly onerous. The bottom area collects all the tasks that drain us of our charge. The ideal job would live always in the top area but also does not exist. Moreover, the middle and bottom areas tend to fill up quickly, and since the work week is finite, they crowd out the top area. If we don't protect our top area, it will shrink. For instance, if working with students is grounding to you, but grading is draining, use the flexibility you have in designing your courses to maximize those interactions.

Create a mentor map. Knowing that we have a mentor in our corner is certainly grounding. Among other things, a good mentor can ensure we have access to crucial information and beneficial opportunities, and they can alert us to red flags they see in us. Research confirms that mentors are essential (Seltzer, 2015). The plural is intentional because experts advise to procure multiple mentors as no one, however knowledgeable, can provide everything we need. It might be wise to have a mentor for teaching and one for research. One mentor might be great with negotiating skills. Maybe the senior faculty member who churns out grant proposals at a record rate might not have much to say on work–life balance. Mentors inside the department have more specific information, but mentors on the outside (even outside the institution) can provide a detached perspective, especially during internal conflicts. The National Center for Faculty Development and Diversity has developed a resource to help new faculty map out the mentors they need. You can access it at www.ncfdd.org/ncfddmentormap.

Invest in professional development. This chakra is about what matters, and the literature emphasizes that one of the things that matter is improvement (Felten et al. 2016). Most campuses offer a wealth of professional development opportunities through their centers for teaching and learning, online learning units, office of research, office of diversity and inclusion, as well as at the college and department level. Some institutions even buy memberships to external organizations through which individual professors can avail themselves of webinars and other resources. Investigate what's available and take full advantage in an area you wish to make improvements.

Understand your fear. Fear can feel like an undifferentiated ball of anxiety, or a hydra with many heads, untamable. But when we pay attention, we can start isolating the specifics. Grace, a physiology professor at a community college whose story we will meet in the heart chakra, shares her approach:

> So many fears come up for me—fear that I am not working hard enough, that I am not good enough, that I am delusional, that I am expecting too much, that the status quo is all we're going to get and I shouldn't push for change. I am learning to listen to that fear and not go where it wants to take me, which is to disconnect. I am trying to learn to honor fear and see that it wants to protect me. What lessons can I learn from my fears?

WORKSHEET 1.1 ARTICULATE YOUR VALUES

Brainstorm a list of values that resonate with you. If you would like help getting started, Brené Brown has compiled a list of possible values, available at https://brenebrown.com/resources/dare-to-lead-list-of-values/.

How many values resonated with you? We are trying to get at your top values. Narrow your list down to three values, and certainly no more than five.

As a sieve to narrow your list down, delete any values that are aspirational (Lencioni, 2012). Maybe you are thinking, I should not always be such a perfectionist and value being more carefree instead. That's a good reflection, but "shoulds" are goals, not values. If that's your situation, right now it sounds like you value excellence more than being carefree. You can repeat this exercise in the future and see what changes.

Write about each of your values. How do these values speak to who you are? Why are they meaningful to you? When did they become important to you?
Value #1:

Value #2:

Value #3:

Copyright material from Michele DiPietro (2026), *The Faculty Guide to a Balanced and Harmonious Career*, Routledge

The true test of values is that they help you make hard decisions. What are some hard decisions you had to make? What values guided them?
Decision #1:

Decision #2:

Decision #3:

Does the list of values you created match with the list of values that guided important decisions you made? If not, reiterate this process until you arrive at a list you are happy with.

Can you stand in your values at work? Which ones? Why or why not?

The premise of this work is that living out your values at work will make you more fulfilled and more productive. What can you do to bring more of your values into your professional life?

References

Ambrose, S., Huston, T., & Norman, M. (2005) A qualitative method for assessing faculty satisfaction. *Research in Higher Education, 46*(7), 803–830.

American Association of Colleges and Universities (2000) Even before the pandemic, many faculty faced food insecurity, housing insecurity, or homelessness. *Liberal Education*, web exclusive, November 1. Accessed online at www.aacu.org/liberaleducation/articles/even-before-the-pandemic-many-faculty-faced-food-insecurity-housing-insecurity-or-homelessness

Baikie, K. A., & Wilhelm, K. (2005) Emotional and physical health benefits of expressive writing. *Advances in Psychiatric Treatment, 11*(5), 338–346.

Barshay, J. (2022) Proof points: 861 colleges and 9,499 campuses have closed down since 2004. *The Hechinger Report*, November 21. Accessed online at https://hechingerreport.org/proof-points-861-colleges-and-9499-campuses-have-closed-down-since-2004/

Berg, M., & Seeber, B. (2016). *The slow professor: Challenging the culture of speed in the academy*. University of Toronto Press.

Boice, R. (2000) *Advice for new faculty members: Nihil nimus*. Allyn & Bacon.

Bronfenbrenner, U. (1979) *The ecology of human development: Experiments by nature and design*. Harvard University Press.

Cable, D., & DeRue, D. (2002). The convergent and discriminant validity of subjective fit perceptions. *The Journal of Applied Psychology, 87*, 875–84.

Cameron, J. (2016) *The artist's way: A spiritual path to higher creativity* (25th anniversary edition). TarcherPerigee.

Centers for Disease Control and Prevention (2023) Benefits of physical activity. Accessible online at www.cdc.gov/physical-activity-basics/benefits/

Cirillo, F. (2018) *The pomodoro technique: The acclaimed time-management system that has transformed how we work*. Currency.

Clark, C. M., Olender, L., Kenski, D., & Cardoni, C. (2013) Exploring and addressing faculty-to-faculty incivility: A national perspective and literature review. *Journal of Nursing Education, 52*(4), 211–218.

Collins, J. (2001) *Good to great: Why some companies make the leap and others don't*. HarperBusiness.

DiPietro, M. (2018) The chakra system as a framework for holistic educational development. *To Improve the Academy, 37(1),* 88–99.

Duhigg, C. (2014) *The power of habit: Why we do what we do in life and business*. Random House.

Erikson, E., & Erikson, J. (1998) *The life cycle completed*. W.W. Norton & Company.

Felten, P., Gardner, J., Schroeder, C., Lambert, L., & Barefoot, B. (2016) *The undergraduate experience: Focusing institutions on what matters most*. Jossey-Bass.

Flaherty, C. (2020) Faculty pandemic stress is now chronic. *Inside Higher Ed*, 19 November. Available online at www.insidehighered.com/news/2020/11/19/faculty-pandemic-stress-now-chronic.

Fledderus, M., Bohlmeijer, E., Fox, J., Schreurs, K., & Philip Spinhoven, P. (2013) The role of psychological flexibility in a self-help acceptance and commitment therapy intervention for psychological distress in a randomized controlled trial. *Behaviour Research and Therapy, 51*, 142–151.

Foucault, M. (1977). *Discipline and punish: The birth of the prison*. Pantheon Books.

Google Dictionary Box (n.d.). Burnout. Retrieved March 6, 2025 from www.google.com/search?q=burnout+definition

Goyal, M., Singh, S., Sibinga, E. M., Gould, N. F., Rowland-Seymour, A., Sharma, R., Berger, Z., Sleicher, D., Maron, D. D., Shihab, H. M., Ranasinghe, P. D., Linn, S., Saha, S., Bass, E. B., & Haythornthwaite, J. A. (2014). Meditation programs for psychological stress and well-being: A systematic review and meta-analysis. *JAMA Internal Medicine, 174*(3), 357–368.

Holt-Lunstad, J. (2022) Social connection as a public health issue: The evidence and a systematic framework for prioritizing the "social" in social determinants of health. *Annual Review of Public Health, 43(1),* 29.1–29.21.

Jaschik, S., & Lederman, D. (2022) 2022 Survey of college and university chief academic officers. *Inside Higher Ed*. Available online at www.insidehighered.com/sites/default/files/media/2022-IHE-Provost-Survey.pdf

Keniger, L., Gaston, K., Irvine, K., Fuller, R. (2013) What are the benefits of interacting with nature? *International Journal of Environmental Research and Public Health, 10(3),* 913–935.

Lencioni, P. (2012) *The advantage: Why organizational health trumps everything else in business.* Wiley.

Maslach, C., Schaufeli, W., & Leiter, P. (2001) Job burnout. *Annual Review of Psychology, 52,* 397–422.

Medic, G., Wille, M., & Hemels, M. E. (2017). Short- and long-term health consequences of sleep disruption. *Nature and Science of Sleep, 9,* 151–161.

Myers, M., & Id-Deen, L. (2023) I need you to survive: Black women resisting white supremacy culture for faculty and student well-being. *Student Success, 14(3),* 53–64.

O'Mara, S. (2020) *In praise of walking: A new scientific exploration.* W. W. Norton & Company.

Padilla, M., & Thompson, J. (2016) Burning out faculty at doctoral research universities. *Stress and Health, 32,* 551–558.

Pang, A. S. (2016) *Rest: Why you get more done when you work less.* Basic Books.

Plouffe, R. A., Ein, N., Liu, J. J. W., St. Cyr, K., Baker, C., Nazarov, A., & Don Richardson, J. (2023). Feeling safe at work: Development and validation of the Psychological Safety Inventory. *International Journal of Selection and Assessment, 31(3),* 443–455.

Pope-Ruark, R. (2022) *Unraveling faculty burnout: Pathways to reckoning and renewal.* Johns Hopkins University Press.

Pressman, S., Matthews, K., Cohen, S., Martire, L., Scheier, M., Baum, A., & Schulz, R. (2009) Association of enjoyable leisure activities with psychological and physical well-being. *Psychosomatic Medicine 71(7),* 725–732.

Sagiv, L., & Schwartz, S. (2000) Value priorities and subjective well-being: Direct relations and congruity effects. *European Journal of Social Psychology, 30,* 177–198.

Schoen, M. (2013) *Your survival instinct is killing you: Retrain your brain to conquer fear and build resilience.* Plume.

Seltzer, Rena. (2015). *The coach's guide for women professors who want a successful career and a well-balanced life.* Stylus.

Sorcinelli, M. D., Austin, A., Eddy, P., & Beach, A. (2005) *Creating the future of faculty development: Learning from the past, understanding the present.* Jossey-Bass.

Tatum, B. D. (2017) *Why are all the Black kids sitting together in the cafeteria? And other conversations about race.* Basic Books.

Twale, D. J., & De Luca, B. M. (2008). *Faculty incivility: The rise of the academic bully culture and what to do about it*. John Wiley & Sons, Inc.

Veage, S., Ciarrochi, J., Deane, F., Andresen, R., Oades, L., & Crowe, T. (2014) Value congruence, importance and success and in the workplace: Links with well-being and burnout amongst mental health practitioners. *Journal of Contextual Behavioral Science*, 3(4), 258–264.

Wersebe, H., Lieb, R., Meyer, A. Hoyer, J., Wittchen, H., & Gloster, A. (2017) Changes of valued behaviors and functioning during an acceptance and commitment therapy intervention. *Journal of Contextual Behavioral Science,* 6(1), 63–70.

Wheeler, D. (2024) Supporting faculty morale. *The Chronicle of Higher Education*. Retreived from https://connect.chronicle.com/rs/931-EKA-218/images/TrendsSnapshot_Morale_MainAsset.pdf

Wickwire, E. (2021) Toward a positive psychology of sleep. In V. Cacho and E. Lum (Eds.), *Integrative sleep medicine* (pp. 195–210). Oxford University Press.

Willet, W., & Stampfer, M. (2013) Current evidence on healthy eating. *Annual Review of Public Health, 34,* 77–95.

Wilson, R. (2012, June 3) Why are associate professors so unhappy? *The Chronicle of Higher Education*. Retrieved from http://chronicle.com/article/article-content/132071/

Woodyard C. (2011) Exploring the therapeutic effects of yoga and its ability to increase quality of life. *International Journal of Yoga, 4*(2), 49–54.

World Health Organization (2019) QD85 Burnout. In *International statistical classification of diseases and related health problems* (11th ed.). Accessed online at https://icd.who.int/browse/2025-01/mms/en#129180281

2
HOW DO WE NURTURE OUR PASSIONS?

The desire chakra

Pulling the trigger

I was a first-generation college student, which means nobody in my family had any experience in navigating academia. When I was in high school, I wanted to be an English teacher, so I was studying English and was considering a minor in education that would have allowed me to teach at high school. It was my education department mentor who recognized my potential and convinced me to get a PhD. My study in graduate school went well. I was at a very good university, had some fellowships, but when I graduated the job market was tough, so I rolled the dice on a one-year renewable contract in Wisconsin. I gambled that my extroverted nature and hard work would make me stand out. And it did. The one-year job turned into a tenure-track one. Tenure-track turned into tenure. It was a ten-year process, but I did it. Pretty great, right? I loved the students I taught there. Many of them were first-generation students, like me, so I resonated with them and felt good about contributing to their growth. But it felt sometimes like my personal life was on hold.

I was fortunate to take a sabbatical in Southern California, and it was an epiphany. It convinced me that I needed to be there—that I owed it to myself to be there. Mary Oliver has a poem, "Invitation," which ends with a line she quotes from Rilke: "you must change your life." So that's what I did. I tried negotiating with my university if they would let me work a more flexible schedule to allow me to divide my time, but they would not go for that. I needed to buy myself time. I negotiated a one-year leave to try the California life. No salary, but at least I had benefits. I only had a few months to figure it out. I knew I had to live in Los Angeles, but how? The year ended, and it

DOI: 10.4324/9781003487371-3

was time to come back to cold Wisconsin. I tried one last effort at negotiating that bifurcated life, but the provost shut down every suggestion I made, every compromise. So I quit. I was 39 and single. I consulted with a lot of people before pulling the trigger: academics, friends, family. They all said move to California. You are competent and hardworking, you'll make it work, they encouraged. After all, I already did it once. I called my parents and said: "I feel like I am choosing sunshine and palm trees over seriousness, and I blame you for that." My dad told me to move to California, to follow my passion. I still felt I needed some kind of permission to do something so dramatic. But once I did it, it was liberating. The provost was shocked. She thought I wouldn't have the courage to quit because who gives up tenure? And yeah, I had so much invested in that place, but it also felt like I was trapped in a bad marriage, and I needed a divorce.

So here I am in California, running out of money, so I turned to adjuncting. At my new institution, somebody in the provost's office assured me this place recognizes loyalty. If you're good to it, it will be good to you, they said. So I tried to be good for them. I networked with several chairs to secure courses. I was teaching in four different departments at one time. Again, the adjuncting turned to a one-year contract, then to a three-year one. Eventually I was fully promoted on the teaching track. It took four years for my living situation to stabilize, and seven years to make a good living. Looking back, Wisconsin wasn't a bad place, but it wasn't a good fit for me. I adapted to it, but why adapt to a situation where you don't thrive? I no longer contort myself to a kind of forced happiness. Life is too short to not follow your passion.

—Lachlan, White gay man teaching professor of English (non-tenure track) at a private research university in California

Granted permission

In grad school I did an interdisciplinary program with a heavy quantitative emphasis. I remember I went to a seminar where the presenter described a new methodology that really fascinated me. It was powerful in terms of what it could allow one to say about an intervention, but it was also very intuitive in how it worked and in its interpretation. I was sold on it immediately and told my advisor. He suggested I do a project using that methodology and write it up in a paper, so I went and looked in the archive for data sets. My advisor pointed out that all the data sets I picked had to do with domestic violence on women. I had not noticed my own interest until he remarked on it. He gave me a paper to read and a challenge. See if you can do better than this analysis, he said. So off I went. Through that project, I realized that I could apply sophisticated methodologies and improve the state of the art on a topic that was absolutely compelling to me. My advisor noticed in me what I could not see for myself. He basically granted me permission to own this professional desire, this passion to investigate and unravel domestic/intimate partner violence.

This topic had a gravitational pull. It captured me in its orbit. In fact, it drove the early part of my career. And I was driven! I myself grew up in violence. I would read these accounts of men beating women, and I would get so mad. I couldn't stop each and every one of them, but I could at least research the topic and use the data to derive interventions, policy, anything. Eventually I had to stop because all this violence became a trigger for me. I ended up being repulsed by the topic. Also, all the emotions that arose in me meant that I could not be objective, and that is bad for research. So I pivoted to other topics, but I am proud of the work I did in this area. And even if I have moved on, I draw an important lesson from this experience. It changed my focus from external to internal. It invited me to pay attention to what I was feeling, what I was passionate about, and not to what others might think I should be doing. So even when I pivoted, I chose another topic that I am also passionate about. I tell this story to my graduate students because they come in wanting to please professors, and instead I want them to flex the muscle of paying attention to their own interests.

—Olivia, White female professor of sociology at a large state research institution in the Midwest

What do you think you're doing?

There are moments by which we measure the rest of our life. While in graduate school for my master's, I was a research assistant for a wonderful professor. I loved research, but I was also interested in teaching and always asked him lots of questions about it. So when he was making plans to travel to a conference, he asked me to cover two of his classes. He didn't want me to go in cold, so he asked me to come observe his class to get a sense of his method. Then we would co-teach one class together, and finally he would let me lead those two classes. He said he would solicit feedback from the students as well. It was a rigorous and intimidating process, but I welcomed the opportunity.

When I watched him teach his class, which was on public speaking, I was struck by the way he gave feedback to the student speeches. Of course we need honest feedback to improve, but it felt a bit harsh. I saw the hurt on some student faces, just a little bit. I could not see myself doing it that way. It was not my style. So when we co-taught, my strategy was to play good cop to his bad cop. I would temper and soften his feedback. And when I got to teach by myself, I leaned into my honest but encouraging style of feedback. I could tell the students loved it. More importantly, I loved it. I remember I was walking to the subway after class, and it felt like my feet were not touching the ground. I knew right then that this is what I was meant to do for the rest of my life.

When my professor came back from the conference and looked at the student feedback, he told me, in his very direct way, "You are a natural. You must teach, and you must go for your PhD." What a convergence to see my passion mirrored back to me by both my students and my professor! So I applied to some programs and got in to the one where the top name in my field was. They gave me a fellowship, plus an additional stipend if I opted to teach a class, an amazing deal. We would have to move to Michigan, which would not be a problem because my husband's corporate job could let him transfer—except at the last minute they sent him to Indiana. Now I had a difficult dilemma on my hands. I wanted to follow my passion, but didn't I have a duty to my husband? My parents certainly thought so, and made it clear I should go with him to be a wife and start a family.

I went to Michigan for my PhD. It wasn't easy, with the distance and the guilt, but I overloaded my schedule so I could finish my coursework sooner and reunite with my husband a year earlier. And I got to have the top guy in my field as my advisor, and I got to teach. The memory of my feet not touching the ground sustained me through the hard moments.

Years later, I was at a conference, and the whole family had tagged along. By then I had a child and was visibly expecting another. All the big names in the field were there, including my PhD advisor. This was the first time I saw him after finishing my degree. I was expecting a joyful reunion. But when he saw me, he only had harsh words for me: "What do you think you are doing? You're having another baby? Are you crazy? Meanwhile, you haven't even written a book yet? Where's your research agenda? How dare you squander all the opportunities we gave you?" He berated me in front of my peers and my child. I responded, "This is what I feel I need to be doing," and I walked away. Guilt washed over me again. How is it possible that I should feel guilty when I chose to prioritize academics, and then guilty again when I chose to prioritize my family? This episode brought me clarity, though. I am sure of my choices. I got to do what I loved. And being a mom, too, made me feel like my feet don't touch the ground.

—Gail, White female professor of communication at multiple institutions (recently retired)

What is going on with these stories?

All three stories deal with desire. Lachlan is so fascinated by life on the West Coast that he does what many academics would consider unthinkable, give up a tenured position. He trades the security and certainty of that role for the risk and uncertainty of adjuncting, trusting that he will make it work. Olivia doesn't even realize what her passion is until her advisor points it out to her and gives her permission to follow it. At that point, that topic takes such hold that it drives her whole early career, until it burns out. Eventually the thing that attracted her so much starts to overwhelm and repulse her. The feelings of excitement and determination she got by delving into her topic give way to frustration and disgust. Olivia still draws a lesson from this arc and tries to inculcate in her students the idea that they don't need anybody's permission to follow their passions. Gail instantly recognizes the moment a life-defining passion takes hold within her. She knows to trust that feeling of her feet not touching the ground. But she is caught between competing passions, academic work and family, and has to make hard decisions that, at least initially, are tinged by a sense of guilt. It doesn't help that there are people in her orbit that cannot fathom why anybody would choose as she does. She feels the need to draw a strong boundary to protect her choices and her family, and she walks away from her former advisor. These stories raise several questions related to pursuing one's passions. What passions are we allowed, obligated, encouraged, discouraged, or forbidden to pursue in academia? What happens when our passions deviate from the narrow path academia has traditionally charted as legitimate? How can we tend to the emotions that our passions engender in us so they don't consume us? How can we draw boundaries to protect our passions, reserve pockets of time to pursue them, and not burn bridges in the process? These themes, and more, are all heralded by the second chakra, the desire chakra. In the next section, we will build chakra theory around it which we will then use to conceptualize the research around these topics and possible strategies.

What does chakra theory say?

In the first chakra, the focus for reflection was on unity. We go inward and drop deep into our foundation, our solidity, our roots, identities and values, the things that make us who we are. This stability and constancy are to be understood in context. The second chakra gives that context. It is situated in the pelvic bowl, by our sexual organs. Its name is Svādhiṣṭhāna, meaning the "dwelling place of the self," alternatively translated as "sweetness." This chakra is represented as a white lotus with six orange-red petals, but in the modern conceptualization it is simply associated with the color orange. Inside the circle of the lotus, we find a crescent moon, prefiguring some of the themes of this chakra, as well as its seed mantra, "*vam*" (वं). Inside the *bindu* (बिन्दु), the dot at the top of the seed sound, there are several deities. One of them is *Varuna* (वरुण), the god of rains and the ocean, riding a *Makara* (मकर), a mythical animal, half terrestrial and half aquatic, similar to a crocodile.

As the numerals imply, if the first chakra was about unity, the second chakra is about duality. After focusing on our inner world, we attune ourselves with the outer world, and we see a universe in flux, where the only constant is change. We see things that are not us, that are different from us. The second chakra brings difference and diversity. Working from these differences, we establish polarities, like hot-cold, darkness-light, masculine-feminine, and so on. In fact, the Ida and Pingala nadis, representing the dualities in the self and in the world, originate in this area, in the *kanda* (कन्द), an egg-shaped area between the first and the second chakra. The half-terrestrial/half-aquatic Makara lives in this chakra as an embodied polarity, containing both opposites. We too aim to rebalance polarities, especially after experiencing an excess. If we get too cold, we seek heat. Lachlan felt the stasis of being "on hold" for too many years in Minnesota, so he gravitated toward the movement and possibilities of California, eventually relocating there. In fact, the second chakra is about movement. Some of the things we see in the world attract us, so we move toward them. Others repel (or repulse) us, so we move away, as Olivia did. This is the pleasure principle in action. We are attracted by what gives us pleasure, and the second chakra is all about nurturing pleasure and cultivating the things that please us. Traditionally, this chakra presides over sexual pleasure (unsurprisingly, given its location in the pelvic area) as well as other kinds of pleasure, including professional passions. In the electric circuit analogy we started in the root chakra, the second chakra brings the spark, the electricity, the charge. It's the energy that courses through our body, getting the atoms shaking, moving, excited, getting us to even take the improbable risks one chances when completely captivated, including giving up tenure.

Fittingly, the element of this chakra is water, heralded by Varuna. Water is fluid and moves along the path of least resistance, guided by gravity. The crescent moon in the chakra also reminds us of water and movement, since the moon influences the tides. Emotions are also traditionally ascribed to the moon, and the pelvic chakra is all about emotions, whose full range Olivia traveled in pursuit of her research topic, from excitement to disgust. Academia has traditionally eschewed emotions in favor of reason, with the predictable result that many academics have blockages in this chakra. Those with a balanced second chakra exhibit emotional intelligence, nurturance of self and others, healthy boundaries, and passion. When this chakra is deficient, we might see lack of passion or excitement, disengagement, or boredom. Conversely, excess energy might present as reactivity and impulsivity in following one's professional desires, starting multiple projects but not following through, and a feeling of being overcommitted, as well as moodiness and poor professional boundaries. To prevent the pursuit of our passions to become all-consuming and pose problems in other areas (e.g., becoming so absorbed in our research as to neglect students in our teaching), one of the Yama is *Brahmacharya* (ब्रह्मचर्य), literally "behaviors consistent with Brahman," the highest universal principle. It is interpreted as moderation, or rejection of excess, originally related to sexual conduct but applicable to all passions.

In keeping with the theme of polarities, a healthy second chakra is able to both express emotions and harness them, so they don't take over. We can think of the first and second chakras working in tandem. If we have done our work diligently in the first chakra, we have built a solid container. Grounding ourselves in our identity includes feeling all our emotions but not being ruled by them. Emotions swirl in our pelvic bowl but don't spill out. Sometimes, our emotions and desires are too intense, and they scare us. Afraid of what will happen if they spill over, we repress them. Repressing parts of ourselves has consequences, however. In our need to be efficient and productive, we may reject the parts of ourselves that want to take it easy and have fun, and thus we may let our inner critic grow stronger until those parts of us become rejected selves. Carl Jung called those rejected selves the Shadow. We try to keep the shadow repressed and chained, the monster in the basement, but the shadow has a tendency to act out and sabotage our life and our work (Jung identified the Makara monster with the shadow). In Gail's story, the extreme reaction of the big shot professor berating her at the conference makes me imagine he was triggered by seeing Gail embrace a self he had actively rejected in favor of productivity and the quest to be the number one in his field.

How do we protect our passions and desires in this sometimes unforgiving academic world? We need to set up boundaries. A crucial boundary for academics is that of protecting their time so that they can advance the projects they are passionate about. Learning to say no is a crucial second chakra skill, not just to others making demands on our time, but to our inner critic as well. This is a surprisingly challenging endeavor for many, and it brings us to the demon of this chakra—guilt. We often feel guilty for wanting to protect our time, for being passionate about the things we love, for having or showing emotions, for choosing paths others disapprove of, like Gail did. Part of the work of this chakra is recovering emotions so that we can be more fully ourselves at work, with joy, excitement, surprise, as well as frustration, sadness, or dread. In fact, the right of this chakra is the right to feel. When we allow ourselves to feel our full range of emotions in our professional endeavors, we create greater possibilities for balance and fulfillment because we bring our emotional identity into alignment with other facets of ourselves.

Faculty insights: Desire and passion

What are faculty passionate about? All areas of faculty performance were mentioned in my sample. Predictably, teaching is the most mentioned passion. There is something inherently satisfying in educating the next generation, and, for many, teaching is what drew them to higher education. Thinking about the content, how to make it accessible to novices, and maybe even the pleasurable feeling of being the expert in the room were mentioned as satisfying payoffs, but by and large people take pleasure in teaching because of the students. As Valerie, a history faculty member at a private R1 in the mid-Atlantic, whose story will be featured in the next chakra, put it: "My desire is to have meaningful

> **BOX 2.1 DESIRE CHAKRA CHART**
>
> Sanskrit name: Svādhiṣṭhāna
> Meaning: Dwelling place of the self
> Element: Water
> Function: Desire
> Color: Orange
> Identity: Emotional
> Right: To feel
> Demon: Guilt

conversations with people. Teaching is how I meet that desire." For faculty like Valerie, it is all about the a-ha moments, the lightbulbs going off, watching students reach insights, passions, and purpose. It's about making a difference through relationships (more on relationships in the fourth chakra, the heart). It turns out that a "web of significant relationships" makes a difference not only for students (Felten & Lambert, 2020) but for faculty as well. It certainly gave some of the faculty I talked with a way to cope with the drudgery of other parts of the job, or with dehumanizing bureaucracy, or downright exclusionary or oppressive practices. Some of the faculty particularly enjoyed working with specific subpopulations of students, such as mentoring LGBTQ+ students or working with first-generation students.

Devlin, the analytics professor we met in the previous chapter, married his passion for teaching to other extracurricular passions:

> I realized some of the struggling students in my class could definitely understand the topic if I went slower and took extra time on each step, but of course there is never enough time in class. So I had the idea of making videos that students can watch, pause, rewind, etc. I made one per class, and I started my YouTube channel. I have a following beyond my institution, and now the students even make requests for what topics to cover next! The videos came in handy during the pandemic. It is only me teaching and no students are featured, so they are compliant with privacy laws in my state. Now I get comments on YouTube on how I saved somebody's life, or at least their midterm, with my video, where they could never understand the same topic from their professor.

From Devlin's story we start to see the power of the chakra approach. The simple principle it is based on is that of alignment. The more our actions create alignment along our chakras, the more meaningful they will be. In this case, Devlin is aligning his passion for teaching (desire chakra) with his values (ground chakra) of improving the human condition through math. As we add more chakras and continue to shape that alignment, our actions will be more and more fulfilling.

Research is another important faculty passion. Faculty in the humanities and the arts spoke of the joys of writing, giving shape to thoughts, problem-solving plot holes, making concepts and frameworks come together, harnessing ideas onto the page, making thoughts visible to others. It captures the spark of learning, of discovery, of continuing to grow and to push the boundaries of human knowledge. Petra, who we left in 1 dealing with her immigration struggles, illustrates:

> My science professor, on Day One, told us we would design an experiment. We got to define our own research question and then investigate it. I came alive! That was the defining moment for me. My project was about blood pressure. It was so much fun measuring it, but the more I measured it the more the results kept varying. Why does it vary so?!?!? I was fascinated. A lecture on variations would not have fascinated me. But we got to do biology the way biologists do biology! So now I structure my courses around undergraduate research and other high-impact practices. My happy place is designing experiential learning. When I see the innate engagement that comes from that, facilitating an amazing learning experience for the students, that's a joy for me.

Part of the reward of research is our autonomy. After all we get to shape our research agenda, what topics we will investigate, which questions we will ask of them, what methods we will use. Some faculty spoke about the joy of working on outside-the-box projects, or transdisciplinary research, especially when this research has ties to anti-racism or topics related to diversity, inclusion, and equity. Several faculty spoke about the importance of knowing their research has an impact as a big part of the pleasure they get from research. For instance, Clara, the part-time faculty member we met in the ground chapter, gives an example:

> I love the pursuit of knowledge but have a hard time with research for research's sake. I am always thinking about action-oriented research. What do we do with what we know? I also want to help the students to make the connection between research and actionable change in the world. I want them to ask: "What does this knowledge mean for me?"

Simon, a Black professor of public health, whose story we will encounter in full in the throat chakra, finds this focus on impact a challenge:

> At the beginning of my career, what drove me was writing interesting papers and networking with relevant people in my field at conferences. But now it's all

shifted to impact, and I don't mean the impact factor of the journals I publish in. I work on HIV! I was drawn to this work because I wanted to make a difference in society! But it's become, I could write four more papers, and who would read them? How many folks is this getting into treatment? It's not worthless, but it's not what interests me anymore. And yet this is what academia values. The effort to make it work in an academic setting is starting to feel like a big lift.

Unlike Devlin, and even Petra, who found alignment between their passions and their work, Simon is finding misalignment between what he values and is passionate about and what the university values, and that is a source of inner conflict.

Service and leadership can be rewarding passions as well. Many participants saw their service roles, official or informal, as a powerful platform to scale their impact and to effect broader and lasting change. Some saw their roles as catering to their love of collaborations across the university, regardless of the project at hand. For Saffron, a White female adjunct professor of English as a Second Language at a variety of institutions, including a for-profit art institute and a community college serving incarcerated students, service roles catered to her progressive improvement orientation:

> I have this deep desire to make things better, in everything I do. A goal in the back of my mind is that of improving processes for the school. If the school runs better, we benefit, and our students benefit. Unfortunately, some institutions are too rigid and lock people in their roles. A supervisor told me: "Saffron, you are an adjunct! You are not paid to have ideas." So I changed school, haha. I guess that's the upside of working part-time. You don't feel too tied to any one place. And the new place is all about welcoming new ideas and creativity!

A specific form of service and administration that some faculty mentioned is faculty/educational development. These are faculty who enjoyed mentoring other faculty and discovered, along the way, that most institutions have a teaching center or a center for professional development, with staff whose job description centers on the passions they steal time for on the side. They became affiliated with their center as mentors or fellows, and one even transitioned to faculty development work full-time.

As people move up into leadership positions, their tasks seat at a higher and broader level. But some faculty's passions cut across multiple levels, as Desiree, an academic activist anthropologist not on the tenure track at a research university in the mid-Atlantic, full professor and administrator, illustrates:

> I love leadership. I love thinking about big ideas and setting the strategic priorities for my lab. I love concerning myself with high-level matters. But

I also love being in the weeds. For instance, I love designing PowerPoint slides. Some of my colleagues offload these tasks to others, but not me. I find them fulfilling at a creative and aesthetic level.

Tim, a Black queer professor of law, who we will get to know in depth in the crown chakra, addresses an additional layer concerning passion:

> One thing I have worked on is to figure out what is *not* my desire. For instance, being an elected politician is not an unusual career for a law professor and, given my personal history, it was always a default, but I now know it is not my desire. It took a while to figure that out. Similarly, I do not wish to be a judge. I value my privacy and my ability to speak too much to withstand the public scrutiny. Also, I do not want to be a dean of a law school. Pruning those branches out allowed me to realize I want to be a scholar and a teacher, the best scholar and the best teacher I can be. I think I have a book in me. We'll see.

So yes, some things attract us, some repel us, and some pull us in opposite directions. Clara gives a great example:

> I was communicating with a full-time colleague about an issue, and I felt condescended by her at every turn. The exchange ended with her calling me kiddo, and I thought, wow, would you ever call anybody else kiddo? Beyond the blatant condescension, it's partly because of the way I choose to carry myself, more informal, more approachable. I do that to be more accessible to students. It bothers me that the strategies that make me effective with the students diminish me with the full-time faculty and make me lose standing and authoritativeness. I do want to be available, but I also want to be respected. Should I be that person, demanding to be called Doctor? But I don't want to be shipwrecked in the morass of the ego.

Clara is hardly unique in that experience. Research defines "warm" (nurturing, approachable) and "cool" (confident, competent) qualities laid across a continuum, with a trade-off between the two. In other words, they create a duality that is hard to reconcile. Gains in warmth are often offset by a decrease on the cool scale, which is exactly what is happening to Clara (Morris et al., 1996). Gender complicates things because it imposes expectations: women should fall on the warm side, and men on the cool side. Should somebody break the rule (as would happen if Clara started demanding to be called Doctor, or otherwise projecting other cool qualities), there are differential social penalties to pay. A man who pointedly demands respect might get away with it, but a woman who does the same will be considered stuck-up, or worse (even by other women, as Clara's experience demonstrates). The Catch-22s women find themselves trapped in are well documented in the scholarship.

Reconciling dualities can be a great source of pleasure and satisfaction. When we work our job to bring together passions from multiple areas of our life (another duality, the personal and the professional), the total satisfaction is greater than the sum of the parts. Dennis, a gay White male visiting lecturer of gender studies at a large university in the Great Lakes region, recounts such a moment:

> As a queer man, I have always been drawn to performance. I started doing professional drag in college, getting booked for shows, and I continued through grad school. I studied gender, and wrote my dissertation on divas as a cultural phenomenon. Fast forward to a recent class in a course on gender in pop culture, during a unit on the Disco era. I decided to get playful. We turned off the light and danced to Sylvester, and I did a split in the middle of class. That's when it clicked—this is what I am meant to do. It was an embodied experience, a perfectly valid pedagogical activity. The students loved it, and I had fun! I found a way to be less buttoned up, and also still comfortable that I have authority from my PhD.

It's not lost on me that, as a man, Dennis might have it easier than Clara, but I love contemplating the fact that, as a drag queen, Dennis is used to bridging dualities.

Faculty insights: Boundaries

Realizing our passions is a great step, and the next step is to protect them. As Damian, the psychology professor who came out during his job interview, explains:

> You have to say no to certain things so you can nurture your passions. As a White man, I have a certain amount of privilege, which allows me to set boundaries and say no, but I see colleagues without that privilege having a much harder time at that. It's not just. Academia always wants more, even after I've given my all. And when I say no, I'm not seen as a team player, but here's the thing. Nobody told me to go home when I was here 16 hours a day. If you don't set the boundaries for yourself, nobody will.

Damian is not wrong. It is very rare in the academy to be told to do less. We have to be the ones to say no. And for many of us, saying no is a struggle. Brené Brown notes that it is hard to set boundaries when you want to be liked (2017). So we say yes but then we resent the task and the asker. This is especially true when the people asking are those with decision power over our career. We need scripts to set boundaries that do not damage our professional relationships. Damian continues with his approach:

> So now I count. Service is 10% of my workload. That comes to 150 hours a year. I keep track of every faculty meeting I attend, every mandatory online training, all the hours spent working on my annual review, etc. And I've discovered I hit 150 hours by midsemester of the first semester of the year. This new frame of mind allows me to consider every additional hour I am asked to contribute as an *extra* hour. The question then becomes: "Do I want to give this extra hour to the university? Or do I want to do something else with it?" And if I don't want to, I go to my chair with my hours count and ask them: "What can I give up, if I am to take on this new thing?"

Brody, a White male assistant professor of management at a teaching university in the Southeast, offers the following advice:

> Even if you feel ambushed by a request, don't give a kneejerk answer. Say, "Let me think about it for a couple days." Then when you circle back around, at least you can say you took the time to think about it, and you can offer an explanation about why you can't do it. Be tactful, be polite. Being busy is not a great excuse, because we're all busy. Your busy-ness is not more important than other people's busy-ness.

Chakra right: To feel

Given that this chakra is about our emotional identity and how it relates us to the external world, it is no surprise that the right connected to the pleasure chakra is the right to feel. However, for centuries the dominant paradigm in the academy has been that of the Enlightenment and Positivism, which privileges one neutral, logical truth. The only route to the only truth, the paradigm posits, is reason, in the form of logical deduction or empirically supported inference. There is no need, let alone room, for other ways of knowing, such as emotions or introspection in this context. Indeed, one must eschew emotions to achieve the impartiality that is proper of the truth. Xander, who we left in the School of Medicine under the pressure of having to raise his salary and that of his graduate students, confirms:

> I have been explicitly told to not bring my emotions at work. They said, how can you be an objective scientist when you have emotions? While I don't agree with this assertion, there is a level at which this advice is helpful, because academia is the most brutal, dog-eat-dog place. It lives on telling

people they are not enough, and they haven't made it yet; and the goalpost is always moving further away, and if you allowed yourself to truly feel the weight of those judgements, it would be very psychologically damaging. You can only survive it if you have numbed yourself to those emotions.

The rude, smug comments of Reviewer #2, enabled by the disembodied peer-review process, are so commonplace that they have become a cliché. One wonders about the rejected selves Reviewer #2 is exorcizing with their cutting comments. But unfortunately, harsh comments happen in person too, witness Gail and Conrad's story. In fact, Conrad is now resolute: "I am no longer showing my feelings to my colleagues. I don't trust them with my feelings, and I will not give them another opportunity to hurt me." Conrad is echoing Charles Feltman's definition of trust: "Trust is choosing to risk making something you value vulnerable to another person's actions" (2024, p. 4). However, he is choosing to not make his feelings vulnerable. In *Daring Greatly* (2012), Brené Brown argues for vulnerability, in the workplace and everywhere else, as the path to an undivided life, but acknowledges that certain circumstances demand that we show up armored rather than vulnerable. All too often, academia demands that armor. This is true especially of minoritized faculty. Grace, the physiology professor we met in the ground chakra, explains: "The right to feel and the right to be are connected, because I can't be me without feeling my feelings. And in academia we often don't have the right to our feelings, especially the right to feel strong emotions like anger for women of color. I've seen firsthand how the world stands ready to ambush us at the first sign of emotionality."

The emotional labor necessary to suppress emotions in an environment that disparages them is astounding, and the toll it takes is deep. The upward path we are walking is a path of wholeness. To find harmony and meaning, we can't leave emotions behind, but we must bring them along, in service of our values, or goals, and our purpose. In other words, what we need is emotional intelligence—the ability to "monitor one's own and other emotions, to discriminate among them, and to use the information to guide one's thinking and actions" (Salovey & Mayer, 1990, p. 189). The pleasure chakra is inviting us to reconnect with our emotions and to build spaces where we feel safe expressing them. It is daring us to feel the pleasure of bringing our whole self to work.

Chakra demon: Guilt

As we get more in touch with our wants and our passions in the pleasure chakra, another current arises. It's that inner voice that tells us that we are wrong to desire what we desire. Maybe the voice goes on to say that wanting things for ourselves is selfish. And it is especially selfish to say "no" to expectations others have placed on us in order to make room for what we want. This is guilt, the demon of the second chakra. Although this is a common human experience, it is especially insidious for academics. We live in a profession built on bottomless devotion, to our students and to our research. There is an old joke about an academic at a costume party, who gets asked: "And what are you supposed to be?" The answer, of course, is: "Writing." The joke resonates because the guilt is ubiquitous. Wendy, a professor of psychology we will profile in the heart chakra, explains:

> It starts from day one. The system is set up to encourage work to such an extent that when you are not doing work you are guilty. Even after tenure, the guilt does not magically evaporate. If anything, it's so instantiated as a way of working that it really takes quite a long time to unravel from.

It strikes me that Wendy uses "are guilty," and not "feel guilty." Under capitalism, if you are not working you feel guilty because you *are* guilty! Many professors feel guilty if they spend "too much time" with students because they should be working on their research. Conversely, Conrad, as a lecturer, feels guilty that he's not working on his teaching when he takes time to write or—heavens forbid!—rest. Deirdre, a White female visiting assistant at a state college in the mid-Atlantic, offers an important insight:

> We say education is a vocation, something some people are just meant to do, and that already evokes a lot of self-sacrifice. Education has such systemic historical challenges, but everybody is out there expecting you to have the magic wand to fix it all. I know in my brain there is only so much I can do, but in my heart I want to do it all and save everybody.

In his book *Becoming a Critically Reflective Teacher* (2017), award-winning educator Stephen Brookfield warned us against problematic assumptions we make about teaching, such as declaring it a vocation or a calling. Those words suggest that education is its own reward, and they are easily co-opted by a system bent on extracting maximum productivity to justify ever increasing expectations without corresponding gains in compensation. I suggest we operate on two levels. On one hand, yes, educators and researchers have a special role in society. We create knowledge, and we help grow the next generation, commendable endeavors. On the other hand, our job *is* also a job, and we get to go home and have a life outside of it. May our delving into the chakra of duality help us to hold on to both these perspectives!

The guilt I've just described, that no matter what we do we should be doing more, is common to many of us. In addition, certain groups experience additional layers of guilt. For instance, many women report feeling guilty for "wanting it all" (e.g., Ward & Wolf-Wendel 2012). Similarly, many faculty of color, often underrepresented at their institution, shoulder a disproportionate advising or mentoring load because students of color gravitate toward the few faculty who can understand their experiences, pitting their desire to help against their need to protect their time (e.g., Porter, 2007).

My interviews also revealed deeper kinds of guilt. Emmett, a lecturer of mathematics who recently left academia, shares one such kind:

> I always received glowing evaluations, but I felt guilty that I wasn't enough to be a great teacher. I was great at teaching, but being a teacher is more than teaching. For instance, one time a troubled student poured his heart out to me for three hours. I could see so many psychological issues that were impeding his progress. I wanted to help him through all that, but I recognize that I am not equipped for it. it's absolutely 100% not my job to be a therapist, but also it is kind of is my job to be there for him. It was too much to reconcile.

Some faculty, such as Gabby, the English professor at a small university, confessed to feeling guilty for having it too good compared to their colleagues:

> I joke I'm a unicorn and won the lottery. Some semesters I have less than thirty students total. But beyond the joke, I look around and see my colleagues crushed under mountains of student papers and faced with daunting standards for tenure and success. I think I have survivor's guilt.

Gabby's words were echoed by faculty who had lost valuable untenured colleagues during rounds of layoffs. Survivor's guilt is a real psychological phenomenon, and one of the symptoms of post-traumatic stress disorder. Grace describes yet another manifestation of guilt: "I feel guilty when I experience joy. When you have experienced a lot of trauma, which I have, the narrative of joy is foreign." If the basic academic guilt is about *not doing* enough, Emmett's version is about *not being* enough, whereas Gabby's version is about *having* too much. And—perhaps most heartbreakingly of all, and most tied to the chakra of emotions—Grace's guilt is about *feeling* joy. In the remainder of this chapter, we will explore strategies for experiencing pleasure at work, owning our emotions, and negotiating with the guilt.

Prompts for reflection

- What brings you pleasure in your professional life? In your teaching? In your research? In your service or leadership? How could you create more of those moments?
- Which emotions come up for you at work? Out of those which ones are you comfortable expressing?

- What dualities come up for you at work? What tensions do you see yourself caught in? What could happen if you shifted just a little toward one pole or the other?
- Where does the shadow come up for you at work? Can you see any of your rejected selves in the people around you that you disapprove of (e.g., colleagues who go home right at 5:00 p.m., colleagues who don't publish enough, or those who don't prioritize their teaching, those who "cross over to the dark side" into administration)?
- How is your right to feel supported in your context? How is it threatened? What can you do to grow the spaces where it is celebrated?
- When and where does guilt come up for you? Can you characterize it? What does it look like? What does it feel like? What are the outcomes of that guilt? Has this trickster taught you any lessons?
- What do you have trouble saying no to? What are some strategies you could try to remind yourself that saying no is an option and to do so in a way that doesn't burn bridges?

Tools, strategies, and possibilities

Because we are in the chakra of pleasure, some of the strategies in this chapter might feel silly. That is expected in a professional culture that resolves the pleasure/duty duality by expunging pleasure altogether. Try them anyway, at least some. At the very least, ponder what rejected selves are operating in the background deciding silliness is not becoming on you.

Take up a hobby. We have already explored in the first chakra the grounding benefits of hobbies. The beauty of a systematic approach is that many strategies act on several levels. From the perspective of the second chakra, embedding a pleasurable activity in our schedule will ensure that this chakra keeps expressing harmoniously, especially when work is not supporting our pleasure and passions. While you will probably get better at your hobby over time, you do not have to excel at your chosen activity to reap the benefits.

Dance. The second chakra is also the chakra of movement, therefore dancing will evoke the kinesthetic dimension as well. If your clubbing days are long past, consider salsa lessons, or line dancing. Throw caution to the wind and join the Electric Slide instead of watching it from the sidelines at the next wedding. Dance with your child, or simply shake your groove thing in the living room by yourself when nobody's watching. It doesn't cost money, and it's fun!

Treat yourself. One of the ways in which we make a habit of denying ourselves pleasure is by not spending money on us. I know it is much easier for me to justify spending money on my loved ones than on myself. I am not advocating loading up the credit card with extravagant expenditures, but I am offering that procuring ourselves pleasure (a massage, a cute gadget) is a valid and beneficial way to spend money, compatible with our budget.

Go on an artist date. We have already mentioned Julia Cameron's morning pages in the strategies from the previous chapter. The other strategy she recommends in *The Artist's Way* (2016) is to take your inner artist out on a date every week. Our inner artist thrives on pleasure and novelty. An artist date could be a visit to the new exhibit at the museum, but it could also be a trip to the fabric store to experience the tactile sensations of various kinds of textiles. The only requirement is that it is just for you. If you bring your children along, that is parent time, not artist time. If you are streaming the latest concert of your favorite band on your television while you are also working on your laptop, that is work time, not artist time.

Bring joy into your teaching. Most of us got into higher education because we loved teaching. It is entirely possible that the bureaucratic aspects of it have dampened its pleasurable aspects, but we can always work to bring back the pleasure. In *The Joy of Teaching* (2005), award-winning educator Peter Filene suggests that the joy comes from focusing on the relational aspects of teaching, seeing it as a conversation with the students rather than a transactional exchange of facts. His book can provide lots of helpful strategies. The next strategies also provide strategies in that same direction based on what some of the faculty I talked with mentioned.

Emphasize connected knowing. Feminist scholars have differentiated between "separate" and "connected" knowing (Belenky et al., 1997). Separate knowing focuses on isolating issues, dissecting and atomizing, translating them into mathematical problems and solving for the optimal solution, often decontextualized and, hopefully, universal. Connected knowing, on the other hand, continually interrogates the issues, asking how they relate to the learner, how they relate to other issues, and how the proposed solutions impact the communities involved. It posits that topics cannot be fully understood without casting them in a broader context, social, cultural, economic, scientific, and so on. Both modes are clearly necessary, but the traditional curriculum has privileged separate knowing. Approaching your teaching from a connected perspective can engage students in new ways and reenergize your teaching. Clara's questions—"What do we do with what we know?" and "What does this knowledge mean for me?"—clearly indicate a connected approach, and the students resonate with it.

Employ experiential learning pedagogies. Petra said experiential learning is her happy place. Not only did it hook her on biology, but she also sees how her students respond to hands-on activities where they discover answers for themselves. Whether we are talking about undergraduate research, internships, study abroad, or service learning, all of these fall in the category of High-Impact Practices (Kuh, 2008). These pedagogies have been documented to produce higher learning and performance gains than traditional lectures, especially for traditionally underserved groups of students. Changing your course to incorporate any of these pedagogies will take effort up front, but it will pay dividends in student success and your own engagement.

Use authentic assessments. Authentic assessments are tasks that ask students to use the knowledge and skills they learned in the ways that professionals in the field use them (Wiggins & McThighe, 2005). These assignments can push the students in ways that traditional assessments, such as multiple-choice tests, usually do not. They can also reduce cheating as they do not focus on a single correct answer and especially if they make use of current events not widely analyzed. Because dealing with academic integrity issues is one of the things that saps pleasure away from teaching, authentic assessments can bring pleasure back, all the more so when students engage with the content at a deeper level.

Build pleasure into your research. Most of us value our scholarship, but we might not enjoy all aspects of it equally. If we break down the tasks involved in our research or creative activity and divide them into pleasurable and non-pleasurable, two strategies arise. The first strategy, when possible, is to take on projects that emphasize more of the pleasurable aspects (e.g., lab work, interdisciplinary collaborations, and mentoring graduate students) and hinge less on the not-so-pleasurable ones. For instance, I do not like dealing with the Institutional Review Board (IRB), so I often choose projects that don't involve research with human subjects. If the less pleasurable aspects are unavoidable, and this is the second strategy, work on them. For instance, many people enjoy their research projects, but dread writing the papers for dissemination. In her book *Writing with Pleasure* (2023), Helen Sword shares a treasure trove of ideas to make professional writing pleasurable. The same is true about many other aspects of research. Many institutions offer professional development workshops about several aspects of the research process, which can demystify them and make them less dreaded.

Build pleasure into your service. People don't generally go into academia to do service, and yet the university would grind to a halt without the work done in committees and task forces. Ernest, the professor of history who learned to feel connected to himself through his sacraments, has an interesting perspective on committee work:

The advice we give and the advice we want to give are sometimes in conflict. We advise younger professionals to do as little service as possible because it doesn't lead to publications. However, from a more holistic perspective, the good advice sounds a lot like service. We advise early career faculty to get to know people outside the department, because they'll feel more integrated into the institution and less siloed. Well, that's serving on university-wide committees. You have to weigh the holistic benefits against the professional drawbacks.

Not all committee work is pleasurable to all people, of course, so our options are to slot ourselves into the activities we find more pleasurable and to minimize the time spent on the others.

Map the terrain of your professional desires. There is a whole landscape surrounding your desires. Study it. Where do your professional desires sit? In teaching, research, service? Do they overlap? What resources (time, authorizations, money, colleagues) does pursuing them require? Where is the synergy with institutional priorities? What support do you have in cultivating them? What challenges do they present? Where are the reasonable attack points?

Embed your passions in your annual review. Faculty evaluation processes usually involve both an accounting of the previous year's activity and a goal-setting process for the next year. With your chair's approval, set your goals according to your passions. That way, you will have to work on them and be accountable for them in a year's time. This will require you to frame your passions in terms that are legible to your chair and the university as advancing their priorities, which is a good practice. The fifth chakra will touch on negotiation techniques, which can be helpful to bridge the gap for your chair.

Set productivity expectations for yourself. Beyond the agreements you make with the department during the annual review process, set expectations. Angel, a White gay professor of English and administrator at a community college in the Northeast, shares his thoughts:

> The guilt definitely is there, when I think that other people are working harder than I am, especially people above me. They are working nights and weekends, so I feel I should too. I had to learn to define what I value as my productivity, independently from how much others work. My strategy was to understand the acceptable level of productivity and do a little more than that. After that threshold, nobody can really complain about how you use your time.

Save time for outside-the-box-tasks. Some faculty shared they reserve a chunk of time, usually on Fridays, for fun tasks. That might involve informal connections with colleagues, going to department colloquia or university lecture series, ideating potential collaborations, and so on. Attending to the social dimension is important for our well-being, as we will see in the heart chakra, and being seen supporting departmental and university activities has a strategic value as well.

Learn to prioritize and contain tasks. Felix, a White straight non-religious associate professor of philosophy at a R1 university in the South, is blunt:

> There are things that need to be done well, and things that just need to be done. Know the difference. Research needs to be done well, lots of committees and reports only need to be done. That's not why I'm here. So my goal is to get those done as fast as possible in a way that is still competent. Save time by not bothering to try to make perfect the stuff that only needs to be done.

Felix is referencing a special case of the Pareto principle, also known as the 80–20 rule. This principle states that 80% of the outcome is determined by 20% of the effort. Often, that is enough, and we can stop there without appreciable repercussions. The implied corollary is that to achieve the last 20% it will take much longer than what it took to get to 80%. Learning to stop when things are good enough is a great way to curb our perfectionist tendencies as well as a great time management strategy.

Carly, the professor of communication we encountered in the ground chakra, adds a practical strategy:

> To contain the non-essential tasks, add a tripwire. Give it a certain number of hours and get an idea of the pace you need. When you get close to the allocated hours it is time to wrap it up. Declare it good enough and move on to things you really want to do.

It will be important to be on the same page as your unit's leadership about which tasks you can save time on or say no to altogether. Sit down with the chair to discuss how to protect your time.

Prioritize passion and purpose. Justin, a philosopher of education who transitioned into administration and taught part-time, offers this advice: "Do the passions first, squeeze the responsibilities in later. I am passionate about anti-racist work, and I know I need to schedule that in first, before my calendar gets full with other things." Justin is referencing Steven Covey's big rock parable (2004). Basically, if you have a vase and you fill it with gravel and sand, you will never be able to put the big rocks in. Instead, start from the big rocks, then the pebbles and the sand will adjust themselves in the interstitial spaces between the rocks.

Start from your values. Your values, which we clarified in the ground chakra, can act like a sieve, as Valerie explains:

> My decision point is: the students get my time, the university does not get my time. On top of that, my child comes first (and I come last, LOL). I have no interest in perpetuating the echo chamber of the institution. If I felt the committee or initiative could make a difference I would do it. But I believe most things at the institution are not worth my time. I don't ask myself, do I have the time? I ask, is this request worth my time?

Make yourself unreachable. Of course, a large part of our job involves being available to our students and our colleagues, but we are definitely allowed to designate some of that time as private, as Grace does:

> I try to protect my time before class. I think of it as grounding time where I am focusing on what is about to happen (teaching and learning) so I can be fully present with my students. Of course, It is hard for me to say I'm not available if somebody needs me right before class, but I arrange my schedule in a way where I am not placed in such a situation. I hide! I close the door and turn the phone off before class even for just five minutes.

Similarly, Angel notes: "If you do not check email on the weekends, people get the message that you do not check email on the weekends."

Learn to say no. A simple online search will surface several books just on the topic of saying no, an indication that many people find this challenging. My interviews brought up several techniques. Some sit with the chair, go over their workload, explain that they are at or over capacity for their service workload, and ask the chair what tasks can fall off their plate in order to take this new one on. Others hinge their answer on the word "however," pointing out how it's a great opportunity that will have an impact at the institution; however, they are not the person to do it right now, listing the reasons why not. Some say they appreciate being asked and the project deserves somebody who can give it the attention it deserves, which they cannot at the moment given how thinly stretched they are. Some suggest a person who would be great, being mindful of who would consider certain roles a career boost for their promotion case. As a last resort when they can't say "no," some will agree to serve on a committee but refuse to chair it, to avoid those extra responsibilities. Consider the possibility Devlin brings up: "A colleague told me, people will respect you more when you start to say no."

Keep track of your time. It is one thing to be asked to step in once because of an emergency, but if you feel chronically overworked, take a page from Damian's book and keep track of your time. Everything you would not have to do if you were not employed counts as time spent working. The next time you are asked to do something above and beyond, produce the spreadsheet and account for your time. Be aware that this strategy will not ingratiate you to your chair and dean. If you have aspirations of leadership in the department and you want to be seen as a team player, you will occasionally have to take on extra work.

Create a "No Committee." Eden, whom we met in the previous chapter emailing the president with resources after the anti-Asian hate crimes, has created a structure to support herself:

> I know myself. I have a hard time saying no. So I created a No Committee. I have three people on it, two are trusted colleagues and one is my partner, to keep me honest on the personal front, since he sees how much I work at home. So, every time somebody asks me to do something major, I take it to them. They review the ask, check if it is in line with my goals, my passions, and my values, and say no. Ha! Because even if an opportunity is completely aligned, I am still overworked! The committee says yes to one thing per year, on average. I also review the opportunities that come my colleagues' way, so it is reciprocal. We remind each other we created this group to support us in setting healthier boundaries. When I get back to the people who asked me, I can offer them all the reasons the No Committee brought up.

Choose discomfort over resentment. When we say yes to things only out of obligation and to avoid the discomfort of saying no, we often fall into the resentment trap later, when we are stuck doing tasks we dislike or do not have the bandwidth for, as Brené Brown (2020) points out. Many of us default to choosing deferred resentment over present discomfort unconsciously, without having pondered the implications of this unexamined position. But the pelvic chakra, the chakra of duality, is a great place to reflect on this polarity.

Learn to say no to your inner critic. It's hard to say no to colleagues, but sometimes it's harder to say no to ourselves. The inner critic is a part of us, but it can take on a theatrical, larger-than-life-tone, similar to Snape, or Regina George, or Iago. To hear them tell it, some of us do not even deserve basic human rights, like rest when we are tired. Get to know them. When do they rear their judgmental head? What do they usually criticize? What are their rhetorical moves? Come up with counters and practice them, ready to deploy them the next time the critic criticizes.

WORKSHEET 2.1 RECOVER YOUR EMOTIONS

Because academia is built privileging reason over emotions, allowing ourselves to reclaim the spectrum of emotions is part of reclaiming wholeness. As you make your way through this worksheet, think of all areas of your performance, teaching research, service. Think of people who elicit certain emotions as well as events (recurring or one-off).

What makes you feel euphoric and excited at work?

When have you felt awe-struck or inspired?

What makes you feel proud?

When do you feel content at work?

When do you feel, or have you felt, playful?

What make you feel hopeful and optimistic?

Copyright material from Michele DiPietro (2026), *The Faculty Guide to a Balanced and Harmonious Career*, Routledge

What makes you feel scared?
When do you feel helpless?
When do you feel inadequate?
When do you feel embarrassed or humiliated?
When do you feel frustrated or aggravated?
When have you felt contemptuous or disgusted?
When have you felt hurt?
When do you feel lonely or isolated?

When have you felt regretful?

What makes you feel neglected?

When have you felt disillusionment?

Review your answers. What patterns are you seeing? What information are these emotions conveying to you?

From your answer to the previous question, is the information you are gathering from your emotions pointing to any actions that would invite more of certain emotions or protect yourself from certain others?

References

Belenky, M., Clinchy, B., Goldberger, N., & Tarule, J. (1997) *Women's ways of knowing: The development of self, voice, and mind* (10th anniversary edition). Basic Books.

Brookfield, S. (2017) *Becoming a critically reflective teacher* (2nd ed.) Wiley.

Brown, B. (2012) *Daring greatly: How the courage to be vulnerable transforms the way we live, love, parent, and lead.* Avery.

Brown, B. (2017) *Rising strong: How the ability to reset transforms the way we live, love, parent, and lead.* Random House.

Brown, B. (2020) *The gifts of imperfection (10th Anniversary ed.)* Random House.

Cameron, J. (2016) *The artist's way: A spiritual path to higher creativity* (25th anniversary ed.). TarcherPerigee.

Covey, S. (2004) *The seven habits of highly effective people* (revised ed.). FranklinCovey.

Felten, P., & Lambert, L. (2020) *Relationship-rich education: How human connections drive success in college.* John Hopkins University Press.

Feltman, C. (2024) *The thin book of trust: An essential primer for building trust at work* (3rd ed.). Berrett-Koehler.

Filene, P. (2005) *The joy of teaching: A practical guide for new college instructors.* University of North Carolina Press.

Kuh, G. (2008) *High-impact educational practices: What they are, who has access to them, and why they matter.* American Association of Colleges and Universities.

Morris, T. L, Gorham, J., Cohen, S. H., & Huffman, D. (1996) Fashion in the classroom: Effects of attire on student perceptions of instructors in college classes. *Communication Education, 45,* 135–148.

Porter, S. (2007) A closer look at faculty service: What affects participation on committees? *The Journal of Higher Education, 78*(5), 523–541.

Salovey, P., & Mayer, J. (1990) Emotional intelligence. *Imagination, Cognition, and Personality, 9*(3), 185–211.

Sword, H. (2023) *Writing with pleasure.* Princeton University Press.

Ward, K., & Wolf-Wendel, L. (2012) *Academic motherhood: How faculty manage work and family.* Rutgers University Press.

Wiggins, G., & McTighe, J. (2005) *Understanding by design* (2nd ed.). Pearson.

3
HOW DO WE GROW OUR AGENCY?

The power chakra

An insane hero

During the second year on my tenure track, an opportunity came my way. One of my senior colleagues encouraged me to apply for an institute at the National Endowment for the Humanities. The National Endowment for the Humanities offers a variety of programs. Seminars are more research focused, but institutes are structured with more freedom with the outcomes. The goal could be a publication, but it could also be related to teaching. That suited me perfectly, given my goals and the mission of my institution. But institutes are a big investment because they are a month-long affair in the summer.

    I knew this would be a solid foundation in my career, but I had great challenges to navigate if I wanted to make it happen. I have three adult children, but at the time they were ten, five, and two years of age, respectively. So I had to figure out a plan for them as my ticket to the institute. The father of my children traveled for work, so he couldn't assist. It was up to me.

    I hatched this wild plan. I flew out in advance, found an apartment, and interviewed students at the local university to help me with childcare. The program for the institute was packed, but I read all the books and did all the work. Out of about 30 participants, I was the only person with young children, and I knew I would be. But I was determined. And the institute was defining, both professionally and personally.

    I had to do things differently compared to other participants, but that was nothing new. Having had children as a grad student and as a young professional made me conscious of having a limited amount of time and needing to be very efficient with it. I learned to make very specific goals because I never had the luxury of time that others have. Children demand all your attention the moment you turn it to them. On the upside, that made me less anxious. I can't worry all the time about whether my paper will be accepted or allow myself to descend in a perfectionistic spiral of endless revisions to it. But I was willing to take on the extra work to make the institute happen because I deemed it important for my children to see their mother doing serious intellectual work. It mattered to me that they saw I was doing something important. Everybody thought I was both insane and a hero.

—Bridget, cis White female professor of English at a regional state institution

The real impostor

I never imagined I'd be a history professor. I majored in French at a big, rural, ag-and-tech university. I yearned for something different but didn't know what, or how to find it. None of my friends went to college, and I had no idea how to pick one. I just went to the state school. This proved to be a terrible fit. Still searching, I studied abroad in France in my junior year. The program required history classes, nothing I would have chosen. Yet the more history I learned, the more France made sense. Although I couldn't put my finger on it then, I was beginning to understand that history–something I had earlier dreaded—was actually about the present, not just the dead past. This fascinated me. I didn't know what to do with my life, so I got certified to teach high school French. As graduation approached, I still hadn't had the college experience I had wanted. Curious about this new thing called history, I decided to go to grad school. I was so clueless. I ended up at a top grad program, being woefully unqualified. It was the only place I got in because the professor overseeing my declared field did not read applications! I was in way over my head. I took all incompletes my first year and dropped out. The vibrant social scene I was now a part of proved far more interesting. I had found what I'd been looking for, a progressive, engaged, liberal arts scene. I'd never experienced one, so I was like a fish out of water, delighted but also feeling very inadequate. I wanted to know what everyone was talking about—who Toni Morrison was, or what the New Yorker was. It was intoxicating, yet also bewildering.

After a year or so, I got curious again, and I began sitting in on a course in an entirely different area of history than what I had applied in. I worked in a group home for people with disabilities, and my shift ended mid-morning. I would leave work and slip into the back of the lecture hall, unenrolled and completely riveted. I never missed a class. It was an a-ha moment: this meant something to me, and I couldn't shake it off. At the end of the semester, I timidly approached the professor, who ended up becoming my graduate advisor and patient mentor— having far more faith in me at that point than I had in myself. I had to reapply, retake the GRE, everything. After all that, wouldn't you know it? I dropped out again, just before doctoral exams, thinking: what am I doing? I'm not PhD material. I still felt like the stepchild of the institution, the black sheep. While other students talked about the imposter syndrome, I felt no comfort, convinced I was the real impostor.

But I came back, again—as I said, I could not shake it. Quitting felt like confirming my inadequacy. I also liked the work. I just didn't believe in myself. Still, I plowed ahead, not because I expected to be a professor. I had to prove to myself that I could. My confidence gained, but I never thought I would pursue an academic job (who would hire me?!). Then, in a moment of procrastination while scribbling my dissertation, I perused some job postings. One announced a position at a liberal arts college out east. I don't know how to explain it. I looked at that listing and said to myself: "That's my job". So I applied. Turns out, my application got lost in the mail. They had my recommendation letters, however, which came separately, and they called, asking me to submit an application. What were the odds? Lo and behold, I got the job!

It was a teaching position, and I fell head over heels in love. I loved the students, the college, the work, everything. I didn't love living in a small town. Still, I was hesitant to try for another job, where tenure standards might require a book. This job did not, which felt reassuring. Certainly, I didn't have that in me. Then a job popped at a research institution in an affordable metropolitan area. I applied on a whim and amazingly got the job. After much crying, terror, and fear, I took it, worried about whether I could write a meaningful book. Heck, it took me three tries to write a dissertation! I applied for grants during my first year, and I won several, again much to my surprise. While I had been shedding the imposter along the way, these residential fellowships taught me there were respected scholars out there who appreciated my work. I also learned that the same respected scholars, who had seemed larger than life from a distance, where just ordinary people, struggling like me. When the book came out, the biggest surprise of all was that I liked it, felt proud even. I had finally gotten out of my own way, earning not only tenure, but a major book prize.

—Valerie, White bisexual female associate professor of history, multiple institutions

Misery loops

I'm a person who lives with depression and anxiety. I've been treated since I was 11 years old, and I'm still being treated right now. I think of myself as someone who's in recovery from depression, because it can always come back. But if I do certain things, it is less likely to come back. This is how, working with my therapist, I arrived at my "sacraments" [eating well, vigorous physical exercise, playing the banjo, keeping in touch with loved ones, and journaling, see Chapter 1]. Academics are not exempt from mental illness, but there is a stigma surrounding it, and we don't talk about it. Maybe it's because we work with our minds, so we are reticent to disclose their flaws. But in fact, academic departments can be misery loops. Faculty are mad at the dean, the dean is mad at the provost, and some programs are always on the verge of getting cut. Academia thrives on misery, and it can exacerbate problems for those already prone to mental health issues.

Well, one fateful day, my university experienced a death by suicide that rattled the whole community. What is going on here? How badly are we treating our people? My university is a research powerhouse, so the pressure is always on, but it shouldn't be fatal. They wanted to address this issue at all levels of the institution, so they created a large committee with multiple subcommittees. I served on it, and I co-chaired two of the subcommittees, doctoral mentoring and mental health.

Because of my role on the task force, I felt empowered to talk to students and colleagues about my own experience with mental illness. I started opening my classes every semester by disclosing my history with depression and therapy. I tell students that I am always happy to talk about my experience if it could help any of them. I don't gloss over the lows. I tell students there were times in my life when I was suicidal. In very practical ways, I owe my life to more than one colleague at the university. At times when I was severely depressed and suicidal, those who knew helped me stay alive. I was on a powerful medication, which I need to take to keep my depression in check and not spiral. But the medication could not be at my house because I would be tempted to overdose on it when I was feeling suicidal. So my colleagues stored it at their place and drove by my house every day to give me my daily dose.

I am grateful to be able to talk about these issues with the students. I am not trying to be anybody's therapist, but I want to highlight the omnipresence of stress and tell students that there are ways to cope. And over the years I've had a lot of students come talk to me after my speech. Often they want to know more, and they ask me to tell them about something I went through when I was their age, as a reality check on their experience. I recognize that it is a measure of privilege to be able to talk freely about these issues. My identities, my age, my tenure status all lower the stakes of these disclosures. But helping to break those misery loops is a whole new aspect of the impact I can have on the students.

—Ernest, White cis gay male associate professor of history at a private research institution

What's going on with these stories?

The one theme that threads through these otherwise disparate stories is that they all center on the participant's agency. For Bridget, a relatively straightforward professional development opportunity would become unattainable unless she figured out well in advance her childcare plan, and even then it presents a challenge. She faces this challenge head on with her strong will, breaking down her task and figuring out all the moving parts that need to click, and being willing to make sacrifices to navigate it. Valerie struggled mightily through graduate school because she did not believe in her own capabilities, and she felt like "the real impostor," in her own words. Even applying for a job generated terror and tears for her. Of course, the irony of the story is that not only is she perfectly capable, but her work also ends up garnering prestige and recognition. Ernest lives with depression, which can at times limit people's possibilities (we saw him contend with writer's block in Chapter 1). The particulars of his situation include the fact that our society doesn't like to discuss mental health. The stigma is real and so is the shame many who live with depression feel. His decision to share his story allows him reclaim his power and to even grow it by becoming a resource for his students who are also struggling.

These stories surface the issues related to building our own power and the questions that arise in that space. What is power, and where do we draw our own power from? What are some practical strategies in which we can use our power in service of our professional desire and in alignment with our values and our foundation? What is the role of our will in building our power? How do our emotions affect our power? What is the role of shame in this context and how can we avoid its paralyzing effect? Agency, will, and shame all pertain to the third chakra, the chakra of power. We will dive into chakra theory in the next section, then we will explore those themes more in depth with other faculty voices and with insights from the research, and, finally, we will introduce strategies to increase our power.

What does chakra theory say?

Our journey so far has involved growing our roots and deepening our foundation in the first chakra and discovering the world beyond us and its pleasures in the second chakra. As we travel to the third chakra, we move up into the belly. The third chakra is called Maṇipūra, translated alternatively as "city of jewels" or "lustrous gem." It resides in the solar plexus, just below the navel. This is where digestion takes place, the process of transforming matter (food) into energy for our body. Therefore, its main function is transformation, and indeed the three opening stories all involve some kind of transformation that generates more power in the protagonist's life. For our purposes, we can define power simply as the ability to act to get things done in the world.

The way we exercise our power is through our will. We are building a strong, trained will that can direct our energies toward achieving our passions and in service of our values. Our power manifests in making choices about how we allocate our time, what we say yes to and what we say no to, making plans,

How do we grow our agency? The power chakra 79

sticking to the plan when we would rather procrastinate, deferring gratification from immediate pleasures toward more fulfilling long-term goals, moving on to the next project when we sense our goal has been achieved and additional effort will not improve the outcome significantly. In our circuit analogy, after creating the system and building the charge in the previous chakras, the third chakra acts as the switches that decide which directions the electricity flows in, so it can turn on the lightbulb or the air-conditioning or the microwave.

Another way to look at the solar plexus chakra is that it represents our ego identity. The second chakra was all about our wants, which would represent the id, but in the third chakra we recognize we can't pursue all our passions indiscriminately at all costs. We recognize we live in a world where there will be consequences if we only act out of selfish motives. The will mediates our passions through a cost–benefit analysis—opportunity costs first, since we do not have the charge necessary to pursue all our desires, as well as social, and even legal, costs. When everything is in good working order, we mostly choose to purse what is valuable to us, what we can reasonably attain, and what will be supported by our context, as theories of motivation predict (Lovett et al., 2023). Occasionally, we might choose to change our context, as Lachlan did in the previous chapter.

It makes sense that this chakra is ruled by the element of fire, the transformative energy that burns matter into energy (heat). The concept of "fire in the belly," or *agni* (अग्नि), is a key concept of chakra-based nutrition and medicine, and agni is the root of English fire-related words such as ignite. Those with a weak agni might have digestive problems and feel sluggish and not experience enough power. Beyond the digestive process itself, people with an open and balanced third chakra will generally read as confident, warm, energetic, and able to take risks when appropriate but still being responsible and reliable. An excessive power chakra correlates with exaggerated competitiveness and ambition, arrogance, hyperactivity, stubbornness, and reckless. Conversely, if the power chakra is underdeveloped, it could result in people lacking initiative and confidence, being risk-averse, or overdefensive in the face of failure. The right of this chakra is the right to act, and its demon is shame, because shame prevents us from taking action. A special form of this shame-based inaction that affects academics in particular is impostor syndrome, as Valerie testifies.

A relevant concept here is that of *Tapas* (तपस्). Tapas means self-discipline, and it is one of the five *Niyama* (नियम) in yoga. We have already encounter some of the Yama, or restraints, the first limb of yoga, in the previous chakras. The Niyama, or observances, are the second limb of yoga, a set of parallel practices to the Yama. While the Yama are framed as negatives (e.g., non-violence, non-stealing), the Niyama are active practices, such as self-discipline (in order to train the will). In the ancient texts, these practices involved meditation and ascetic techniques. The root of this word, *tap* (तप्), means to burn, bringing in once again the idea of fire burning away our weaknesses through practice and discipline.

For visualization purposes, the solar plexus chakra is represented as a yellow lotus with ten petals. Inside the circle of the lotus is a red downward pointing triangle symbolizing fire, and inside the triangle is the seed mantra of this chakra, "*ram*" (रं). As with the other chakras, there are several deities inside of it, including, fittingly, *Vahni* (वह्नि), the god of fire, as well as *Rudra* (रुद्र). Some texts refer to Rudra as the "mightiest of the mighty," and our might is certainly what we are trying to awaken in this chakra. But one of the possible roots of this name is connected to the English word "rude," and indeed one of Rudra's moniker is "one who makes all beings cry at the time of cosmic dissolution." Out of all the gods in the power chakra, I am emphasizing this particular one because it connects to the dark side of power as a terrible force. When the third chakra's will is in service of the second chakra's anger, we see the destructive effects of our power. Whether that is a good thing depends on whether our angry will is in alignment with our values from the first chakra or not.

The first three chakras bundle together and are referred to as the lower chakras. An imperfect but effective mnemonic for this triad is Newton's second law, $F=ma$. Mass, the solidity of the first chakra, combines with acceleration, the movement from the second chakra, to create force, our power in the third chakra. As a group, these chakras map well onto what Maslow (1954) defined as the D-realm, characterized by deficit-driven needs. Rahul trying to survive in academia after his liver transplant, Honorine spending a month in bed just to recover from a taxing semester, Valerie dealing with her crippling self-doubt, are examples of people descending in the D-realm in those moments. In his book *Transcend* (2020), Scott Barry Kaufman introduces the metaphor of a sailboat. The D-realm is the hull of the boat. If it has holes, it will sink, so one needs to patch the holes to even begin to set sail. Indeed, a professional life ruled by the demons of the lower chakras, fear, guilt, and shame, functioning at a suboptimal level to the tune of "I'm not enough" is a life under deficit, where the very right to exist and have our needs met, the right of the first chakra, is threatened—let alone the right to act.

Faculty insights: Power

So where do faculty draw their power from? And what saps faculty of their power? These are complex questions that elicit a large set of responses. Some of them reveal a great deal of wisdom. Many of my respondents were quick to say that we can't hang our power on title, rank, or external recognition. And yet other answers, sometimes from the same person, reveal that we crave those recognitions, and we feel more powerful when we gain them, or, conversely, that we feel less powerful when we are not appreciated. Sasha, whom we met in

> **BOX 3.1 POWER CHAKRA CHART**
>
> Sanskrit name: Maṇipūra
> Meaning: Lustrous gem
> Element: Fire
> Function: Transformation
> Color: Yellow
> Identity: Ego
> Right: To Act
> Demon: Shame

the first chapter wrestling with campus carry laws and her decision to move to a different state, admits that there were other factors at play too:

> There was also an ego aspect to it. I rose through the ranks, from faculty to interim then permanent chair to associate dean to interim dean to dean. I questioned my internal promotions. Did I get them because I was well liked and part of a club, or did I truly deserve them? How valuable would I be outside of my institution? I have to say I was curious. So I took my curriculum vitae on the outside to people who didn't know me. In addition to removing myself from an unsafe situation, landing a good job was a nice pat on the back.

Sasha's confession is astute in its awareness. She correctly named the ego as the current at work. That's what our ego does; it works out its calculus to reassure itself. That's why the process of aligning the ego force with all the other forces is so important. The downward pointing triangle visually represents the process of drawing down the energy from the upper chakras as well, including, in Sasha's case, the consciousness (see Chapter 7) that she was worthy of a work environment where she didn't feel constantly unsafe. She looks back on her decision to leave as ultimately positive. By being aware that the ego is always at play, we can guard ourselves from decisions made solely as ego strokes that ultimately won't bring fulfillment into our lives.

Sasha offers us another insight about our power that we should keep in mind as we unpack the rest of this chakra:

> When I became department chair, I had a lot to learn. Look how important I am, I remember thinking. All these people report to me, and I can move them to accomplish so many things. But the department was quick to remind

me nobody moves them if they don't want to be moved. There were days when I went from feeling most powerful to least powerful in the span of 15 minutes.

Power, like all other chakra energies, ebbs and flows by nature. We don't need to be a department chair to have experienced the same thing. Faculty who have taught back-to-back sections of the same course, with identical content, know the disorienting experience of an inquisitive, engaged group of students that makes us feel on top of the world followed by a stony wall of silence in the next section that won't break no matter how hard we try.

Faculty were certainly aware of spaces where they could feel their power in action. The most common space cited was teaching. Respondents feel powerful when we can have an impact with their students and make a difference in our lives. Like with Ernest, the impact does not have to be related to our subject matter to count, and it could happen, and often does, out of the classroom, in mentoring situations. The power of mentoring extends beyond students, as faculty also report feeling powerful when they can make a difference with other faculty, either in a one-on-one peer mentoring situation or in broader faculty development projects.

Research is another space where faculty could readily see the effects of their power, in the knowledge generated, works of art created, theories applied to find solutions to social problems. But before even getting to the outcomes of their work, faculty feel their power in the scholarly process itself. Vivian, the English professor who narrowly escaped her student's wrath, explains: "Writing is the first thing that comes to mind. That's when I feel most powerful. I feel strong and I feel free! I believe it's because writing is part of being in conversation with others." Emmeline, a White female professor of psychology at a medical university in the South, adds:

> I feel powerful when I get something done. Sometimes I feel more powerful when I declare the project finished than when it comes out in print, because I can clear my plate and move on to the next one. I get a rush from clicking the submit button.

And finally, many faculty mentioned feeling powerful in their service roles, either while holding administrative appointments or while serving on university committees and task forces. The transformation achieved could be small but significant, or in some cases momentous, like in Bridget's case:

> While I was serving on the senate, we had a new president with a vision of teaching and of the university antithetical to mine. His vision was all about quantity, increasing numbers. He wanted the university to grow as big as it

could possibly get. His strategy involved leveraging our 800-seat auditorium and have classes taught in there. Classes of 800 students are unthinkable to me in our context.

The one thing we have going for us as a university is the ability to have personal relationships with our students and treat them as full persons and not just numbers. He would have dismantled this point of pride for us in a few years. I knew my views were shared by most of the faculty. So I allowed myself to be elected as the executive officer of the senate. We mounted a vote of no confidence against both president and provost. I was the face of that movement. It was incredibly stressful, but the source of my power was that I was speaking for my colleagues so I was a lot braver. We are a public university, so this had resonance far beyond our institution. The state officers ended up sanctioning him. He changed his behavior toward faculty afterwards.

Bridget's story, while confrontational, is situated within university structures, such as the faculty senate. But quite a few respondents said they feel powerful, or even most powerful, when organizing and advocating beyond those university structures, like Dennis, the lecturer of gender studies from the previous chapter:

The moment I felt most powerful was definitely in graduate school, when we went on strike. I remember that back then, when I would talk to faculty and the subject of change came up, there was a sense of despondency about the state of higher ed. The more they had progressed and entrenched themselves in the institution, the more their idealism hit reality. It's like hitting your head against a brick wall, higher ed is never going to change. But we forced change! We won the strike! Even though going on strike for two weeks was very scary, we made it happen. So in a small measure we got to see the university move in the direction we wanted to. The university had refused to put language that would protect tuition waivers connected to teaching assistantships, but eventually they relented. The graduate student union also won dependent coverage for health insurance. The word dependent had never been in the language. There are quite a few graduate students who are parents so this was very significant!

As satisfying as these victories are, this was an area that some faculty also cited as being the one where they felt the least powerful. Wendy, the professor of psychology who described her guilt in the previous chakra, speaks eloquently to this aspect:

I remember feeling ungrounded and burned out at mid-career. Lots of women at this stage experience the same, and we know this from national research but we also had lots of institutional data at my university to back this fact up.

> You see the limit of what you are allowed to do in academia. The system is not set up in your image. So we rolled up our sleeves. My colleagues and I organized and dedicated ourselves to activism. We have status at the university from tenure and rank, and the security that comes with them, so let's try to make changes! We poured lots of uncompensated energy into the institution. We were happy to do it, because we saw it as helping the women in the next generation, and ultimately the institution by moving it into a more equitable space that would allow it to attract and retain the best faculty. It was completely dispiriting to find out the institution was not interested in this change. That was the only way for me to read the roadblocks they mounted against us at every turn. The burnout I felt initially that moved me to embark on this work was nothing compared to the burnout I felt after years of unsuccessful efforts. My solution was to change institutions, with the opportunity to come in as a senior person who is valued and recruited rather than stay at my old university and keep bumping up against the same limitations.

Wendy's story reminds us that, while a big part of burnout is the sheer exhaustion that we discussed in the ground chakra, another crucial part is the loss of agency, which is of course part of our power. I am not suggesting that the institutional limitations that burn us out could simply be solved by focusing on our solar plexus chakra. Rather, we need to keep cultivating our power because the system is refractory to change, and this stubbornness drains many of us of our power. Jackson and Hardiman's model of multicultural organizational development (1994) explains this phenomenon. The model describes a continuum of stages from completely exclusionary and discriminatory organizations to organizations that have rethought their identities and practices to embrace all members equally. Contemporary higher education is in the intermediate stages. It wants to embrace and not exclude people, certainly a significant advance from its exclusionary past, but it is not yet willing to change all the practices necessary to do so. It expects all its members to function in the system as is, with minor changes around the edges. This of course creates the disempowering frustrations Wendy and others experienced. Some cited the lack of transparency at their institution. Some came up against the lip service paid to data-driven decisions and felt very frustrated when they couldn't sway leaders from decisions that merely reproduced the inequities of the system, despite bringing plenty of empirical evidence to the table. Several mentioned dehumanizing policies and processes at their institution.

Felix, the philosophy professor who prioritizes tasks according to how well they need to get done, brought up financial considerations that often feel taboo to mention in academia:

> As for least powerful, there have been moments years ago when I looked at my assistant professor salary, and weighed that against the credit card debt

I had amassed during my post-docs. I struggled to get out of that debt for years. And I would think, WTF am I doing this for? Why am I struggling?

Olivia, the sociology professor who started her career studying domestic violence against women, offers another disempowering context:

> When we had faculty meetings about who to hire I felt least powerful. Faculty were ruthless when they assessed candidates. I would read their application materials and go to their talks and meet with these candidates. Of course I had my favorites, but only very rarely did I think a candidate was completely unviable. But everybody else was very critical. I would leave those meetings thinking, thank God I'm already here because they would never hire me today! It made me feel small.

This story is an important reminder that we, as academics, are very skilled at the "doubting game," and we draw power from it, but sometimes we are disempowering others in the process. And the flip side of this lesson is that there is as much power to be gained and shared by playing the "believing game" (Elbow, 2009).

Tim, the law professor we met in the desire chakra, invokes a very powerful disempowering experience that should have no place in society, let alone at a university, but that continues to make news, that of "existing while Black":

> The time in my career where I felt least powerful was the beginning. I was 27 when I started. Some of my students were actually former classmates that had not graduated yet, so I worked very intentionally at performing and projecting a professorial aura. Because of administrative reasons, I officially started in March, so I was brand new when Spring break came. The university had closed the building to students for the break, but professors were allowed to be there. I went there to work and ran into this woman who was the deputy chief of operations for the building. She didn't recognize me and started questioning me. WHO ARE YOU WITH? I didn't know what to say back without sounding a smartass. So I simply said that I worked here, and she was like, YOU ARE NOT SUPPOSED TO BE HERE! The intersection of my race and age came together. I was not legible as someone belonging there. I went to my office and called an older Black female professor who was a mentor. She took care of it, and that person apologized profusely, but it left me shaken and upset because the interaction recapitulated countless similar experiences.

For all the work and messaging and dollars universities spend on "sense of belonging" campaigns, there are still many who too often receive the opposite message, of not actually belonging. Those experiences are profoundly disempowering, and this is not even counting the times they can have lethal consequences.

Against all these disempowering experiences that burn people out, how do faculty build back their agency? Many people mentioned that they build their own power through connections, and we will explore relationships and connections in the next chapter, dedicated to the heart chakra. For now, let's consider the insights of Alfred, a White gay male assistant professor of medicine on the clinical track at a large public research university in the Midwest: "I have power in part because other people believed in me and lifted me up. They brought me to a seat at the table so I try to do that for other people too." Paying it forward is indeed a way to exercise our power and to build more of it in ourselves and in others. When we find ourselves in a position to be able to benefit others, especially those from groups who have traditionally been barred from power and resources, and we do so (as mentors, as sponsors, or in other ways), we apply subtle shifts to the whole system, not just the people we help. And we benefit from strong multiplier effects, as Desiree, the anthropologist professor passionate about leadership and PowerPoint, illustrates:

> I'm at my most powerful building a team that does good work. It took me a while to feel like I was leading them effectively, but now that we are a well-oiled machine I feel I have all their power behind me. And we produce deliverables that are beautiful and effective.

Unpacking Desiree's statement, feeling part of something greater (a task related to the crown chakra, see Chapter 7) is a great booster of personal power, both in a psychological sense and a practical one. She is simply able to achieve more. And achievements were indeed mentioned as a source of feeling one's own agency, often with the caveat of being careful to disentangle one's success from one's identity. Some mentioned challenges as a mighty motivator—acting with defiance in the face of challenges, feeling most energized backed against the wall with nothing left to lose. Others mentioned their superpower, like Olivia:

> When I am in meetings, the topic sometimes makes my heart start racing because I get this clarity about what's happening in the room. Usually there will be a lot of mixed signals, people saying different things, getting hung up on side issues. But often, when I weigh in and describe what I am seeing, we are able to move past an impasse. I feel powerful when I can bring that clarity.

Not all of us can bring clarity like Olivia. But we each possess our own gifts. Cultivating our gifts, and actually gifting them to the world, grows our power.

Grace offers an example of building power from drawing down a higher consciousness from the crown chakra:

> I draw power from my prayers and from the wisdom of people who came before me, our ancestors … from their poetry and stories. For example, for a whole year during the 2016 election cycle, every single day I listened to a speech by Dr. Martin Luther King, or read something from James Baldwin, or Toni Morrison. I found community in their books and words. I felt less alone in the world and that is empowering.

The wisdom Grace drew from the peaks of consciousness these great thinkers gifted the world is a reminder of the things that matter to her. That is to say, a central part of our power comes from living in alignment, from our values in the root chakra to our thoughts in the crown chakra, and from building practices that remind us to do so. This is another way of saying that our power might be visible to us through our accomplishments and the ways we act in the world, but its source is internal. Several faculty mentioned their internal core as the source of their power, including Cyrus, a White gay male assistant professor of art, at an R2 arts-oriented public university in the South: "Power comes internally. I have this internal core that so far can't be broken. It helps me deal with homophobia in academia and other inequities—you know, people talking equity, but not actually doing equity."

As we build our power, we need to be mindful of how we wield it, and whether we act proactively or reactively. Several faculty spoke of their anger. Anger is an emotion, so it belongs in the second chakra, but it comes up again in the power chakra because of the consequences of when we act in anger. In fact, anger delivers us very useful information, if we listen. We get angry when the things that matter to us are violated—our values, our boundaries. Understanding who exactly we are angry at, and what the anger is about, can point us to meaningful changes that we can enact in our lives. But anger is often a secondary emotion, and it covers a primary one. Often, we are angry at somebody, or at the institution, because their thoughtless actions hurt us. Focusing on the anger saves us from dealing with the hurt, but from a holistic perspective, it does not promote wellness or alignment among the chakras. Ernest offers a cautionary tale about acting out of anger:

> Before I had tenure, my faculty mentor raked me over the coals for something one day. I felt humiliated. I got angrier and angrier overnight and next day I decided to go confront him. I was driving to work, and I was rehearsing in my mind all the things I was going to say to him, and I got so lost in my own thoughts that I got in a car accident. Nobody was hurt except my dog, whose back was broken. It was anger, but it was fear and shame and guilt processed as anger. In no situation of mine has anger ever helped.

On the other hand, there is a long history of advocacy and activism fueled by anger, for instance, in the wake of the AIDS crisis, where LGBTQ+ organizations such as ACT UP and Queer Nation made anger their manifesto. Taking a page from their book, Donna is fully in touch with her anger:

> Anger and even rage are crucial for me. They are the fuel of a lot of the work I do, and it shows. An alum said to me, I appreciate your activism because it shows your love of the institution. It revealed to me that anger is the flip side of love, and it was an important part of my understanding.

Colin, the professor who had his promotion case thwarted by his president, acknowledges his anger but looks for alternatives:

> I feel anger at the aggressive and unrelenting ignorance in society, and the embrace of racism and other isms. But that's not a pedagogical response. Because guess what? There is a lot of ignorance in the classroom. And if your response to it is anger, you're not gonna get very far. So you have to rein in your anger and approach people with empathy and compassion. For instance, I had students who refused to wear a mask in class, and at my school they were free to do so. My first response was real anger. But I didn't lead with that; I pulled them aside and talked to them. It was for my own good to try to understand. What's their truth? What's their emotional state? And once you do that, the anger dissipates. There's understanding, and there's a possibility of learning. My only job was in correcting basic fallacies of thinking, which is a professor's duty, especially in philosophy and political science.

When we acknowledge our anger and dig deeper to uncover the primary emotions and the threats to our values, we can use that information to realign our actions and our values, like Colin did with his student, or to set boundaries with those who violate them.

Chakra right: To act

If power is the capacity to act in the world, the right guarded by this chakra is logically the right to act. Faculty generally agree that academia wants us to act, be active in research, to be dynamic and engaging in our teaching, to innovate and transform. However, some pointed out that this encouragement does not extend to all parts of academic life. For instance, some of the faculty experience a climate that discourages actively confronting sedimented dysfunctions of the institution. Devlin confided that he does not feel safe acting against the grain for fear of intimated repercussions. Wendy agrees and goes one step further, saying she acted anyway, but there were consequences. Colin certainly experienced the consequences of his agitating in the faculty senate when he applied for promotion.

Olivia spotlights a different situation:

> When my research on domestic violence on women became overwhelming for me, I had to pivot to a different area. I chose another area that was also meaningful to me and important to society, where some of the work I did before could reasonably translate. It didn't, but it generated a new research question: why do the strategies we use to address domestic violence work in that situation but fail in my new area? I found this question fascinating and energizing. My new topic is also of great importance to society, so I was still working within the standards of quality and significance for research, but some faculty in my department were not happy. They felt victims of a bait and switch. They hired me for something and then I abandoned my commitment. But did I not have the right to move in this new direction? I certainly felt their disapproval. It was so palpable that I felt I needed to do something to remedy. I ended up taking on significantly more service to prove, and feel, that I really belonged in the department.

What Olivia is talking about is a psychological contract (Rousseau, 1995): individual beliefs in a reciprocal obligation between the individual and another party. Olivia's colleagues wished to hire somebody working on intimate partner violence and hired her because they believed she was the best applicant in that area. There is no legal contract obligating Olivia to publish in that area forever and ever, but if she switches too soon, they will feel betrayed, and they will feel that they "wasted" that hire—and treat her accordingly. The insight from the research on implicit contracts is that even though they are not legally binding, once the expectations are fully formed in somebody's mind, violations will have predictable effects, almost as if it was an actual contract violated. Of course, Olivia's expectations when she decided to accept the hiring offer was that the department was invested in her and would treat her collegially and support her academic freedom to grow over time, especially if the reasons for pivoting were sincerely held (recall she ended up feeling triggered and repulsed by her research topic). She too feels that a psychological contract has been violated, and eventually she left that institution.

Other times, the struggle with the right to act is internal. Kendrick, a Black queer research assistant professor of statistics whose story we will learn in the third-eye chakra, elucidates:

> I struggle with the right to act. I find myself paralyzed with fear thinking about things that could go wrong, so I procrastinate. It's not work that is doing this to me, it's me. I am trying to learn that it is ok to not know what will happen but still strive toward a goal.

Angel, who we met in the previous chakra discussing the guilt of not working evening and weekends, has never met Kendrick, but it's hard to believe his comment is not in dialogue with him:

> I study Christopher Isherwood, and he talks about a Hindu belief: I am entitled to the work but not the fruits of the work. That's where the value is, in the labor, not in the fruits of the labor. The scholarship is the value, not the accolades, the grants, the royalties etc.

Angel is correct. The Hindu belief Isherwood references is *Īshvarapraṇidhāna* (इश्वरप्रणिधान). Literally, this means "devotion to the Lord," which by extension means regarding our actions as offerings to the divine, or the universe. In other words, dedicate the effort and surrender the outcome. Īshvarapraṇidhāna is another yoga Niyama. Indeed, yoga sutra 2.45 says that "by observing Īshvarapraṇidhāna, Samādhi is achieved" (Bryant, 2009). *Samādhi* (समाधि) is the last limb of yoga, the earthly stage of enlightenment, or liberation, and it is indeed a special kind of freedom to be able to act without worrying about the result.

Chakra demon: Shame

If the right connected to the power chakra is the right to act, then it follows that its demon is shame, because shame paralyzes us and prevents us from acting. Shame is the fear that we are not enough. We might know in our mind that nobody is perfect and everybody is flawed, but feeling shame means being afraid we are flawed in a particularly damning way that makes us unworthy. As Valerie said, others might have impostor syndrome, but we are truly the impostor, and we will be found out. So another element of shame is the struggle to conceal our flawed parts so that we will pass as worthy for one more day. Some faculty disclosed (a great antidote!) shame around their degrees. Some with master's degrees worked in an environment where they felt judged for not having a doctorate—and eventually internalized that judgment, another component of shame. Some with doctorates felt shame for having the wrong kind of doctorate, for instance, an EdD instead of a PhD. But some PhD holders also felt shame, some working in medical schools for not having an MD, others for having their degree in the "wrong" field. Emmett, the lecturer who left academia, offers an important distinction:

> Not being enough is definitely one of the reasons I left academia. Impostor syndrome is feeling like you are not enough. I never had that. I knew what I brought, and I have the student evaluations to prove it. It was my peers who felt I was not enough, because I didn't have a PhD. That's not shame, that's a toxic work environment.

This is a very important difference that we should keep in mind as we discuss shame in the rest of this section. A powerful Hindu myth applies here, that of the *Nīlakaṇṭha* (नीलकण्ठ). Nīlakaṇṭha is one of the appellation of Shiva, which he earned when he came to the rescue after a great poison had spilled all over the land, poisoning everything and threatening all human and divine realms. Shiva aspirated all the spilled venom into his mouth, but it was so powerful that it would have been fatal even for him. His consort Shakti helped him by choking him at the throat so that he would not swallow. The trick worked and saved the world, but the substance was so virulent that it turned Shiva's throat blue. Nīlakaṇṭha means blue-throated and is a great reminder that even if our environment is toxic, we do not have to swallow.

But many of us swallow the poison and internalize the fear or belief that they are not enough, and that their accomplishments are inconsequential or merely the product of luck or other external causes. In fact, as many as 82% of people report feeling like an impostor (Bravata et al., 2020). Psychologists call this the impostor phenomenon because it is not listed as a pathology in the Diagnostic and Statistical Manual of Mental Disorders (DSM) and therefore it is not technically a syndrome. Still, impostor feelings affect our power, our ability to take risks, our self-esteem, and ultimately our well-being. This phenomenon is characterized by a vicious cycle: impostor anxiety drives the approach to an achievement-oriented task, leading to overpreparation, or procrastination and then panic. When the task is executed well, the accolades soothe the anxiety, but because the success is not internalized, their effect is short-lived. This renews the anxiety, which can only be quelled by more accolades, and the cycle continues.

Even tenure, one of the most coveted rewards in academia, might not be enough to convince the impostor. Research has shown that, after the initial euphoria and in addition to the newfound freedom to take risks protected by rank and title, many faculty can develop a "mid-career malaise" (Matthews, 2014). Desiree, who was recently promoted to full professor, confirms: "I feel I have to work even harder to PROVE I deserved this promotion and that it wasn't a charity pass: it's impostor syndrome on crack." This perverse reasoning is so common that faculty stress—already high for a profession without intrinsic physical risk—is higher for associate professors than (untenured) assistant professors (Jaschik, 2012; Wilson, 2012)!

If positive feedback provides only momentary relief, every little criticism can trigger shame. Desiree voices a sentiment I have witnessed countless times in my consultations:

> For me, it's linked to my perfectionism, which is the flip side of impostor syndrome. For instance, I know on paper that I am a good teacher. But every time I get student evaluations at the end of the semester, even just one mean

comment is enough to make me ashamed. It feels intolerable. Over time, my internal voice has become less harsh but it is still there.

What is it about teaching that a single bad evaluation has so much power over us? A negative comment from a reviewer might sting a bit in our research, but we roll up our sleeves for that revise and resubmit and accept it as part of the game. We are used to treating research as public property, and in fact are all on board with the principle that our research is no good until it has been peer reviewed. But teaching is more private, intimate. It happens behind closed doors. Many faculty are reticent to open the doors of their classrooms for peer visits and observations. That secrecy might actually aid the shame. The Scholarship of Teaching and Learning movement aims to make teaching community property, go public and create the teaching commons (Chick & Friberg, 2022), and one of its side effects is that it can decrease the shame of teaching failures for the faculty who get involved in it.

Vivian mentions another situation, both particular and universal:

> I took a position at a university abroad for a couple [of] years. They perceived me as "the loud American." Before even taking the job, I was aware of the stereotype of how Americans are seen in the world and the behaviors that feed that narrative, and worked so hard to not project those vibes, yet that's who I was to my colleagues. I was ashamed that I changed my behavior for them, and I was ashamed that it didn't work.

While few of us have held positions abroad, most of us know the effects of a stereotype hanging over us. The research on people under stereotype threat (Steele, 2011) is clear. When a stereotype is hanging in the air and we are at risk of confirming the stereotype with our actions (failures, often), minimal activations of the stereotype are enough to impact performance. For instance, merely saying "Good luck everybody on this math exam, especially the women" is enough to depress women's performance on the exam compared to control groups. Notice that the stereotype of women being bad at math has not even been mentioned explicitly. It is enough to know that the person in charge of scoring the exam is aware of the stereotype and that it might influence how they grade for women to score worse than men or than women in the next room taking the same exam, sans stereotype—even if those women know the stereotype is complete bunk! The activation of the stereotype is enough to unground us in the first chakra, generate negative emotional interference in the second chakra (in particular anxiety), and diminish our power in the third chakra. It is a sinister alignment of energies.

Audre, an African-American professor of English and self-identified recovering administrator on the West Coast, highlights an aspect of academic life that calls us to overcome our shame:

> The expression that comes to mind is SHAMELESS self-promotion. Being shameless is generally a bad quality, but it is a necessity for academics trying to disseminate our work. It is simply part of creating something new. People don't find our work magically, you have to leave at least bread crumbs for them. And shame is the demon that comes up. Who are we to demand that our colleagues pay attention to our work, out of all the interesting things they could pay attention to? It feels very conceited. I am still working through that issue.

The dissemination of our work is crucial. It completes and renews the scholarship cycle. It puts us in conversation with other scholars, and from this process new insights and hypotheses are generated, which propel forward the next cycle. The answer to Audre's question—who are we?—is that we are experts! We have spent years developing our expertise in a particular area. We are the ideal people to add to the academic discourse in that area! We owe it to the world to free ourselves from the clutches of the shame demon and share our gifts freely!

Prompts for reflection

- When do you feel most and least powerful? Where does your own power come from? How do you gain it back after feeling disempowered?
- What is your superpower? What do other people say is your special gift?
- When is your will strong? And when do you fall into procrastination? What strategies work for you to get you back in your groove?
- Do you ever feel like an impostor? That your accomplishments are insignificant, or dumb luck? Are you ever caught in the impostor cycle? What triggers these feelings and how does the phenomenon manifest for you? How can you soothe yourself out of it?
- Consider a situation that made you angry. What happened? What information did the anger bring you? Which of your values were violated? What emotions hid behind the anger? How did you express that anger in the moment and later? What changes was the anger prompting you to make? How easy or hard was it to not behave reactively? What could you do next time to get some distance between your anger and your actions?
- How is your right to act supported in your context? How is it threatened? What can you do to protect it?
- What makes you feel ashamed of yourself? What do others try to shame you about? What lessons have you learned from this demon?

Tools, strategies, and possibilities

This section considers the issues brought up from the faculty stories and offers strategies to grow or remember our power, at work or in the rest of our life. As a rejoinder from previous chakras, remember that one of the manifestations of burnout is the loss of agency; therefore, as we build our capacity back, we are also healing ourselves from burnout.

Right charge your third chakra. The physical and the energetic realm are connected. It is hard to take the world by storm when we are feeling sluggish. Fight the inertia by generating energy with a physical activity. Go for a run, or a powerwalk, or a bike ride, or do jumping jacks, anything to get the juices going. Conversely, if you feel hyperactive and frazzled, slow yourself down so you can focus. Do some breath work, try meditation, or get a massage.

Take stock of the energy systems you are a part of. Are you in situations that lock you up in a specific role? Are you the one they always ask to bring treats for the department social? Perhaps you take on most of the emotional labor in a relationship. Or you are the one expected to compromise during conflict. Maybe they expect you to take the lead while they wait to be told what to do. Maybe you are fine always playing the nurturing role, or the leadership role, or being the one voicing the uncomfortable truths. But if you are not, this exercise will help you pinpoint the contexts that trap you in certain roles so you can start imagining and demanding alternatives for yourself.

Study your resistance. While the eventual goal is to move past the resistance, you can also treat it as a laboratory. Collect data on yourself as if it was a research study. Notice when you start procrastinating. Notice what you do to keep avoiding tasks. Notice the excuses you tell yourself. Revisit findings about the habit loop from the ground chakra. As you map this space out, you can also gain insights to anticipate and predict your resistance and to be prepared to counter it.

Take a risk. A well-balanced power chakra will know when to take calculated risks. Pushing yourself out of your comfort zone can shake things up in other areas of your life. Join Toastmasters and sign up to give a public speech. Throw your name in the hat at a Moth story slam or other storytelling night. Sing at a karaoke bar. Channel Eleanor Roosevelt and do the thing you think you cannot do. Always be safe and don't overdo it.

Create a visual representation of your power. Art is a great on-ramp for transformation. Inspired by Woody Guthrie's New Year's resolution to "keep hoping machine running," Gabby created her "Hope Machine" artwork, a collage of the reminders in her world to keep a positive outlook on the future. When she relayed that story in her interview, I was in turn inspired to create my "Yes I Can" machine, a contraption that absorbs all my past proud accomplishments and transmutes them into a manuscript on the chakras. On days when I was mired in self-doubt, the artwork stood as a visible reminder that I have overcome much more daunting challenges in my life than writing a book, and I certainly have the capacity to see this project through.

Inventory your areas of power. To create my "Yes I Can" artwork, I had to decide what to feed the machinery. I had to spell out all my accomplishments. Some are on my CV and some are less tangible but still significant. The act of sifting through my life to trace my powerful moments was significant in and of itself, before even rendering them into art, and a great remedy when I struggled with self-confidence.

Backward design your projects. In pedagogical theory, we use the concept of backward design. When designing a course, we advise instructors to start from the end and work backward. Start from what students should be able to do by the end of the semester, and use that anchor point to determine step by step how they will get there. A similar approach works in other contexts, and indeed designers and engineers will confirm that this is the standard design process and that there is nothing backward about it. Start from what your project (grant, website, award application, symposium, etc.) needs to look like by a certain date and work backward, developing a timeline of tasks and people involved.

Calendarize all tasks. The devil is in the details, especially for faculty pushed and pulled in many directions. If a task is necessary for the completion of your project, it must find its way onto your calendar, and must be assigned a reasonable amount of time. This is the place to put those pomodoro sessions from the ground chakra to good use. If an emergency happens and the task cannot be attended to, it is not the end of the world, but it needs to be moved to another time slot. This suggestion might feel trivial, but it is crucial for those with attention issues or struggling with procrastination. This is how we exercise the will to make choices and prioritize some things and give up others.

Prioritize tasks by urgency and importance. Inspired by a President Eisenhower maxim, Steven Covey (2004) created the Urgent-Important Matrix. His advice is to categorize our to-do list according to two dimensions: whether a task is important or not and whether it is urgent or not. This will give us a heuristic for prioritizing. Urgent and important tasks are the crises to attend to right away. Important but not urgent tasks are things that will always drop to the bottom of the list unless you schedule them. Urgent but unimportant items are interruptions, and you might delegate them off if possible, or get them done quickly. And non-urgent unimportant items are distractions. Eliminate them or save them for when you need a break from other tasks.

Eat the frog. Another way of prioritizing comes from Mark Twain. He famously said that if you must eat a frog, you should do it first thing in the day. After that, your day can only get better. These frogs might be the important things that trigger your resistance. In my center, we sometimes schedule eat-the-frog meetings first thing in the morning. If somebody has an unpleasant task, they might message the team saying they have to eat a frog and if anybody else also does, let's do it together for mutual support.

Join an accountability group. Expanding on the previous idea, the task doesn't need to be unpleasant. A morning spent working with a colleague at the local coffee shop, each on their own project but together for motivation, might do wonders for your scholarship. We call those mornings Ugena days, in honor of the first colleague who started that tradition. We offer those container meetings weekly for faculty. We call those time slots "Write Here, Write Now." We take turns hosting them, which consists of simply asking people to write down (in the chat if it's a virtual event) their goals for the time slot, setting a timer, and prompting people at the end to share in the chat how far along they got toward their goal. The purpose for these meetings can be short term (e.g., meet once to write a conference abstract) or long term (e.g., commit to meet for a semester with the goal of writing a paper). Many institutions offer versions of these groups so you can likely find something that works for your needs.

Study your attention thieves. Jenny Odell points out that in the attention economy we live in, we can regain control by reclaiming our attention (2019). What are your attention thieves? Make a list. If the list does not come easy to you, study your patterns for a week. Once you have a rich picture, come up with a plan to deal with each one. If these thieves grab our attention so easily, there might be something in there for us. They might point to our passions or our values. For instance, we might spend lots of time on social media because we value feeling connected with our loved ones far away. Therefore, the goal might not be to eliminate them altogether but to find ways to be intentional and efficient in our usage. We might forgo endless scrolling in the hopes of finding a status update by somebody we miss in favor of scheduling a video call with them at a convenient time.

Check the stories you tell yourself. We are hardwired to fall into predictable grooves when we recount the occasions that left us feeling disempowered, as Grenny et al. (2021) demonstrate. Two common stories we tell are the Victim and the Villain. In the first, bad things just happened to us, through no fault of our own. In the second one, there is an evil mastermind villain orchestrating all manners of cruelties against us. While these stories are occasionally true (and the faculty in this book relayed a number of stories about bullying, sexual violence, blatant racism, and more), when we use those as the defaults for our mental processing, they don't leave us with anywhere to go. Are we truly completely never at fault, or was there something we could have done to deescalate a conflict? Is our interlocutor truly Dr. Evil? Could we possibly look for common ground on anything? As we check our stories and come up with better archetypes (see the third-eye chakra chapter for more on this), we reshape our mindset to a more action-oriented one.

Don't give up your power. The third type of story that Grenny et al. (2021) consider is the Helpless story, characterized by the refrain "There is nothing I can do." Audre offers very sage advice to pivot away from a helpless mindset:

> Don't say there is nothing I can do. I have not been in a circumstance where I have not recognized my power. I've felt my power even in situations designed to disempower me. The power structure wants you to believe you don't have power. But when you say you don't have power you are giving away what power you have to the structure, because you always have some agency. Power means recognizing you always have choices. Even when the choices are difficult you always have a choice, even if the choice is to leave.

Rather than saying, "I have to do what the chair/dean/publisher demand because I have no choice," adopt a game theory approach. Consider all the moves you have, the possible countermoves of the other player, and the benefits and risks of each combination. If it turns out, your best bet is to do as you are told, reframe the stance as "At this time, I am choosing to go along with their request because I value the benefits I get from complying."

Avoid invalidators. Part of building power is letting it accrue and simmer and distill until it becomes a compelling vision guided by our values, passions, and goals. What this process does not need is people who invalidate our goals, or our process. Be intentional who you share plans and passions with, and cultivate those relationships that support you.

Realize you are not alone with your impostor feelings. Characteristics of the impostor phenomenon are reported by as much as 80% of people. Academics are especially prone to this form of self-doubt. This means feeling like an impostor is normal and expected, and you are not alone. Chances are that if you open up to other colleagues they might reveal a similar predicament, and you can find common ground and build mutual solidarity. Normalize having these conversations.

Recognize your achievements. Even though we all know that academia does not give charity passes, we often fall into the insidious habit of discounting our own accomplishments relative to other people's. The irony is that others are probably devaluing their own achievements and putting yours on a pedestal. Use this tendency to your advantage! Acknowledge and celebrate your own accomplishments. Publish them on social media, where your network will shower you with accolades. Don't forget to return the favor as often as you can!

Write the ways you make a difference. Publications, awards, and other academic accolades are certainly worth recognizing, but we should also remind ourselves how we impact others. Remember that burnout is characterized by a loss of agency. Therefore, it is important to recognize all the ways in which we make a difference, to our students, our colleagues, our profession, our institution, our families, and ourselves.

Get comfortable with failure. The impostor phenomenon also thrives on exaggerating our own failures. Some of us explicitly teach our students that failure is part of the process and really a learning opportunity, but we often forget to take our own advice. Expect failure, plan for it, acknowledge it when it happens, learn from it, celebrate what you learned, and move on. Some people build their "failure CV" to represent visually to themselves how many jobs they applied for before they got the offer, or how many rejections before their paper got accepted, and so on.

Incorporate High-Impact Practices (HIPs) in your courses. We already mentioned HIPs in the desire chakra, as an innovation that could make your teaching more pleasurable. The beauty of a lot of these strategies is that they hit on several chakras. In this particular case, HIPs can make your teaching more impactful (it's in the name itself!) and help you build agency in your teaching.

Take a leadership assessment. Knowledge is power. Whether we occupy a formal position of leadership or not, we all lead, be it a research group or students in a learning expedition, a committee we chair, and so on. If you are feeling not very powerful as a leader, these instruments might help. I should mention that, as a statistician, I am skeptical of viewing these instruments as oracles because their validity and reliability are suspect. But they are great starters for reflection and discussion. As an example, when I took the DISC leadership assessment, I scored as an I, which means I lead by inspiring people. At the time, this was an epiphany for me. I considered myself defective as a leader because I wasn't directive enough (that would be a D). That experience affirmed my style, allowed me to see myself as powerful in my role, and gave me a language to talk about my approach.

Build collective power. A friend of mine likes to say that a university is an elephant—that is, it is considerably hard to move. That is certainly true if we try pushing it on our own, and we might get trampled, but there might be strength in numbers. Parker Palmer (1992) has studied the civic movements from the 1960s on, with the goal of understanding what made them successful. He outlines four steps. The first step happens when people make the individual decision to stop leading divided lives (e.g., lives that compartmentalize our work apart from our values). If you are working your way through the chakras, on some level you have already decided that. The second step is when like-minded people find each other and come together for mutual support. In the third stage, groups develop a language to translate private problems into public concerns that others can get onboard. And in the final stage, with enough momentum, the system is forced to reckon in some ways with these public demands. None of this is easy or quick (as the civil rights movement demonstrates) but this insight can be your sign to start finding your people.

WORKSHEET 3.1 BUILD A STURDIER SAILBOAT HULL

We have traversed the lower chakras and confronted their demons—fear, guilt, and shame. Before we move further up, let's make sure to consolidate their lessons.
In the first chakra, we considered the fears that make us coil in instead of expanding out and taking the space we deserve.
In the second chakra, we considered the guilt we feel when certain emotions arise or when the thought of following our passions comes up. When you think about these concepts in relation to your job, what issues come up?
In the third chakra, we considered the shame that paralyzes us when we want to orient our will to certain actions. When you think about these concepts in relationship to your job, what issues come up?
What selves have you rejected in your attempts to be successful at work? What would you like to say to those selves now?
What does your inner critic sound like? A valley girl with vocal fry? Janice from *Friends* with the nasal Oh My God? Stewie from *Family Guy* with the British accent? Maybe your dissertation advisor? Maybe your dad? And what do they say?

Put all these insights across the lower chakras in relation to each other. What patterns do you notice?

What actions are you inspired to take from this analysis? Make a plan.

References

Bravata, D., Watts, S., Keefer, A., Madhusudhan, D., Taylor, K., Clark, D., Nelson, R., Cokley, K., & Hagg, H. (2020) Prevalence, predictors, and treatment of impostor syndrome: A systematic review. *Journal of General Internal Medicine, 35*(4), 1252–1275.

Bryant, E. (2009) *The Yoga Sutras of Patañjali: A new edition, translation, and commentary.* North Point Press.

Chick, N., & Friberg, J. (Eds.) (2022) *Going public reconsidered: Engaging with the world beyond academe through the scholarship of teaching and learning.* Routledge.

Covey, S. (2004) *The seven habits of highly effective people* (revised ed.). FranklinCovey.

Elbow, P. (2009) The believing game or methodological believing. *Journal for the Assembly for Expanded Perspectives on Learning, 13*, 1–11. Retrieved from https://scholarworks.umass.edu/entities/publication/d08b95ac-7ba2-4e70-b25f-f3de6a1373db

Grenny, J., Patterson, K., McMillan, R., Switzler, A., & Gregory, E. (2021) *Crucial conversations: Tools for talking when stakes are high* (3rd ed.). McGraw-Hill.

Jackson, B. W., & Hardiman, R. (1994). Multicultural organization development. In E. Y. Cross, J. H. Katz, F. A. Miller, & E. W. Seashore (Eds.), *The promise of diversity: Over 40 voices discuss strategies for eliminating discrimination in organizations* (pp. 231–239). NTL Institute.

Jaschik, S. (2012, June 4) Unhappy associate professors. *Inside Higher Ed.* Retrieved from www.insidehighered.com/news/2012/06/04/associate-professors-less-satisfied-those-other-ranks-survey-finds

Kaufman, S. B. (2020) *Transcend: The new science of self-actualization.* TarcherPerigee.

Lovett, M., Bridges, M., DiPietro, M., Ambrose, S., & Norman, M. (2023) *How learning works: Eight research-based principles for smart teaching* (2nd ed.). Wiley.

Maslow, A. H. (1954). *Motivation and personality.* Harper and Row.

Matthews, K. (2014). Perspectives on midcareer faculty and advice for supporting them. In *Collaborative on academic careers in higher education* (COACHE). Harvard Graduate School of Education.

Odell, J. (2019). *How to do nothing: Resisting the attention economy.* Melville House.

Palmer, P. (1992) Divided no more. *Change Magazine, 24*(2), 10–17.

Rousseau, D. M. (1995). *Psychological contracts in organizations: Understanding written and unwritten agreements.* Sage.

Steele, C. (2011). *Whistling Vivaldi: How stereotypes affect us and what we can do.* W. W. Norton & Company.

Wilson, R. (2012, June 3) Why are associate professors so unhappy? *The Chronicle of Higher Education.* Retrieved from www.chronicle.com/article/why-are-associate-professors-so-unhappy/

4
WHAT IS THE ROLE OF LOVE IN THE ACADEMY?

The heart chakra

Hostess duty

When I was still a graduate student, my mentor had a visitor in town from Europe. My mentor was one of the biggest names in the field, and this researcher had flown all the way to the United States just to talk to him because he admired my advisor's work so much. Well, it turns out my advisor wasn't as excited about this meeting of the minds. Even though he had agreed to the visit originally, by the time the guy showed up, he had gotten busy, there were deadlines, and he could not be bothered.

So my advisor pawned the visitor off on me. I had to take on hostess duties. I took him to lunch, we talked about differences between the United States and his country—pretty mundane stuff. We discussed research for sure, but I did not have the breadth and depth of knowledge my advisor had. I can tell you he got an earful of my dissertation, ha ha. All along, I was questioning myself, should I be doing this? I am busy too! I needed to work on my research, I had experiments to run, and I wasn't too keen on losing a whole day chitchatting with this stranger. But since I was stuck with him, I made the best of the situation.

Fast forward to a couple of years later, when I had just taken a position at another university as a new assistant professor. I was busy setting up my lab and getting my research agenda going, when the European visitor contacted me out of the blue. He was working on a grant application that specifically stipulated an American collaborator, and he thought of me. Not my mentor, but me! Of course I accepted, and this grant was amazing. It launched my lab, and allowed me to visit his gorgeous country regularly. But most of all, it allowed a fulfilling relationship with him, personally and professionally. I did not enter this

DOI: 10.4324/9781003487371-5

relationship with ulterior motives, in fact I was a bit put off in the beginning at being my advisor's stand-in. But I did it because I was asked, and then I had this human being in front of me so we connected.

Now I ensure to tell my students to not be naïve and underestimate the importance of interpersonal connections in academia. Just last night, I was reminded. I am on a board of an international conference, and we're trying to choose speakers. Having done this a number of times, I know that the way people choose is by asking themselves, who do I know, who can I think of? And last night was no different. And of course when that's your process, all sorts of biases come up because people know people like themselves for the most part. So if you want to fix that problem, you have to network very intentionally beyond your circle of sameness. You can indeed build ways of connecting that are not transactional. Put the relationship first, and the opportunities will follow.

—Wendy, White female professor of psychology at a research institution in the South

Daughter beats dean

I haven't felt the brunt of oppression and discrimination personally, but as an educator and as a human being, I always felt very strongly about being inclusive and welcoming to all. I got the opportunity to put my beliefs to the test when my teenage child came out as trans in 2015, and we started our journey of becoming an LGBTQ family.

For the first few months, our main goal was to get her into counseling to give her a safe space to process her experience with a therapist. Shortly after, we enlisted the help of a medical professional to ensure she had the healthcare she needed. And of course we wanted a safe environment for her at school. Frankly, we were worried about school. It was startling to feel the intensity of the hate against my daughter. Knowing with your brain is one thing but feeling it in your heart and soul is a completely different experience. It was heartbreaking.

We asked her to do online schooling for the next year to buy us some time because my husband and I did not believe she would be safe. But around that time is when the national hysteria against trans kids started exploding. Multiple states passed bathroom bills. We watched with bated breath to see if our state would pass one as well. It was devastating to contemplate that my daughter would have to contend with the hate from the state now, on top of the hate from her peers—to know that the last safe space at her school, a locked bathroom stall, could be taken from her. We found relief when the federal administration released the guidelines for school systems to clarify that all civil right protections attach to transgender students. But our county was wishy washy about it, and our state attorney general declared they would sue the federal government to challenge those protections. They ended up passing their own version of a bathroom bill.

I knew in my heart right away that the bathroom bill and the campus carry bill (see Chapter 1 for the rest of Sasha's story) made it impossible to care for my loved ones. I told my husband, and he agreed. We will find another job in a different state, he enthused! I loved his optimism, but deanships don't grow on trees. And yet we had blinding clarity: our daughter's wellness beats being a dean. I ended up taking a job in another state as Associate Dean, a step down. I didn't care. In a couple of years, I was promoted again. But that is inconsequential in the bigger scheme of things. What truly mattered was protecting the people I love.

—Sasha, White female professor of communication in a variety of leadership roles at multiple institutions

The heart of my teaching

When I look back over my career there is one day that stands out—the day after the 2016 election. I had to teach a 7:00 a.m. class, which was never easy, but that day felt especially heavy. I had a vortex of emotions swirling inside. I felt fear, sadness, anger, frustration, and confusion. Most of all, I felt grief.

I had to get my head in the game, but I couldn't shake my worries. What will this election mean for me, an immigrant woman of color, and people like me, which is most of the students I taught? Oh yes, the students. That morning after the election, when I walked into my classroom, the energy was high, but not in a way ready for learning. Students were animated, gesturing to each other… they seemed to want to talk about what happened. I didn't know what to do. Business as usual seemed so inadequate. But it's not like I felt I had the tools for a meaningful discussion. I decided to proceed and teach my lesson, but I felt numb and, at moments, speechless. I was avoiding eye contact with students who I knew were really struggling. In the middle of the class my blood pressure dropped precipitously, and I almost passed out. My students ran to the front of the class, some gave me water to drink, others helped me get back up. I often go back to that day and how I should've acted or what skills I wish I had. And, the reason why I still go back to that day is the lesson it taught me. A part of me didn't want to act like it was business as usual and only focus on the content. But I didn't have the tools. I was afraid that I was going to sound unprofessional if I talked about the election. My body did not let me.

We as a society have been fed and pushed this lie that we can simply go on after a campus shooting or other traumatic events, but we are not just brains processing information. We are whole persons, with a social, an emotional, and a spiritual dimension. The events of that day made me pause and ask myself, what am I doing? What am I trying to achieve with the students? What is at the heart of my teaching? What is the purpose of education? What does it mean to struggle together, process contradictions, and pain with students? It was a turning point because I realized I was perpetuating this culture of stoicism and fragmentation.

I was well versed in the holistic approach from a theoretical standpoint, but that day taught me I wasn't embodying what I knew to be true. This is when I started digging deeper and deeper about how important all the layers of the self are for learning. In 2017 I did a large research study, asking students what matters to them in their college years. Love, beauty, all the affective stuff were at the top. I teach physiology. So I started taking baby steps. For example, before I teach the physiology of the heart, I put my hand on my heart. I feel my heartbeat, or take my pulse. I developed a relationship with my heart, listened to what it had to say. When it was quickening, I began slowing down. When it felt constricted, I breathed in to expand. When it was bursting with joy, I let it express. I gave myself permission to ask uncomfortable questions so that I can equip myself with the skills needed to be comfortable incorporating the affective dimensions in my teaching. For a long time I was teaching like the content exists over there, when in reality it is within us, all of us. For learning to be meaningful, it must be embodied.

—Grace, woman of color, immigrant professor of physiology at a community college in the Southwest

What's going on with these stories?

All three stories clearly deal with the heart. Wendy decides to connect genuinely with a stranger who crosses her path, and professional opportunities flow from it. That experience was so determinant at a crucial time in her career that it informed her philosophy of intentional networking, which she deliberately passes on to her students. Sasha sacrifices her job out of love for her daughter and a desire to keep her family safe, moving out of state to escape the devastating effects of legislated transphobia. And Grace's turmoil teaches her to put the heart first in her teaching and to care for herself and for her students beyond the content, an insight confirmed by her large-scale research project.

These are stories of relationships, connections, and ultimately love, for self and for others. Love may sound like a weird topic for a career book, but it is actually the heart of the matter (pardon the pun) if we wish to work in a way that is fulfilling and purposeful. What does it mean to love in the academy, an institution that was built on the split between the head and the heart? That is the question this chapter will center. And when we ask it that way, it already points us in a productive direction. Loving in the academy might just mean healing that split and working toward balance, as all three protagonists discovered. Of course, when we talk about the heart, heartbreak and grief are always lurking in the background as a possibility, as Grace's story reminds us. In the next section we will build the machinery from the chakra theory to properly address this question. We will then flesh out the themes with quotes from other faculty as well as theory and evidence from the educational development literature.

What does chakra theory say?

Moving up the liberating current so far, we have worked on our values and our foundation in the first chakra, our passions in the second chakra, and our power in the third one. We have faced the demons of fear, guilt, and shame. This work sets the stage for the next leg of the journey, as we move up into the heart chakra. The fourth chakra is located in the cardiac plexus, and its element is air, the oxygen we breathe into our lungs to oxygenate the blood the heart pumps there, or energetically, the life force or prana. Its name is Anāhata, translated as "unstruck," or "sound made without any two parts touching." Reminiscent of the Zen koan, "What is the sound of one hand clapping," this name is a reference to the fact that we need the friction of two forces to produce sound (e.g., sticks beating on the drum, plectrum strumming the guitar strings). While that kind of friction can produce soul-stirring music, the ancient philosophers imagined a pure world where that friction is no longer necessary for beauty to emerge. In this chakra, polarities are no longer working as agonist and antagonist but harmonize together.

Love is precisely this integration. In the second chakra, we had a kind of love. If we are passionate about something, we love that thing. The love in the heart chakra is a love that does not need an object. Love is who we are. Love is our stance, what we put out in the world, as self-love and as love of others. With a healthy heart chakra, we are able to love all of ourselves, from our ego to our shadow, and we welcome back all our rejected selves. An apt word is "beholding." The goal of the heart chakra is the ability to behold, to really see ourselves and others in our wholeness. Imagine a parent beholding their daughter as she comes down the stairs into the foyer in her prom dress ready for her big night, basking in how radiant she looks, holding in their gaze all the ways in which they are proud of her without forgetting her stumbles and imperfections, embracing the path that got her to this evening, hopeful for her future and mindful of the struggles she'll have to face. Now imagine beholding ourselves that way, and everybody else, our students, our chair, our colleagues, reviewer #2. That's the kind of love we are talking about. Unfortunately, the most common blockage in the heart chakra is the absence of self-love. In my interviews, an expression I encountered commonly was that of "not knowing my worth," as an explanation for staying in a job that took the interviewee for granted or was downright toxic, or even referring to the colleagues who were able to leave as those who "knew their worth." This kind of worth is not of the head only. Everybody can look at a resume and be impressed, but knowing one's worth is an embodied wisdom, a knowing of the heart that pulls from all of the chakras. Therefore, the work of this chakra is to restore that self-love and compassion.

In the lower chakras, we have cultivated our physical, emotional, and ego identities. In the heart chakra, we nurture our social identity, the part of ourselves that comes from and grows by being in relation with others—the intentional connections that Wendy talks about. In her online course, Priya Parker (n. d.) defines connection as an energy exchange between people who are paying attention to each other. This approach meshes well with the energetic approach we are taking with the chakras. Focusing on connections and on this energy exchange represents a pivot. Up until now, we have worked on internal pieces of ourselves. From here on, as we travel up the liberating current, we will strengthen pieces of identity that transcend our individual experience, as this journey takes us from the individual to the universal.

Fittingly, people with a balanced hearth chakra come across as content, caring, empathetic, and kind. Like all other chakras, the heart too can be excessive or deficient. If the idea of an excessive heart chakra, of too much love, sounds strange, just remember we are talking about energies. If too much energy is trapped in this chakra and spinning on itself with no way out, that means it's taking away from other chakras, and our values or our power, for instance, are not being nurtured. This scenario results in the person acting like a people pleaser, a martyr, always sacrificing, requiring some satisfaction by feeling needed but never truly an equal in the relationship. Conversely, people with a deficiency in the heart chakra will appear cold, critical, intolerant, isolated, or lacking in empathy.

Visually, this chakra is represented as a lotus with 12 petals. Traditionally, each part of this lotus has a different color including a "smoky" center, but in the modern depiction the color is green. Inside the lotus is the *ṣaṭkoṇa* (षट्कोण), the six-pointed star, which is made up of two triangles, upward- and downward-pointing, symbolizing the two energies meeting in the middle. Inside the ṣaṭkoṇa is the seed mantra of this chakra, "*yam*" (यं). Each petal of each chakra, as well as the total number of petals for each lotus, has a meaning but, for brevity's sake, we haven't discussed those so far. The petals of this chakra, however, are worth mentioning, because they refer to the following qualities: bliss, peace, harmony, love, understanding, empathy, clarity, purity, unity, compassion, kindness, and forgiveness. All these aspects are strong components of deep relationships with others and with ourselves.

As always, several deities are represented in the heart chakra, but its dedicated one is *Vāyu* (वायु). In keeping with the air theme, he is described as smoke-like and worshipped as prana itself. One of his incarnations is *Hanumān* (हनुमान्), the monkey god who jumped from India to Sri Lanka in one leap to go rescue *Sita* (सीता), who was held prisoner there, according to the *Rāmāyaṇa* (रामायणम्) epic. He was able to take the leap because he needed to, that's how myth works. But while we humans can't leapfrog over the ocean simply by believing it, the multiple leaps of faith that Sasha took out of love for her daughter come from a similar fortitude of heart.

The heart chakra has a second manifestation of its function, conferred by its position in the system. The heart is the middle chakra, the center of the system,

> **BOX 4.1 HEART CHAKRA CHART**
>
> Sanskrit name: Anāhata
> Meaning: Unstruck
> Element: Air
> Function: Love
> Color: Green
> Identity: Social
> Right: To Love
> Demon: Grief

the midpoint between the gut and the head, the individual and the universal. As such, it brings forth the idea of balance. Its job is to balance out the polarities we encountered in the desire chakra and reintegrate us into wholeness. The guiding principle of the fourth chakra is equilibrium. If we want to ascend to the upper chakras, this balancing is key.

Unsurprisingly, the right associated with the heart chakra is the right to love, and its demon is grief. Grief makes the heart heavy and closed to love, rather than light and open, like Grace's experience of feeling numb.

Faculty insights: Love

Talking about the heart in the academy is no easy feat. We have built academia as a celebration of the life of the mind, the pursuit of knowledge, on the gamble that divorcing the mind from the heart will yield more powerful, accurate, and generalizable knowledge. We have predicated the whole academic enterprise on removing the personal from it in search for the universal, the "university." The positivist paradigm eschews subjectivity, feelings, as not only irrelevant, but also damaging to the pursuit of the truth. It is only recently that we have started to heal that brokenness, with the acknowledgment of multiple, subjective truths and of the importance of our positionality to academic inquiry. We are still collectively fumbling our way around the question of what it means to find the love in higher education. In my interviews, when we arrived at the heart chakra, I simply asked: "How do you nurture the heart, love, and relationships at work?" The answers were often tentative. "I don't know if this is what you have in mind," people would preface. There were no such preambles to questions about other chakras. For instance, people knew immediately when they felt powerful/powerless in their professional life, and they could map their power into all areas of faculty performance, teaching, research, and service/leadership.

In an environment that privileges the mind, we are still unsure about the heart. Nevertheless, mining the faculty answers reveals several interesting ideas.

An easy starting point to unpack love in the academy is teaching. After all, many of us got into higher education because we love to teach, and the best teaching is relationship-rich (Felten & Lambert, 2020). How can we create relationships that foster learning and growth? For Lachlan, the English professor who moved to California, the starting point is openness and vulnerability:

> I am very open with my students. I believe in telling the truth and sharing vulnerability. I don't pretend to know everything. If I'm teaching a poem, I'm happy to admit that I don't know what some parts of it mean. I talk to my students about choosing material because of an emotional truth that I find in it. For instance, I love teaching Mary Oliver. I teach A New Yorker essay that talks about how Mary Oliver is sometimes view[ed] as too "Hallmark," rather than a serious poet. I don't overvalue a certain kind of rigor that tends to be favored in academic environments. I don't know if I am a better teacher but I'm a more openminded, by which I mean openhearted, teacher than I was 10 or 20 years ago. I talk with my students about using first person in their papers. Of course you have to be present in your writing! Being the hardest professor is not something I'm at all interested in.

Emmeline, the psychology professor at a medical university, describes another aspect of loving the students:

> I started meditating two or three years ago, and it changed my conception of teaching. I don't fight my students anymore. I assume the students and I are in this together. Part of it is acknowledging that I might be more invested in my course than they are, and that's okay. It is my baby, not theirs. Maybe they just need to get through the graduation requirement. Maybe they are overwhelmed, and it's all they can do to just pass the class.

Emmeline is unknowingly referencing one of Parker Palmer's five habits of the heart (2011). They are as follows: an understanding that we are all in this together; an appreciation of the value of otherness; an ability to hold tension in life giving ways; a sense of personal voice and agency; and a capacity to create community. Valerie, the history professor who meandered her way through college and graduate school, articulates her love for her students as follows: "I feel I am now the professor I needed as an undergraduate."

Angel, the English professor in the community college system, offers another expression about love: "We have a saying in the community college world—Loving our students to success. It's not a paternalistic approach. It's about understanding your students and their needs so you can better support them."

This is how Cyrus, the art professor who spoke about his unbreakable core in chapter 3, operationalizes this attitude:

> I work in the first public integrated university, intentionally created as that in the fifties. I know many of our students are first generation. They don't have the support at home that comes from parents having familiarity with this world. They don't know if they belong here. One thing I do is I use readings from a diverse group of authors. Students can see themselves in the curriculum, and it connects them to art. I also know that students are so much more than a brain to fill with knowledge. They always come to me with their challenges, relationship problems, deaths in the family, and more. They are overwhelmed. I try to be supportive. I tell them everybody starts with an A, and I want everybody to keep their A. They know early on I am invested in their success.

Cyrus's attitude is in contrast to many professors I have worked with, whose main preoccupation is catching potential cheaters. I do not mean to minimize academic integrity concerns, and I have certainly had my share to deal with, but, like Emmeline and Cyrus, I'd rather stay up late dreaming up more ways to connect with the students than ways to entrap them. Chakras are about energy, and the energy we nurture is the one that will more easily expand.

Faculty talked about the heart, love, and relationships in the context of their scholarship as well. For instance, Brody, the professor of management who talked about giving thoughtful nos in chapter 2, does research on different kinds of relationships in the workplace:

> I'm all about relationships. My dissertation was about workplace ostracism, the intentional withholding of connection, and the consequences to the person. Good management and leadership are all about connecting with people, so I find a way to weave the importance of relationships in the course. At the end of every class I talk about the power of kindness. We are developing future business leaders, and I want to leave an impression with them that regardless of intelligence and leadership skills, you have the opportunity to be kind to people. I use actual business stories to make that point.

Beyond the subject of the scholarship, Audre, who we left in the previous chapter discussing how to hold onto her power, describes a heartful stance in her work:

> Early on in my career I made a commitment that my work, my poetry, would not be just an aesthetic exercise. I decided it should be culturally and communally responsive. I had a job teaching in a women's prison. Many of my students were pregnant women. At some point they were going to deliver and the way this worked is that when they went into labor they would

be shackled hands and feet to be taken to the hospital, deliver, and then the county would take the child. Having witnessed the dehumanizing ways systems treat human beings, I can't just write about flowery things. I have to speak out.

Audre is echoing Alexis Gumbs's concept of the community-accountable scholar (described in Brazzel, 2020), which underscores the connection between love and accountability. Acting lovingly toward something involves being accountable to that thing. We are always accountable to something or somebody in our scholarship. For instance, we have to meet our departmental metrics for output, quality, and significance. But when we ask ourselves who we really want to be accountable to and how, the answer reveals our heart's stance, and that will inform our choices.

Donna talked about the importance of emphasizing the heart in fields that traditionally eschew it, and one way in which she does that:

> Engineering is very disembodied. It's a foil. It makes it obvious that emotion isn't there. It cries out for it. And I've always been the person that will bring it. I'll cry first. I'll express the emotion for the group. In the corner of engineering I've cut out for myself, people get it.

Eden goes back to emphasizing scholarly conversations as a means of cultivating the heart:

> My approach is to use our disciplinary tools to have heartful conversations, and psychology gives us a wealth of those. For instance, a few years ago the American Psychological Association passed a resolution of apology to people of color for its role in promoting, perpetuating, and failing to challenge racism, racial discrimination, and human hierarchy in the United States. It [is] easily searchable on their website. It is grounded in historical facts and empirical evidence, and chock full of references to peer-reviewed articles. I discuss this apology with my students, and it is so helpful. I recognize that our identities and biases are always at play, but this official document grounds the conversation so that it is not just my opinion. It is the beginning of community and solidarity.

Many other faculty spoke about community and relationships as a way to nurture the heart. Carly, a communication professor and administrator, follows her natural inclination to connect with people:

> Academia is so siloed. I try to break out of that on purpose. I've always been that one, like in high school cafeterias where you have the jocks at one

table, then the nerds, then the theater kids, and all the cliques. I was the one who was sitting with a different group every day. So I do the same here at the university. At this faculty renewal retreat, I met a biology professor. His course is challenging, so the students nicknamed him "Heartless," which is a pun on his last name. I got to know him. [It] turns out [that] he has a special needs child he's devoted to. And he told me stories from his childhood, when his father took him fishing and working with animals, and that's how he discovered his love for nature and science. Not at all heartless. I believe everybody's got a story. And I know that finding the heart in other people is where I get my heart.

Alfred, a clinical assistant professor of medicine, relates a similar attitude:

In medicine you often work as teams. I try to find value in the human connection as well as the work. You have to spend time working on the relationship before working on the task. I do small talk before I do big talk. And I find that personal narratives help, getting to know people and the things that matter to them. It's rewarding on its own, but it also helps later with disagreements. If you've showed you value the person, they will know you are only criticizing their idea and not their whole self.

What are some of the connections faculty intentionally nurture? Several faculty spoke of their mentees, including Olivia:

My intention is to honor my mentees and be fully present with them. I talk to them as somebody who cares a lot about them. I try to do with them what my advisor did with me. The most important message they need to hear is: you belong here. We selected you. You don't have to continually prove you are smart to us. You *are* smart enough, even if you are still learning a lot of things.

When we start from the person in front of us rather than from the content we need to pass on, we are nurturing the heart, ours and theirs. A group similar to graduate student mentees is younger, early career faculty. Damian describes how he stands up for them:

Despite the challenges at my university, I still love my profession. And I want to protect the faculty in it, especially younger faculty. That's why I raise questions others won't in faculty meetings, like questions about workload, hours, expectations. Or why I serve on the T&P committee. I want to make sure everybody gets a fair and compassionate shake.

Damian continues by describing another professional connection that nurtures his heart:

> I participate in a weekly writing accountability group. I love it. It nurtures me. Usually, the purpose of those groups is to hold you accountable to the university. Finish this paper so your tenure case is safer. But this group helps me [to] be accountable to myself. For instance, this week's goal is to stop work at 5:00 p.m. Do the work you need to be doing and do it efficiently so you can be done at 5:00 p.m. Also, I am the only White person in that group. And that is important to me because of the different perspectives I get and the checks on my privilege.

Damian offers several themes. One is the idea to use whatever influence we have, or whatever safety we feel, maybe from our tenured status, in service of protecting those in more precarious positions. The second one is to reimagine structures so that they are not simply in service of productivity (the power chakra) but of our heart and well-being as well. The third is to break out of our comfort zone. We tend to associate with people who are similar to us, but when we consciously seek out connections across lines of difference, we open the door to growth, both of the mind and of the heart. While Damian is talking about racial differences, Felix describes nurturing connections across disciplinary lines:

> My best, most emotionally warm connections are not in my own department, but with people who work on the same issues I work on. Many are not even in the same field! I have deep connections from fields like psychology or anthropology that have become the best sorts of friendships.

Vivian goes even further to highlight the importance of connections outside the professional sphere:

> I get my need for connection satisfied by belonging to groups outside of work. For instance, groups of yogis and runners. I've moved around a lot and everywhere I've gone I've been part of a group like that. The best part is that, with those people, my job doesn't matter. They don't even know what I do, or what my title is!

Connecting around our passions helps us unplug from work and nurture parts of ourselves that work does not usually attend to. When the passions are about physical activity, like in Vivian's case, these connections also add all the health benefits stemming from them.

Conversely, seeking sameness can also nurture our heart. Simon, the professor of public health we met in the desire chakra, talks about a peer group that matters to him:

> I nurture the heart by forging and maintaining relationships with colleagues I like and trust. I have a text message thread with other Black gay academics, not even at my institution. I'm fortunate that I have found friends who understand what I go through as a Black man and also share an academic background. Race is a crucial lens of analysis in public health. Some of my papers were fueled by my gut reaction to things I was experiencing, and then I took my training to translate all that in academic ways that my colleagues can hear and process and see if it resonates with them.

In her best-selling book *Why Are All the Black Kids Sitting Together in the Cafeteria?* (2017), Beverly Daniel Tatum explains the importance of these affinity groups for people who experience racism (or other isms). People who share our background and experiences make us feel seen, validate our gut feelings or give us a reality check, empower us to speak up, and much more. Developmental psychologists call experiences such as belonging to Simon's text thread "immersions" (Cross 1995) and point out that they are essential for our social identity development.

Faculty insights: Balance

As we already mentioned, the heart serves a second function, conferred by its position as the center of the system—that of balance. Some even say that that is the main function, as balancing all the chakra energies in harmony with each other is the whole point of this work. And yet, this puzzle is tenaciously hard to solve. When I asked faculty how they find balance, the most common answer was "I do not. I don't have strategies to share, but I can't wait until the book comes out so I can find out what others said." The spontaneous convergence to this answer to my open-ended question shocked me. Some even admitted they ended up in therapy due to their lack of balance. Emmett gave a sharp description of his unbalanced state:

> I found balance by quitting academia. The first month at my new job, my manager was like, Why are you online? It's 8:00 p.m. in your time zone! Go be with your family! It threw me for a loop. I didn't find balance in academia. I felt more like I was being torn into pieces than I felt like I was being held in place.

Academia is a notoriously high stress environment, with educators reporting stress levels just below doctors, who deal with life-or-death split-second decisions, and above construction workers, who face significant health and safety risks (e.g., Statista, 2016; Vivian Health, 2023). Simon argues that imbalance is a feature, not a bug of the neoliberal university:

> The mythic quest to achieve work–life balance is ridiculous. I never figured it out. For a while I tried very much to do it, work 9–5, not check email on the weekends, and it didn't work. I have no problem disconnecting. But without working on weekends, I couldn't maintain the productivity required. The structure is designed with the expectation of not having balance, you could not get tenure without all that.

Sasha's story ends with an important insight:

> As a faculty member I figured out how to be great. Then I had two kids and suddenly there was so much more to balance and I was awful at it. When my daughter was three, she once asked me: What are you doing here? Sweetie, I *live* here! No, mom, you live at the office! #WorstMotherEver No one will come to you and tell you to do less and slow down. It's always up to you.

Over the years, I have worked with so many amazing women, smart and productive academics and devoted parents and wives, who have confessed to me at a low point that they felt like the worst mother ever. So if you are feeling that way, I am here to say no, you are not. The competition for worst mother ever is very stiff. But Sasha is right. It is up to us to find our balance. Nobody will come and save us.

Other times, the lack of balance can be symptomatic of deeper issues, as in Tim's case:

> I used to have these periods of hyperfocus, which I referred to as being in the zone. I loved them but they were followed by long stretches of not being able to focus at all. With the help of my doctor, I realized that was a symptom of ADHD, so we got that under control with medication. I also suffer from depression, and I have observed that having my ADHD managed has also helped with depression. All of that has been tremendously helpful in balance. Now I can grade with focus through the day then have dinner with my husband.

So how do the faculty that feel at balance create it? Petra focuses on strong boundaries and a powerful heuristic:

> Even as an administrator, I opted to stay on a ten-month contract. In the summer I have to go see my family and friends in the UK. I do not get

paid, so I am very clear that I need to unplug, except for a couple of hard administrative deadlines.

But even during the school year, at a basic level I plan my time, all of it. Every day, I say: what are the three things I *have* to do today? And I do those. Everything comes later, if I have time to do them. If not, that's what tomorrow is for. I won't even look at that today. It comes down to your core values. My filter is: what's going to make the biggest difference today? Some days it's teaching, some days it's administration, some days it is time with the kids.

Olivia, too, focused on setting strong boundaries and letting go of the outcome, which helps her have a strong sense of identity:

I told myself, if I get tenure I'll be set, but if I don't get tenure I'll be okay. I didn't want to get stuck into the mindset of I must get tenure or else. I promised myself I would only work on things I enjoyed doing, and I would not work weekends or evenings. I wanted to have a life. I don't identify as a professor. That's what I do for a living. I identify as other things. I don't even hang out with academics.

Olivia did get tenure and kept her balance, as well as her detached attitude. In fact, that might be one of the secrets for those who find balance, as Angel articulates:

Balance is hard for academics because our identities are tied up with our work. Many faculty can do big chunks of their work from home. When you have whole days where you don't go to campus, setting boundaries can seem impossible. Understand you are not your work. Do the work to decouple your identity from your work.

Others found a workable path for themselves by making peace with the demands of academia, Wendy being one of them:

Balance is sort of overrated. A common theme I keep hearing from my colleagues is that the newer folks emphasize balance without understanding that academic work is not the traditional nine to five. It allows you to organize your life in a way that makes sense for you, but you do have to be careful not to let it overrun your life. It looked different in my life as a single person, than as a coupled person, and now with kids.

In other words, Wendy focuses on the affordances of academic work, for instance, the ability to work from home some days, and she keeps reworking her arrangements in a dynamic fashion as her life circumstances change.

Several others reframed the whole goal, like Eden:

> A colleague advised: don't think about balance but integration. Balance implies separation. Work for reunification instead. For instance, I schedule walking meeting so I can integrate work and nature/wellness. I adopted a dog the day after I submitted my tenure portfolio. She reminds me of staying in the moment, and that the purpose of life is joy.

Interestingly, she was not the only one to mention animals as reminders of wellness, presence, and balance. Serena, the professor of fashion marketing who discussed moving through her fear of not having all the answers for her students in chapter 1, credits horses:

> Horses are the ones who taught me about slowing down. There is so much in front of us and when we are so busy running around, we miss all of it. We don't see it, or we don't feel it, because we suppress feelings. But being with my horse, I awoke to that awareness of the world outside of me. That's when everything took off at work in terms of the depth of the relationships I was able to build, and the trust I could create. I learned to be attuned to my students' emotional energy for instance. I would be like, something does not feel right, let's turn away from the monitors and make a circle and talk about it. Students loved it, and asked if we could do this again when we feel we need it? I was bracing myself. I thought I might make a fool of myself but instead I made a difference.

The idea of slowing down is echoed by others, in particular, by Grace:

> How do I find balance? I slow down. When I feel stuck with bolts of hopelessness, I know I need to slow down so I can step back, gain perspective, have the opportunity to imagine, to dare, to create. When there is no pause, there's no chance to imagine, and then it's a vicious cycle.

What other strategies do people use to invite balance in their life? Bridget echoes the Pareto principle we invoked in the power chakra: "I am an '80% is good enough' kind of person. I'm not a perfectionist and that has helped me with balance." Honorine goes back to her foundational value—her family:

> I find balance by reminding myself that my first ministry, my calling, is my family. They have to be okay before anything else. No publication could come before them. Balance came when I started to say no and being clear how my decisions would affect my time with them. I know I'm in danger physically and emotionally when I don't do that.

Colin quips, but his strategy is to cultivate self and community:

> I tell people, drink more! Go to the pub with friends (do not drink by yourself at home)! Academia can be lonely, so you need to counter that. I play music with friends once a week. I just got back from Europe. My wife would tell you I work too hard, but I have many other interests. Also, sleep! Academia is stressful, but the idea that you cope with that stress by working insane hours is a joke.

Lachlan keeps the big picture in mind:

> I operate on a reward and punishments system for myself, and I always have the rewards lined up before the punishment starts, so I can minimize the punishment I go through. My bad day teaching or my long day at work is paying for my vacations, for the day I saw the baby elephant in Africa or the fine dining lunch I had in Paris.

Vivian holds on to an epiphany she had years ago:

> One day, I was in my backyard in my hammock and was looking at my feet and had a moment when I realized I was doing nothing. It occurred to me I couldn't remember a single point in my life that I was "doing nothing"—always thinking or worrying about a project versus just being, fully present in the moment. It was an epiphany. From there, I consistently work to carve out time in the evenings or weekends when I am doing nothing.

Cross-cultural scholars distinguish between "doing" and "being" cultures (Kluckhohn & Strodtbeck, 1961) and classify the United States as a decidedly "doing" culture. That impulse is always there because capitalism measures our worth by our productivity. Vivian's epiphany and reclaiming of doing nothing is quite radical in this optic. In her book *How to Do Nothing*, Jenny Odell (2019) unpacks the radical power of doing nothing as resisting-in-place, and argues that it requires discipline (the subroutines from the first chakra), desire, and will—naming healthy lower chakras as the foundations of this rebalancing act. Doing nothing allows us to appreciate what we already have instead of always looking at the next thing.

In yoga philosophy, contentment, or *santosha* (संतोष), is one of the five Niyamas, or observances, and it should be intentionally cultivated. From a chakra perspective, the right to be is an expression of the ground chakra, while the right to do relates to the power chakra. It is no accident that, in a doing culture, the thought of an afternoon on the hammock doing nothing fills many people with shame, the demon of the power chakra. But balance is a property of the heart, the center of the system, which is another way to say it is a function of the whole system. And in fact, looking at the quotes, we can see that balance happens with healthy expression of all the chakras in alignment. Spending time just being, an energy of the ground chakra, is important, as is keeping our values at the forefront, also from the first chakra, as Honorine's story demonstrates. Setting strong boundaries, from the second chakra, is also crucial, as Petra's and Olivia's experiences highlight, so that we can nurture our passions, as Colin does. Bringing in the will from the power chakra allows us to make plans, decide on the trade-offs we are willing to make, and stick to them, as Lachlan suggests. As we integrate the upper chakras in the discussion, it will be evident how those, too, contribute to balance.

Chakra right: To love

Unsurprisingly, the right connected to the heart chakra is the right to love. According to lifespan development, every age is characterized by an identity crisis. The main developmental crisis through one's 30s is characterized by the tension of intimacy versus isolation, and its guiding question is "Can I love?" (Erikson & Erikson, 1998). Most of this developmental work is carried out in one's personal life, through relationships, marriages, parenting, revisiting one's relationship with their parents, and so on, but a slice of this will organically happen at work. Is academia a good context to elaborate this crucial question? For the most part, it is. Judging from my interviews, participants didn't feel their right to love was particularly challenged. Nevertheless, some people brought up interesting points. Here is Ernest's take:

> Can you love at work? It's been well over 20 years since I met with a student with the door closed. Even when they come to see me to talk about mental health challenges. It's unfortunate, but it is a strong boundary that I have to set.

Of course, there is a reason why we keep the door open—to dispel any doubts that anything untoward is going on in the office. Power dynamics matter and ensuring that students will not be taken advantage of is crucial, but for somebody like Ernest, whose goal is to support students through their mental health crises, it affects how he can provide his support.

Amy, a White female associate professor of neuroscience and administrator, in transition between universities, discusses the related right to be loved: "This can be challenged too, because it's hard to feel appreciated for everything you are beyond dollars brought in grants and number of students taught. The holistic consideration is threatened." This is the heart of the issue. Some institutions are great at making faculty feel appreciated as human beings, while others are not. Felix gives an example of this problem:

Academia can be very critical. Its critical side leads to the failure to celebrate people, express joy in other people's accomplishments. I was up for a prestigious fellowship. The night before the deadline I pulled an all-nighter in my office. My mouse battery ran out on me. So I went out to the admin workstations and grabbed a mouse on the admin's computer. The next day they made such a big deal of it: you took Felicia's mouse! The scolding about the mouse took center stage and nobody congratulated me for making the deadline for submitting the fellowship application.

Small acts, like congratulating a colleague, cost us nothing and go a long way toward making them feel valued. And yet we often forget them. If academia does not make that a priority, we need to make it our own priority to create moments when we heap love on each other.

Chakra demon: Grief

Grief is a natural part of life, and academic life is no exception. Beyond literal deaths, faculty grieve a variety of metaphorical ones. For example, some mentioned mourning the fact that their jobs did not live up to the expectations they poured into them in grad school, realizing that we won't save the world one peer-reviewed paper at a time. Faculty who did not make tenure grieved leaving behind friends, colleagues, and a familiar life. Even those who left positions or institutions of their own accord grieved that separation. As Deirdre put it: "It's like a relationship, even if you are the one who broke up, you grieve what could have been."

Grief becomes a demon when it separates us from our heart, as Grace experienced. We have to go through all the stages of grief—denial, anger, bargaining, depression—to get to acceptance and meaning (Kübler-Ross, 2014). Clara shares a poignant story about keeping her heart open through her grief:

> In 2018 I was pregnant. All my students knew because I was showing. Then my husband and I went to a routine appointment on a Tuesday and found out the baby had passed away. I had to have surgery that Friday to remove the tissue and to make sure I was okay. I was heartbroken. I had classes on Monday and decided not to take time off. I thought the students deserved it, and it would keep me busy. I did not anticipate how hard it would be to tell my students. I had four classes, so I had to keep retelling the story through the day. I was a complete mess by the end. But I also experienced an outpouring of support from the students. They shared their stories with me. They brought me my favorite snacks. I was already comfortable being vulnerable, but this was a game changer. I have since incorporated that experience in my teaching, and now I do a unit where they can ask questions anonymously

about pregnancy and miscarriage and birthing, all the things society never talks about. It's a very successful unit. It pushed me to dedicate myself to this openness, this vulnerability, this honesty.

While Clara's heartbreak is not something that happens every day, her story highlights how grief can open us up to love and connection, if we embrace the vulnerability.

Prompts for reflection

- How do you nurture the heart, love, and connections at work?
- How do you practice self-love and compassion? Are there parts of your (professional self) that you struggle to embrace?
- What dualities have you reconciled within yourself (e.g., giving/receiving, success/failure, masculine/feminine, collaboration/independence, order/chaos, mind/body, professional/personal, being/doing and so on)? Which ones remain in tension?
- As you build your professional community, who do you want to be accountable to? How will you build this accountability in your work?
- The academy is a challenging balancing act. How do you cultivate balance? Conversely, which areas of your life feel imbalanced? What can you do to foster integration?
- How is your right to act supported in your context? How is it threatened? What can you do to protect it?
- What professional grief have you experienced? What lessons did the grief demon teach you?

Tools, strategies, and possibilities

As usual, in this section we will build a repertoire of strategies and suggestions to activate the heart chakra, some general and others specific to academia. Recall also that balance, compassion, and connection are three of the four pathways out of burnout that Rebecca Pope-Ruark (2022) identified, making the heart chakra an indispensable piece of the healing puzzle.

Breathe. Recall that the element of the heart chakra is air, and that the blood pumped by the heart oxygenates the whole body from the lungs. Intentional breathing that expands the lungs' capacity, as opposed to the shallow breathing we do on autopilot, contributes to general wellness. In addition, there are several established breathwork techniques to produce specific outcomes. Box breathing is grounding. Alternate nostril breathing is calming. Lion breathing, bellows breathing, and breath of fire are energizing. Ocean breathing is refreshing. And so on. A vibrant pranayama practice is a great companion to yoga and meditation.

Practice backbends. We have already mentioned the benefits of a regular yoga practice. In particular, backbends are heart openers. There are several beginner backbends that can serve as the foundation for deeper backbends, which in turn push us to the growing edge of our practice, inviting courage and vulnerability.

Practice loving kindness meditation. Meditation is a great tool for grounding, and we mentioned it as such in the ground chakra. One specific type of meditation is loving kindness, where after finding a comfortable cross-legged position and stilling ourselves, we focus on generating positive feelings. The practice starts with a focus on self-love, then the energies expand to people we love, then people who we feel neutral toward, then difficult people, and finally all the people in the world. The meditation can be focused by repeating simple mantras. A classic one is "*Lokaḥ Samastāḥ Sukhino Bhavantu*" (लोकाः समस्ताः सुखिनो भवन्तु), translated as "May all beings everywhere know kindness and peace."

Practice giving. Arms and hands are connected to the heart chakra and, as the saying goes, arms and hands are the wings of the heart. Generosity is certainly part of a well-developed heart chakra, and we can use the practice of giving as a laboratory. Study what happens when you give of yourself. Decide to give money to every unhoused person you meet for a week. Or to say yes to your chair's requests for a month. Or to your students' requests for extensions. Notice what happens to your sense of self when you give. Notice when it does and doesn't feel safe to give. Notice when you feel that you can't say no. Notice when requests run up against your boundaries and which ones do not. Treat this as an opportunity to learn about your heart.

Practice receiving. Conversely, if you are always quick to give but struggle asking for what you need, practice receiving. You are certainly worthy of other people's generosity. Again, treat this practice as an experiment and notice what happens when you allow yourself to receive, or when you push yourself to ask for what you need. Ask for deadline extensions if you feel overwhelmed. Ask more experienced faculty to mentor you on a grant proposal. Notice when asking feels uncomfortable and look for patterns. Notice if shame or guilt arise when you ask for help, and notice what happens when you work through those demons. Notice when receiving feels uncomfortable, and also notice when people are happy for the chance to do something for you. Remember this is a learning opportunity.

Practice forgiveness. Forgiveness is one of the 12 petals of the heart chakra lotus and an essential component of a balanced heart chakra. Our culture presents a distorted view of forgiveness, and so it is good to get clear on what forgiveness is and what it is not. It does not mean forgetting the harm, or not protecting ourselves from future harm, or not seeking restitution. It is not decoupled from accountability. In his book *The Book of Forgiving: The Fourfold Path for*

Healing Ourselves and Our World (2015), Desmond Tutu explores the practice of forgiveness and its spiritual and psychological benefits, now empirically verified by science. It would be impossible to do justice to that book here, so I will just recommend it for further reading. For our purposes, forgiveness is governed by the belief that letting go of the grudges we nurse in our heart is healing for us first—even when it comes to the PhD advisor who put his name first on our paper even though we did the great majority of the work, or the committee who did not endorse our application for promotion.

Focus on relationships as the core of your teaching. Recall Emmeline, who doesn't fight her students anymore and instead assumes they are all in this together. What would happen if we made that the point of departure of our pedagogy? Not the content, not standards and rigor, not the gatekeeping and the punishing of the cheaters, but hearts and relationships, doing our best to learn our students' stories, being the professors we wish had taught us, as Valerie said. There's room for the rest too, but when we lead with relationships, from relentless welcome to warm hand-offs, we can unlock extraordinary results, as Peter Felten and Leo Lambert document in *Relationship-Rich Education* (2020).

Adopt contemplative pedagogies. Contemplative pedagogies is an umbrella term describing several contemplative practices that can be adopted into our teaching. At first glance, this is a haphazard collection: pedagogies of movement (yoga, walking), of stillness (silence, meditation), ritualistic (vision quests, altar making), activist (volunteering/service, vigils), relational (deep listening, storytelling), and more. But the red threads linking them all are *connection* (to others, to nature, to our deep self) and awareness. These pedagogies shift "the focus of teaching and learning to incorporate 'first person' approaches which connect students to their lived, embodied experience of their own learning" (Contemplative Pedagogy Network, 2017). Through these practices, students can connect their learning to their values (ground chakra) and their sense of purpose (crown chakra), mediated by the heart chakra, producing more meaningful learning. In their book *Contemplative Pedagogies in Higher Education* (2013), Barbezat and Bush provide a rich account of all these pedagogies with multiple examples of faculty who have integrated some of them into their courses. This is an excellent starting point for those wishing to learn more.

Plan nano conferences. Learning from her experience with the European visitor, Wendy has made professional connections a cornerstone of her approach:

> The beauty of academia is that it connects us with people all around the world. I have colleagues who have become friends that I have only met in person twice, but we are super connected virtually for our work. One of the ways I cultivate those connections is through *nano conferences*. It's two to four

faculty getting together in person to work deeply on something for a few days at least. We do them on a shoestring budget. A couple have been at my house, with people passing through town. We also build that into grants when possible, a line item in the budget for in person meetings.

Nurture connections through storytelling. Storytelling is a way to build authenticity. When we tell our story, we present ourselves to the world exactly how we wish to be seen. Neuroscience has discovered that multiple areas of the brain activate when listening to a story, an unsurprising finding since stories activate emotions, meaning, and even bodily responses. But, amazingly, the brain patterns of the listener synch up with the storyteller's brain patterns (Stephens et al., 2010). The connections start at a molecular level! Storytelling is a very versatile tool. It can be employed in teaching. My center has structured new faculty orientation around storytelling, asking participants to share the story that brought them here, and the story they want to tell about themselves in one year or five years. We then simply share knowledge and resources to help people realize their stories. It is not an accident that this book is organized through faculty stories. Many other uses of storytelling are possible, with a little creativity.

Participate in social events on campus. Most campuses schedule several social events through the year. It is natural to feel that we can't spare the time, but the benefits of getting out of our silos, reconnecting with colleagues we rarely see, and reset our brain bring balance to the time spent in the office, the lab, or the studio. Alternatively, schedule your own social events. I know of several faculty groups who go out to lunch periodically, where the only stipulation is to not talk about work. They describe these moments as recharging their batteries.

Slow down. As Sasha remarked, it is up to us to slow ourselves down. Nobody will do that for us. What are the professional areas where we can afford to slow down? What would that look like? It certainly might involve setting boundaries and saying no, so all the strategies from the pelvic chakra apply. In their manifesto *The Slow Professor: Challenging the Culture of Speed in the Academy* (2016), Maggie Berg and Barbara Seeber offer several strategies for slowing down our teaching, our research, and our service.

Do nothing. Building on the previous strategy, sometimes slowing down is not enough and we need to screech to a halt. Try scheduling times where the goal is not to produce and do, but to be. Work them into the rhythm of the semester. For instance, orientation is a charged time for my center, so I schedule an off-the-grid vacation right after. For others, the stress might be at the end of the semester. If a vacation is not possible, maybe an hour on the hammock might do wonders for you, like it did for Vivian. Jenny Odell's book (2019) elevates these ideas from intentional rest to a political consciousness.

WORKSHEET 4.1 WRITE YOUR BALANCE MANIFESTO

Let's start by reflecting on how balanced some of your polarities are. If this applies, how happy are you with the balance between teaching and research in your job? giving/receiving, success/failure, masculine/feminine, collaboration/independence, order/chaos, mind/body, professional/personal, being/doing

Are you able to balance the short-term urgent demands of your job with steadily advancing your long-term priorities?

Does the effort you exert to support your department feel proportionate to the support you get back from your department?

Does the ratio of time spent at work with time outside of work (including sleeping) feel appropriate to you?

Are there other polarities in your life that should be included in this reflection? What are they and how do you feel about their balance?

Write your balance manifesto. Don't write it as aspirational (e.g., I wish I did more of this and less of that). Instead, write it from the viewpoint of having already achieved that balance and describing what it looks like (e.g., I integrate my hobbies into my work by making them the subject of my scholarship. I protect my time on the weekends to spend it with my family, but I dedicate a half hour on Sunday to getting organized for the week so I will feel ready on Monday and not overwhelmed).

Copyright material from Michele DiPietro (2026), *The Faculty Guide to a Balanced and Harmonious Career*, Routledge

What would you need to make your manifesto a reality (e.g., time, money, recognition, resources, and hard conversations)?

Create a plan to bring more balance in at least one of the areas you listed.

References

Barbezat, D., & Bush, M. (2013) *Contemplative practices in higher education: Powerful methods to transform teaching and learning.* Jossey-Bass.

Berg, M., & Seeber, B. (2016) *The slow professor: Challenging the culture of speed in the academy.* University of Toronto Press.

Brazzel, M. (2020) Community accountable scholarship within a critical participatory action research model. In D. Bendix, F. Müller, & A. Ziai (Eds.), *Beyond the master's tools? Decolonizing knowledge orders, research methods, and teaching.* Rowan & Littlefield Publishers.

Contemplative Pedagogy Network (2017) *What is contemplative pedagogy?* Accessed online at https://contemplativepedagogynetwork.com/what-is-contemplative-pedagogy

Cross, W. (1995) The psychology of nigrescence: Revising the Cross model. In J. Ponterotto, J. Casas, L. Suzuki, & C. Alexander (Eds.), *Handbook of multicultural counseling* (pp. 93–122). Sage.

Erikson, E., & Erikson, J. (1998) *The life cycle completed.* W.W. Norton & Company.

Felten, P., & Lambert, L. (2020) *Relationship-rich education: How human connections drive success in college.* John Hopkins University Press.

Kluckhohn, F. R., & Strodtbeck, F. L. (1961) *Variations in value orientations.* Row, Peterson.

Kübler-Ross, E. (2014) *On death and dying: What the dying have to teach doctors, nurses, clergy, and their own families.* Scribner.

Odell, J. (2019). *How to do nothing: Resisting the attention economy.* Melville House.

Palmer, P. (2011) *Healing the heart of democracy: The courage to create a politics worthy of the human spirit.* Jossey-Bass.

Parker, P. (n.d.) The Art of Gathering Digital Course for Teams. Priya Parker. https://course.priyaparker.com/products/the-art-of-gathering-digital-course-for-teams

Pope-Ruark, R. (2022) *Unraveling faculty burnout: Pathways to reckoning and renewal.* Johns Hopkins University Press.

Statista (2016) Percentage of working adults in the U.S. who say their current job is bad for their stress level, as of February 2016, by sector. Accessed at www-statista-com.us1.proxy.openathens.net/statistics/642765/workers-with-stressful-jobs-in-us/

Stephens, G., Silbert, J., & Hasson, U. (2010) Speaker–listener neural coupling underlies successful communication. *Proceedings of the National Academy of Sciences of the United States of America, 107*(32), 14425–14430.

Tatum, B. D. (2017) *Why are all the Black kids sitting together in the cafeteria? And other conversations about race.* Basic Books.

Tutu, D., & Tutu, M. (2015) *The book of forgiving: The fourfold path for healing ourselves and our world.* HarperOne.

Vivian Health (2023) *New survey ranks healthcare as most stressful career.* Accessed at www.vivian.com/community/wellness/new-survey-ranks-healthcare-as-most-stressful-career/

5
HOW DO WE CULTIVATE OUR VOICE?

The throat chakra

Can the postdoc speak?

I was involved in an interesting project toward the end of my postdoc, as I was transitioning to becoming a faculty member. My mentor had a prestigious grant with the National Institutes of Health, and I was helping out with it, with the understanding that I would become a Co-Principal Investigator (Co-PI) once I was officially made a faculty. The project involved engaging with Black queer communities.

As a queer Black man who does research on HIV and racism, I know quite a lot about engaging Black queer communities. In particular, researchers can't just go in and expect people to give them time and access to information and data collection. Marginalized communities are skeptical of academia. Too many times, they have been subjected to these extractive practices, where researchers come in, make promises to the community to gain access, get the data they want, and then bolt, walking back on their promises. So the community is now suspicious, wondering why these people are here, what their motives are, and if they can be trusted. And the thing is—this is all reasonable. For those of us who do research on public health topics, the motivation has to be to actually help the communities we work with. If it's only to get the data we need so we can write a paper so we can get a grant so we can get tenure, that is disingenuous, not to mention exploitative when you think the paper wouldn't exist if it wasn't for the cooperation of these marginalized communities. I have a lot to say about this, hahaha! And I decided I would say it. People warned me not to say anything because I was only a postdoc. First of all, I did not want to start my faculty career by silencing myself. And also, I did not want to be Co-PI of a flawed project.

DOI: 10.4324/9781003487371-6

There were so many issues to address that it would have been hard to address them well verbally, but I knew I could do it better in writing. I was an English major as an undergraduate, and I am confident in my ability to write a reasoned and persuasive argument. So I organized my arguments. I gathered all my evidence. I distilled all the guidelines for community-based action research. I addressed all the points of mismatch with the project, but I maintained an optimistic tone, and I made sure to not blame individuals. And when I aired my grievances, people listened! I knew they were good people who wanted to do the right thing. It turns out the right thing was hard to do. For instance, one of my suggestions was that we needed more Black people involved in the project to send out into the community to collect data. Knowing that the research team shares a cultural background with the community they are researching positively influences trust—this is a well-documented fact.

My colleagues were willing to hire more Black students into the project as data collectors, but our institution was so White that they weren't many, so now what? The lack of imagination to think outside the box versus the path of least resistance working with the existing structures was frustrating. But I kept at it and eventually we got it right. We managed to establish a relationship of reciprocity and trust with the community, and as a result we collected better data and did a better project overall. I am proud to say my advocacy made for better science!

—Simon, Black gay male assistant professor of public health at a global public research university in the South

Becoming the problem

I fell into the academy accidentally. My mom and my sister are both professors, so I knew the traditions and the rites of passage, the tenure and promotion process. I thought I could do it and did it. But I had been unraveling since tenure (see Chapter 1). The exhaustion was the symptom, but the roots were many. My salary was a big sore spot. It was unequitable and yet every time I voiced my concerns, they were dismissed. The university should have focused on the problem of salary compression and even inversion, instead they branded me the problem because I kept bringing those up. So instead of talking about salary, I started talking about leaving. When I speak things out into the universe, I am being accountable to myself. When I say things, I feel I am done with the thinking stage and into the implementation and action stage. By serendipity, I met the chair of the leadership studies department of a Catholic university at a conference and things fell into place from there.

I moved institutions, but I was clear the next position would not be a place of permanence for me, just time to figure things out. My plan was simple: at the new place, I was going to do the work but be detached. I wasn't going to let the issues affect me. I would do my job and go home. That plan was doomed.

Excellence is such a core value of mine that I could not stay detached. I would point things out and try to make them better. As a leadership scholar, I spent a lot of time reflecting on these concepts. My strength is in making things better. I thrive in that space, particularly helping people to discover their leadership capacity and to use it to enhance the environments they are in—seeing a need, figuring out the resources, and making a plan to fix that need. My hope is that I use my strengths and my talents to make things better. When I am critiquing things, it's because I am trying to make them better.

And yet, once again, I became the problem when I drew attention to the dysfunction. A big issue for me was that I saw the students were seriously unprepared compared to my previous institution. We are admitting these students, and then they can't graduate because they don't have a strong foundation. We keep taking their tuition money knowing that such a large percentage of them will not graduate. That is wrong to me. It's a serious misalignment of values, especially at a religious university.

What I learned from all these experiences at multiple institutions is that I cannot be direct in my speech. When I do, I am described in terms I don't claim. If I am direct, they say I'm blunt, I'm harsh, I'm mean. So I learned I cannot be honest. I have not been able to use my voice in the way I want to use it. As a Black woman in the United States, my voice is tied to my racial identity, and I have to navigate all those complexities.

Needless to say, this is not working for me. In a few months, I will be leaving this institution too, and academia altogether actually. I am okay with it as I knew from the beginning that I was only biding my time here until I had more clarity. But I also know I had to prepare my mother before I could break the news to her. I had to be very careful. I had to do it face to face, sit her down, and choose my words carefully. And I know that, as careful as I was, it still broke her heart when I told her. As an emigrant from southern Africa, being in academia is a measure of success to her. Me? My measure of success is being in an environment where I can speak in my full voice, standing in my values.

—Honorine, cis Black woman from the diaspora, associate professor of leadership studies at multiple institutions

The 40-year-old virgin

I came to academia late. I used to work for a lighting design firm, and I supported my husband while he got his education. When it was my turn, I was 40, so I always joke that I was the 40-year-old virgin to college. And truly, I had no idea how it all worked. I got my bachelor's and my master's degrees, and they asked me to teach for them as soon as I graduated. I thought they must be crazy to want to put me in charge of a course. But as soon as I was in the classroom, with the students hanging on my every word, I loved it. So that's how I became an adjunct faculty.

Faculty who teach part-time face a lot of challenges. My colleagues and I are no exception, but it would be unfair of me to blame my institution. The problems are systemic. I actually have a great relationship with the president of the university. They all wish they could do more with the resources they have. That's why advocacy is so important.

I have been fortunate to have some great mentors and champions—Dr. Amos for one. He was a senior tenured faculty member and was respected across campus. He saw the challenges adjunct faculty were facing and made that his cause. He started making the case to the administration that part-timers needed their own council to be able to present issues and solutions in ways that made sense for them. He drew a group around him, including young full-time faculty, to represent the face of changing times and attitudes. As soon as I got wind of this project, I told him that I wanted to be involved. The president was not opposed to this idea, as long as the faculty senate was on board.

Truthfully, back then there was a minority of full-time professors who felt that adjunct faculty were less credentialed overall, and as such it was only fair that they didn't have the same level of say in university affairs. We had to keep making the case, and eventually we were able to be heard. The senate supported us, and the Part Time Faculty Council was founded.

I ran for president of the council, was elected, and served several terms. I am proud of our accomplishments. We advocated for raises and used data to make convincing arguments. The university prioritized our needs, and we received several raises over the years. We were also able to get the parking fee eliminated for part-timers. Parking is a thorny issue. Many part-timers are only on campus to teach one course, then they race off to the next university they teach at, where they also have to pay parking, and maybe a third one too to make ends meet. Being charged for parking at the same rate as full-time faculty is not equitable. We didn't get everything we asked for, naturally. That's how negotiations go. I take negative answers as "not now," and look for the right situations to bring my request up again. I am comfortable and confident asking for things from my background in sales. But I don't open my mouth unless I know what I am talking about and have figured out my messaging. Years ago, my mother-in-law gave me a cartoon with this quote: "Tact is making a point without making an enemy." I stuck it on my fridge.

I also started a newsletter, which was a great way to get the word out on issues that matter to faculty who teach part-time. One could see this as a small feat in the bigger scheme of things, next to salary raises and parking fee waivers. But it is the tool that most contributed to creating a sense of family, camaraderie and belonging. It gave us a group identity, instead of a bunch of people who show up after hours to teach general education courses in the evening. I have been in conversations with faculty at other institutions who want to adapt this model to their context. Not bad for a clueless 40-year-old virgin without a PhD!

—Calliope, female part-time instructor of English at a research institution in the Southeast

What's going on with these stories?

The common theme running through these stories is that of voice. These faculty members are all navigating the complexities of speaking up and expressing their truth. All of them are trying to be heard by somebody in a position of power and authority over them. Simon is only a postdoc and does not have the years of experience that senior faculty members possess, but he knows a lot about marginalized communities. He is advised not to speak up, but the issue is too compelling for him. He is persuasive and the project improves because of his contributions. Honorine is advocating for fairness and justice, key values of hers, but she is branded as mean and stereotyped as the angry Black woman, simply for bringing up issues that everybody else notices. The lesson she abstracts is that it is not safe for her to speak her truth in academia, even when her arguments are well reasoned and corroborated by evidence. In fact, she becomes the scapegoat when her colleagues decide to shoot the messenger. Even the process of communicating her decisions to her mother confirms that, at times, the most thoughtful and impassioned arguments can't spare somebody from disappointment. Calliope is already comfortable speaking up, but the changes she's working toward are so momentous that they require years of advocacy (and somebody in a position of privilege as a tenured faculty advocating side by side with part-time faculty). Even after the council was founded, she has to lean on all the savvy from her corporate days to steer the negotiations in a positive direction, make her arguments with tact, take rejection with grace. In the process, she also discovers the power of communication to share experiences and to form community.

These stories surface several important questions. How can we use our voice in a positive way? Is it safe to speak our truth, especially to people in a position of power over us? How do we argue our way with integrity through a conflict? How can we advocate and negotiate for our needs? How can we be heard and not dismissed? Where is the line between being direct and being labeled rude, or worse? How can we engage in dialogue when the other party stonewalls or lies? Voice, truth, and lies are all concepts related to the fifth chakra, the throat chakra. In the next sections, we will explore the philosophy of the throat chakra, add insights from the faculty interviews, corroborate them with evidence from the research, and finally present some strategies to protect and grow your voice in the academy.

What does chakra theory say?

After building a strong foundation in the ground chakra and creating the container for the passions and emotions of the pelvic chakra, we have grown our power in the solar plexus chakra and added love in the heart chakra. To reprise the metaphor of the sailboat borrowed from Kaufman (2020), we built a robust and secure hull. In the upper chakras, we are now ready to unfurl our sail and start cruising. Maslow (1954) talked about the B-realm, driven by "being" goals, as opposed to the D-realm and its deficit-based needs that characterized the hull and the lower chakras. When we are secure, we can devote energies to our growth and self-actualization. The sail is metaphorically also our canvas, which we can paint with creativity, imagination, and purpose, the functions of the upper chakras. Our sailing takes us now to the throat chakra, the nexus between the body and the head. The location at the throat and the vocal cords suggests this chakra's primary association, which is the voice.

The Sanskrit name of the throat chakra is Viśuddha, which translates to "especially pure," or "the purifier." It is represented as lotus flower with 16 petals. Inside the circle of the lotus is inscribed a downward pointing triangle, and inside that triangle is inscribed a smaller circle, symbolizing the ether element, or the sky, *ākāsha* (आकाश). Inside the smaller circle we find this chakra's seed mantra, "*ham*" (हं). The resident deity of this chakra is *Sadāshiva* (सदाशिव), the ultimate manifestation of Shiva. Traditionally, the lotus is white, the triangle is sky blue, and the petals are purple, or smoky, but in the modern representation, the color associated with the throat chakra is bright blue. The traditional element is ether, but, to underscore its function, sound is also considered its element (even though it is not technically a physical element but a vibration).

Vibration, in fact, is the principle of this chakra. It's the vibration of the vocal cords that allows us to express our voice. People with a healthy, expressive throat chakra will exhibit clear communication with a resonant voice, as well as the ability to listen. If this chakra is deficient, people will have difficulty speaking up, saying what they mean, or even putting thoughts and feelings into words. Conversely, those with an excessive throat chakra might be prone to gossiping, unable to keep confidentiality, or talk more than listen. But the concept of vibration goes beyond sound waves. Every physical object vibrates at a specific frequency. We even say, metaphorically, that people "vibe," and there is much truth to that. Two people walking together tend to synch up their gait. People listening to a story even synch up brain waves with the storyteller, a phenomenon known as neural coupling. Indeed, neural coupling is essential for successful communication (Stephens et al., 2010), as we intuitively affirm when we say we are on the same wavelength as somebody else. On a more cosmic level, vibration is the creative principle of the world. In Hindu cosmology, *Om*, or *Aum* (ॐ), is the primordial sound which created the world and persists as *nāda* (नाद), the cosmic vibration. When we speak, or chant, or otherwise use our voice, we tap into that cosmic vibration, and we co-create by participating in that creative act—speaking things out into the universe and moving from thinking to action, as Honorine said.

The creative aspect is so constitutive of the throat chakra that all creativity belongs here, not just spoken but written, visual, musical, etc. In fact, the identity we grow and nurture in this chakra is our creative identity. Our creative expression is the next step in which we grow our identity from individual to universal. Our scholarship and creative activity will survive us on the internet long after we are gone. And when others encounter it, it will enrich them because communication expands our experience. If I listen to a friend telling me about the northern lights, it might not be as if I experienced them firsthand, but it will certainly be more than not knowing about them at all. Back to the neural coupling, the mirror neurons that activate are the same ones that would fire if I was indeed experiencing the northern lights myself.

The power of our voice can also be destructive, as the opera singers who can shatter glass with their voice demonstrate. Simon, Honorine, and Calliope all took risks with their voice. But while Simon and Calliope were successful, Honorine's words shattered the fragile status quo, at both her institutions. The glass breaks because the singer's pitch catches the frequency at which the glass naturally vibrates and amplifies its intensity to the point that it strains the glass beyond its vibrational capacity. Similarly, when we ask our context to stretch farther and faster than it is capable or willing to do, something has to give, and, unfortunately, it is often the messenger.

From a chakra system standpoint, good communication happens at the intersection of several energetic currents. The upward current traveling from our values and passions has to meet the downward flow from our higher consciousness and purpose. As they meet in alignment at the throat, we can speak our truth. At the same time, the chakras take energy in from the environment and express it back out; therefore, a balanced exchange is essential. When we have imbalances, we can either reduce the intensity of how we express ourselves, often resulting in the feeling of walking on eggshells; vibrate at the same frequency of the group, which might feel like groupthink, or selling out; help the environment grow its capacity to receive our requests, as Calliope did; or deem our context's inability to hear us as unsafe and toxic and flee, as Honorine did. A key yoga and Hindu belief is that of *satya* (सत्य), truthfulness. As we weigh our options, yoga reminds us that lying is not one of them. Satya is one of the five Yamas, the restraints which constitute the first of the eight limbs of yoga. It is second only to ahimsa, nonviolence. Indeed, lies are the demon of the throat chakra, both the lies we are told and the lies we tell ourselves and others. It only makes sense that the right associated with this chakra is the right to speak and be heard.

> **BOX 5.1   VOICE CHAKRA CHART**
>
> Sanskrit name: Viśuddha
> Meaning: Especially Pure
> Element: Sound
> Function: Communication, Self-expression
> Color: Blue
> Identity: Creative
> Right: To Speak and Be Heard
> Demon: Lies

The throat chakra has also another function, that of purification. *Saucha* (शौच), purity, is another central concept in yoga philosophy. It is the first of the Niyama, the observances. Yama and Niyama are to be practiced always, but Saucha naturally comes up in the throat chakra ("the purifier"), because it receives the *amrita* (अमृत), the nectar of immortality, which splits into a pure and poisonous forms. When the throat chakra is closed, the poison filters down into Manipura, the power chakra, where it is assimilated as poison and produces decay. An open and balanced throat chakra is able to purify the poison so that we absorb its wisdom. For this reason, purification practices are traditionally undertaken when working on this chakra.

Faculty insights: Voice

How do faculty build their voice? When is their voice strong? When is it weak? The interviews reveal complex, even opposite, approaches. Echoing the three opening stories, the polarities that emerged from my interviews are between speaking and not speaking, and internal versus external factors that build or dampen our voices. Gail, who we met in the desire chakra being berated by her superstar advisor for becoming pregnant before having written a book, describes the power of her audience in shaping her voice:

> My voice is powerful when I sense that people believe in me. It doesn't matter if they agree with me or not, but I need to know they have an inherent respect for me. That interaction with my mentor at the conference really shook me. He did not support me and had no respect for my choices. That has shaped me.

Similarly, Emmeline declares: "Voice is a verb. I use it, I voice my truth, if I feel I am going to be heard. I want no part of a group that will not hear me. They do not deserve my voice."

Conversely, reflecting on the time she sent resources to discuss anti-Asian hate to her president, Eden moves from a different point of departure: "It's ok if my voice isn't heard in the way I want it to be heard, but it's important that I speak it. Silence is not neutral." Audre elaborates on this point:

> I feel a responsibility to speak the truth. I would be remiss if I walked into a room and did not do that. When I was younger emotion crept into my voice a bit, now I can take the higher view and not judge people by the moments in which they are not being their best selves, but it is my duty, my dharma, my purpose in life to speak my truth.

Dharma (धर्म) is one of those expansive concepts that doesn't have an immediate equivalent in English, but in this context it refers to righteous, moral, lifelong duties we feel we are called to. Charlene, the professor of French who we met in chapter 1 scheduling walking meetings, offers a rejoinder between speaking and not speaking:

> You learn to see when it is worth speaking. Silence can also be a way for me to use my voice, because sometimes not saying anything is also saying a lot. I usually speak, so when I don't speak, people notice. And I have used that as a strategy. In my field, we use the concept of marronage—the process of extricating oneself from slavery, forming maroon communities. I see my voice as part of my ongoing process to free myself from societal oppression.

Moving away from the binary of to speak or not to speak, a related question is when to speak, as Brody's story highlights:

> At my previous institution, I was brand new on the faculty, but I had been on staff in an administrative role there for years so I was friendly with everybody. So at the first faculty meeting, when the chair brought up a proposal I felt very comfortable offering feedback. I thought nothing of it, as I was simply contributing my expertise. But a few days later, a colleague who was a good friend pulled me aside and told me a lot of people got upset that I spoke up. Who does he think he is? It's his first day here. He doesn't know the first thing about how the department runs! They saw my speaking as arrogance. At first I wondered, just how fragile of an environment is this? It is not my first day! I've been here for years! But as I thought about it, I realized sometimes you can be part of an institution for years but see a very different slice of it from a different vantage point. For all my seniority, I was actually inexperienced as faculty, and there is a lot to be said for observing and listening first. Initially I wanted to find out who said that and confront them, but really it was good feedback for me. So at my new institution I listened, I took notes, and it was a while before I spoke.

For an institution founded on the premise of creating new knowledge, disseminating it in society, and teaching it to students, my interviews reveal an agonizing soul-searching process. Age, experience, seniority, tenure can modulate the intensity of this process, but the decision to speak or hold your tongue is generally a charged one when the stakes are high. In addition, Carly reminds us that other individual variables can affect this process:

> When I am afraid to speak up, I interrogate the reasons for that and ask myself, do those reasons really matter more than the things I have to speak up about? Do those things have to be said here and now, and do I have to be the person to bring them up? I feel less in control in those moments, and that's scary because I want control. I do have generalized anxiety disorder, and a lot of my anxiety is about control.

When faculty speak, what moves them to do so? Wendy articulates the most frequent reason stated in the interviews:

> In her book, Linda Babcock says it's easier to advocate on behalf of other people than of yourself. So as you go along in your career and have more security, it becomes easier. Pay it forward and speak for others too.

The excellent book Wendy is referencing is *Women Don't Ask* (2007). Many faculty, and particularly women, admit that they find it hard to ask for themselves, but are willing to step up to advocate for other people and amplify their voices, particularly for those in more precarious positions—much like Dr. Amos did for Calliope. Among those, Damian:

> My POC colleagues have helped me understand my voice better, so I now use it when they cannot, or when they ask me to because they are tired. I say things like, I sure hope a bunch of the new hires will be POC, because we have more than enough White people in the department. I can say that as a White person, they can't. In large meetings, I write down what I am going to say so that I am clear when I say it.

As if in conversation with Damian, Tim, expands on this point:

> I was known as a measured nuanced voice, so when I spoke with a strong voice, people pay a lot of attention. I'm grateful for those with the strong voice. The one in our department left, which means I have to occupy that space more often. It's a bit uncomfortable. If I was the only Black person in the department, I would have no choice but to be that all the time. But people get sick or scared of you if you are always exposing inequality.

When we look at the factors that make faculty's voice strong, they are disparate, but a pattern emerges. Bridget says her voice is strongest when her deepest core values are violated. Petra feels her voice is strongest when she is passionate about the topic (talking to students about health, fitness, and well-being, in her case). Desiree knows her voice is resonant when she is confident, and she builds her confidence through her expertise, knowing what she is talking about. Lucien, a nonbinary transmasculine lecturer whose story we will explore in depth in the next chapter, the third-eye chakra, declares their voice is strong when their heart is engaged. Donna knows her voice is strong when she is grounded in community. These comments together trace the liberating current, from the root chakra and its values to the passions of the pelvic chakra, through the confidence of the power chakra and the connections of the heart chakra. They reinforce the point that a resonant voice is the intersection of the energies rising up from the root chakra and the charge coming down from the crown chakra, meeting and expressing at the throat chakra. Even without having delved into the crown chakra yet, it is easy to see that a full consciousness of ourselves—the quality of the crown chakra—helps us speak our truth, as Colin's comment demonstrates:

> The key for a strong, resonant voice is having self-knowledge, including both my strengths and my limits, and not letting them define me. Otherwise, you are speaking from a place of hubris, arrogance, and you will look foolish. This is Plato's message in "The Apology." Socrates's wisdom comes from knowing what he knows and what he doesn't know.

Having this self-awareness is particularly important as we work to find our voice, because the pressure to just vibrate at the same frequency as everybody else is always there, as Valerie tells her students:

> My advice is to be true to yourself. Say what you know you want to say. Don't bend your voice to fit what you think the powers that be want. I tell my grad students this all the time. They are all trying to figure out what they need to say so they can have and keep a job. I would say, keep your head down, do your work, but be true to yourself, and speak up when it matters. Decide what matters. Decide which battles you will fight because you can't fight them all. Decide what is meaningful to you. Decide the price you are willing to pay for your voice, because there will, at times, be consequences.

The theme of being true to oneself was echoed by others as well. For instance, Felix discusses it in the context of writing for publication:

> In the publication process there are pressures that tend in the direction of making you lose your voice and make you write in a way that is stereotypical

for the discipline. You have to respond with confidence and bend the arc of the reviewer's thinking from their position to yours.

The idea of being true to oneself needs an important clarification, offered by Desiree:

> I'm not very good in upper administration spaces, full of corporate speak and leadership speak, so I stay away from those. I couldn't be true to myself there. But at the same time, I reject the idea that there is only one self to be true to. While those spaces are definitely not me, I am many other things at once, as all of us are. We toggle back and forth these selves, and we code switch all the time.

As a Black queer professor, Tim is also regularly code switching:

> I grew up engaging in public speaking at church from the age of three, getting on stage and reciting bits from Dr. Martin Luther King's speeches. It's great training for being in front of the classroom or giving a presentation at a conference. But it's a little trickier how to be in a faculty meeting. You have so many decisions to make—how strong you want to communicate, who is going to be turned off by this language, who is going to be pulled in? So I deploy different registers strategically.

Speaking of faculty meetings and consequences, the following story is a reminder of the long-lasting ripples that surround some faculty when they use their voice. Aretha, the professor of mathematics in chapter 1 who retired when she sensed a mismatch between her values and her institution's, explains:

> In my second year I stood up to an extremely powerful colleague, and people thought I was crazy. But I thought it was she who was poisonous and rude and petty. She always undermined the chair and went around him to the dean. One time during a faculty meeting she was doing her high school whispering to the person next to her, being purposely disrespectful to the chair. So I turned to her and said I'M SORRY, WHAT DID YOU SAY? She later called me into her office and told me I needed to respect her leadership because she was more powerful than the chair. Wow. In retrospect, that branded me as a loudmouth and affected my attempts to get into leadership because that's how people saw me.

Far from putting the disrespectful professor in her place, Aretha's words colored her image in the department for years, long after the senior professor retired. This is one area that faculty highlighted as a challenge—managing conflict without either unloading on the other person or caving in. As another example, Gabby related her struggles to start a new program:

> For a long time now, I have been advocating for a new track for grad students. Many of them won't end up on the tenure track, but in other jobs in academia, like in a writing center, a center for teaching and learning, or other administrative roles, commonly referred to as alt-ac. I believe we owe it to our students to prepare them for the jobs they actually get… but it's not going well. For some reason I can't get traction. So now I am in a vicious cycle, because I am angry, and my anger doesn't win people over. My son just listened to Dale Carnegie's audio book and told me I can't lead with anger…I need to find something we all value and build from that, but it is a challenge.

Gabby's son is obviously referencing Dale Carnegie's book *How to Win Friends and Influence People* (2021), one of the most popular self-help books since its publication in 1936. Gabby sees what she is doing wrong, but she can't find a way out of it. A related challenge that faculty reported is negotiation, particularly negotiating salaries, course load, and service load, as Donna indicates:

> I do struggle with things like negotiation. I have to let go. Make your best case, and it yields what it yields. For a long time I thought that, since I can't get what I want, I must be a bad negotiator. But understanding that you don't always get what you want made me a better negotiator, because I try to see the other person's perspective.

Voicing our truths and needs can be quite challenging. The section on strategies will include communication strategies for high-stake situations.

Chakra right: To speak and be heard

Predictably, the right associated with the throat chakra is the right to speak and be heard. But interestingly, and alarmingly, the right to speak is the right the majority of faculty singled out as the most challenged right in academia. Some remarked that this predicament wasn't unique to themselves but a reflection of the national state of affairs about freedom of speech and academic freedom in higher education, particularly when it comes to heated topics like diversity and inclusion. Pointedly, many of the faculty who reported this challenge were women, or faculty of color, or international, or visiting lecturers, or faculty who teach part-time. Many of them explicitly attributed their challenges in being heard at least in part to systemic biases and the hierarchical structure of academia, which all work to discount those particular voices. Some remarked that their suggestions are simply not heard, but others, like, Devlin, report censoring themselves: "The right to speak is simply not there. I don't feel safe saying what I think so I often don't out of fear of reprisal." Rahul was quite blunt in his take of the landscape:

> I felt I had no right to say anything because they wanted me to be so grateful that I even have a job. You are owned by the university. They own your work. They pay you and you should obey. That's how I felt at the end.

And Emmett, having left academia for industry, encapsulates his feelings in a scathing comparison:

> I had been at my new job for 6 months and I disagreed with somebody who had been there for 10 years. They listened to what I had to say and did not dismiss me out of hand. Here, they listen even if I am wrong. In academia they wouldn't listen even if I was right.

To be sure, many other faculty did not report this right as challenged, but Deirdre offers an astute observation:

> Things that have happened politically nationally gave me a sense of impending limitation on my right to speak. I don't do research in equity and social justice so I can only imagine what it's like for colleagues who do. Processing the tensions around me, when I see that my colleagues' right to speak their truth is being compromised, I realize that my right to speak is conditional. It is only there because my speech doesn't challenge the powers that be. They are not stopping me now, but they have no problem stopping other people from speaking, which to me says they could stop me too if my words were deemed controversial.

Gail reminds us that we can also forfeit our right to speak if we are not careful, or trade it for academic favors: "If you allow yourself to become too beholden to others, you can't have self-advocacy, and you deny those rights first to yourself and then to others."

After a chapter dedicated to building our voice, listing so many ways in which the right to speak is threatened is a bit demoralizing. Acknowledging that this is a complex issue and that the challenges are real, the strategies section will offer some tools that can help us get our voice heard more.

Chakra demon: Lies

Quite unsurprisingly, the demon of the throat chakra is lies because lies are the enemy of the truth. Not many people singled out this demon specifically in their interviews, but several more mentioned in their stories people who had lied to them, colleagues, advisors, administrators, and others, using omissions, falsehoods, downright gaslighting. There is not much to say about that because we can't control what other people do. All we can do is cultivate our own trustworthiness, which is the currency of relationships, and be shrewd about who we place our trust in.

However, we also need to mind the lies we tell ourselves. For instance, Honorine describes her own situation:

> For a long time, I didn't distinguish between perfectionism and excellence. If I'm not perfect I will be discovered and kicked out. I was chasing perfectionism. The biggest lie I told myself is that I was a fraud if I didn't do it perfectly.

The lies we tell ourselves span all the chakras and connect to other demons. We lie about our worth, our power, to protect ourselves from shame or guilt, or we lie out of fear, and so on. As we work through the other chakras, we are better able to see through the veil of illusion (see Chapter 6).

Beyond these individual lies, a metanarrative emerged across the interviews. The biggest lie that academia tells about itself is that it is different. Academia is about knowledge and truth. It will use logic, the scientific method, critical thinking, epistemology, to arrive at the truth. Because it is about rationality, it does not concern itself with the petty gossip and power grabs and conniving. Its decisions are data-informed and evidence-based, so they are effective and efficient and bring the most good to the most people. The strength of your argument carries the day, not your status or title or salary of the speaker. Because it is built on reason, it is immune to human biases, in particular racism, sexism, homophobia, transphobia, ableism, xenophobia, and so on. As the French philosopher Lyotard (1984) argued, we should be suspicious of metanarratives, and indeed the stories in my interviews generally disprove each component assertion. Realizing that academia is just like every other human environment was quite sobering for some of the faculty, as Honorine kept discovered at multiple institutions when she spoke up, or Colin, or Rahul, or Donna, or Gail, or several others.

Prompts for reflection

- In what ways are you vibrating in synch with your professional environment? In what ways do you feel out of synch? What's good about either situation? What's bad?
- When is your voice strong? When is it weak? What happens in charged situations, such as conflicts or negotiation?

- What truth(s) are you trying to express at your institution?
- Which less-heard voices have you been able to amplify? Are you trying to do more in this space? What could help you build your advocacy?
- What purification practices could help you polish your lenses and clean your filters so that your perceptions are finer?
- How is your right to speak and be heard supported in your context? How is it threatened? What can you do to protect it?
- What are the lies that have plagued you, either told by others or by yourself? What lessons has this demon taught you?

Tools, strategies, and possibilities

After laying out the issues, it is now time for strategies. As we venture into the upper chakras, it is worth noting the correspondences between upper and lower chakras. In some ways, we are revisiting similar issues through different lenses. The metaphysical principle "as above, so below" definitely applies here. Therefore, it makes sense that a number of strategies that we introduced in previous chapters would be mirrored here as well. This is great news because it means those strategies do double (or triple, etc.) duty and work toward multiple chakras. In other words, we do not have to apply an infinite number of strategies to see the impact. For the sake of brevity, we will only mention strategies multiple times when we wish to highlight a new facet of the same strategy.

Commit to a purification practice. As mentioned earlier, the throat chakra is connected to purification. As we ascend through the chakras, we need to purify ourselves to access the more refined levels. Purification practices in yoga do not have a penitential purpose; instead, they serve a clarifying one. If the lens through which we look at the world is dirty, we will not be able to see clearly. Purification practices are how we clean the lens. Giving up liquor, caffeine, sugar, sex, are examples of such practices. It doesn't have to be forever, and you can treat it like an experiment, noticing how your energies shift during that period.

Engage in creativity recovery. The throat chakra is the chakra of creativity but many of us are blocked in that area. Writer's block in particular can hinder our success as it impacts our productivity. If, like Ernest, you are experiencing writer's block, there are several processes to unlock your creative juices. A very famous one is *The Artist's Way* by Julia Cameron (2016). That process is simpatico with the chakra system, as it works to recover, among other things, a sense of safety, identity, power, connection, and compassion, key concepts in our journey so far.

Practice talking. So much of what academics do involves talking: in the classroom, at conferences, in faculty meetings, on zoom, etc. We engage in a variety of speeches (e.g., informative, persuasive, and ceremonial). And yet many of us aren't comfortable with public speaking. Deliberate practice is the key to improving. Part of it is becoming comfortable with an audience, and another important part is to get feedback on our strengths as well as areas for growth. Some faculty have reported that their local Toastmasters group has helped them be better speakers.

Practice listening. The full right of this chakra is to speak and be heard. Therefore, active listening is crucial. Listening without judgment, without interrupting, without planning or rehearsing what we are going to say next, making eye contact, and paying attention to the non-verbal are some of the elements of active listening in academia, which favor a "high-considerateness" communication style. Those of us more used to a "high-involvement" conversational style, characterized by jumping in and interrupting, or speaking loudly, might be seen as rude and not really listening (Tannen, 2005). A different conversational style can be mastered with practice so that we are comfortable codeswitching depending on the situation, as Desiree remarked.

Practice writing. Written communication is a crucial part of our expression. We have already discussed the benefits of journaling, one of Ernest's "sacraments." And earlier in this chapter, Damian mentioned how writing down his points or argument before speaking helps him be clear and concise. In addition, academic writing spans many genres. A narrative for promotion is different from a syllabus, which is different from a grant proposal, which is different from a research article, which is still different from a research article in the scholarship of teaching and learning. We don't use all genres with the same frequency, so we won't be equally effective in each of them. Deliberate practice is key.

Take advantage of institutional services and opportunities. Again, a part of deliberate practice is constructive feedback. Many institutions offer considerable opportunities for feedback, and it would be wise to explore and take advantage of them. For instance, many offices of research offer guidance on grant proposals. Educational development centers also offer several services. For instance, at my center we offer mutual mentoring groups for those submitting portfolios for tenure, promotion, and other multilevel reviews, where participants have the opportunity to read drafts of each other's narratives and receive feedback. We have also offered writing accountability groups, grounded by the resource *Writing Your Journal Article in Twelve Weeks* by Laura Belcher (2019). Writing centers usually work with students, but sometimes they will serve faculty as well, or postdocs. Some institutions offer services for non-native English speakers. I even know of institutions that have engaged theater faculty to offer workshops to enhance public speaking with theatrical techniques. What is available at your institution might surprise you.

Cultivate your own trustworthiness. Truth is central to the throat chakra and goes hand in hand with trust. While some of the stories in this book show a great degree of trust with senior colleagues and the administration, others document broken trust. We cannot control whether other people trust us; we can only work on our own trustworthiness. Angel connects our trustworthiness with living in our values: "Your values are how you sustain yourself. If others are telling lies, do not tell lies. If others are gossiping, do not gossip."

Invite other voices into the conversation. This is a general principle, but it has wide applicability in teaching. Showing our students that we value their contributions works wonders for engagement. It is particularly important to invite student feedback early on in the semester, when we can course-correct and address issues brought up. Many universities provide templates for feedback forms, but other formats are possible as Serena, the recently retired fashion marketing faculty, demonstrates:

> I kept an anonymous comment box in class. Anybody can put a suggestion in the box, or even a frustration. That's a great way to open up discussion and realize there are more things in common than differences if you just take the time.

Amplify other voices. Building on the previous suggestion, we have seen from Calliope's story and Damian's comments how important the support can be from faculty with more power and security. If you are in that position, pay it forward, as Alfred suggested in the power chakra. That kind of allyship will benefit others, but it will also strengthen your voice.

Challenge microaggressions. Whether they are directed at you or at others, microaggressions dim the potential for constructive communication. It's hard to know what to say in the moment, especially since they might happen out of ignorance rather than malice, and we don't want to look like we are overreacting. Ganote et al. (2016) provide a simple but effective script, Open The Front Door (Observe, Think, Feel, Desire). After witnessing a problematic act, provide a descriptive, nonjudgmental observation of what happened. Add your thoughts about why this is important. Add how this makes you feel. And finally request a change in behavior. For instance: I notice in our discussion that when women speak they are often interrupted, but that doesn't happen when men speak. This differential treatment signals that women's contributions are less valuable. I personally feel uncomfortable with this dynamic, and I'd like to request moving forward that we honor all voices equally by not interrupting.

Cultivate motivating feedback. One of our most important speech acts as academics is giving feedback (e.g., in the classroom, on a tenure committee, and in the faculty senate). Yet many dread giving (negative) feedback, and the conflict it might herald. A quick Google search reveals countless listicles of techniques to give effective feedback. I recommend Therese Huston's *Let's Talk: Make Effective Feedback Your Superpower* (2021) because it emphasizes relationships and connections, as well as the values and goals of the giver and receiver of feedback, an approach in line with chakra theory.

Understand your conflict management style. Our empathy, assertiveness, and flexibility shape our conflict management style—accommodating, avoidant, compromising, competing, or collaborating (Killman & Thomas, 1977). You might have a sense of your style or you can take an online assessment at kilmanndiagnostics.com. From this awareness, you might decide you want to cultivate more assertiveness, more empathy, or more flexibility in your approach.

Separate the relationship from the conflict. Remember the cartoon Calliope taped on her fridge. In the heat of the moment, it is important to remember we are trying to resolve a conflict, not make an enemy. Serena shares her way of doing just so:

> I engage others with I statements—I feel, I believe. I do not use blaming statements. Blaming others is not expressing your voice. Even when in conflict, I try to leave a space open for others to put their ideas on the table.

Assigning fault, or labeling people ("You always complain!") is a quick way to make an enemy.

Understand both your goals and your interlocutor's. Sometimes people get hung up on their positions ("I do not support your proposal") without getting at their underlying goals and interests ("I am worried that we will all be overworked"). Focusing on positions gets us stuck. Focusing on goals and interests moves us toward problem-solving and inventing options for mutual gain. As Xander puts it:

> What am I asking for? What am I trying to achieve? I try to get really clear on that, then I craft my message around the concerns of my colleagues. What do they care about? Why are they bringing this conflict?

Don't be seduced by the dynamics of the conflict. During hot moments, our reactive nature can be activated. If we don't keep our goal in mind, pretty soon we are seduced and led astray on a side quest, where the goal becomes to win the argument, or to prove the other person wrong, or put them in their place. We don't need to rebut every point made, and keeping our eyes on the larger goal helps us focus our will and manage our emotions activated in the lower chakras.

Focus discussion on shared values. In an impasse, it can be helpful to take a step back. Alfred uses this tactic as a jolt to decision-making processes that are stuck: "When actions and values don't match up, I'll say, Hey, we say we have these values, but we're not acting on it so it's not really important."

Remind people that you are all on the same side. When possible, it is helpful to frame discussions as disagreements of strategy toward a shared purpose (e.g., student success, excellence in research, and shared governance). Using contrasting statements can help clarify your aim ("The last thing I want to do is dilute the rigor of our major and the value of our degree. Rather, I want to make sure that students with unique needs are adequately supported.")

STATE your path. One of the reasons discussions get derailed is because our usual path is counterproductive. We observe a behavior and immediately tell ourselves a story to explain it. ("She did that because she's selfish.") We attach feelings to that story, so now we are angry. And then we act, or rather react, accordingly, escalating the situation. Instead, Grenny et al. (2021) suggest a heuristic they call STATE your path. After observing the behavior, start by sharing (S) what you saw and telling (T) your story ("X happened, and when I see that I immediately worry about FERPA violations"). Ask (A) for other people's paths ("Am I the only one that worries about that?") to check consensus and allow for minority reports. As you advocate for a specific resolution, it is very important to talk tentatively (T) ("I wonder if we could do Y instead to avoid even the appearance of impropriety"). And, finally, encourage (E) testing ("Would that work for everybody? Or does anybody else have an alternative solution?").

Negotiate well. Negotiations are another example of high-stake communications. Whether it is negotiating salary and perks during a job interview, or a research leave, or any other request, asking for what we want can be daunting. Schneider and Kupfer (2017) have studied negotiation strategies in academia, and they offer several recommendations, grouped under the categories of Preparation, Assertiveness, Empathy, Flexibility, Social Intuition, and Ethicality. The worksheet at the end of this chapter will loosely take you through these dimensions and help you map out your strategy for a sample negotiation.

Write your values. We discussed and clarified our values in the ground chakra because they are the foundation for everything else. For instance, metanalyses show (McQueen & Klein 2006) that value-based self-affirmations can come in handy in high-stake situations, such as conflict or negotiation, or any other situations that feel like a threat to our identity—including a job talk or taking a test, which means this is advice you can also share with your students. This particular process is shared by Therese Huston in *How Women Decide* (2016). Before engaging in the discussion, find a quiet space by yourself, set a timer for 15–20 minutes, write one of your values at the top of a piece of paper, and spend the time writing about that value—why that is a value for you, how it came to become one, how holding that value has shaped your life, and any other reflection. You can choose any value you hold, not necessarily tied to your career. While this strategy doesn't guarantee a higher salary or the corner office, it reaffirms your identity, allowing you to walk into your high-stake situation with less anxiety and more confidence.

WORKSHEET 5.1 READY YOUR VOICE FOR NEGOTIATION

Identify a goal you would like to negotiate toward (e.g., a course release, additional funds for graduate students, a certain salary during a job interview, working remotely, etc.).
Vet your goal. Is your goal specific? How can you make it as specific as possible?
Is your goal reasonable? Can the department support it? What data support your ask? Do your research and show your work.
Is your goal aspirational? How will this goal make a difference for you and take your work to the next level? How will the department, college, and institution benefit? Is it anchored in the strategic plan, an institutional priority, or the long-term vision for the department?
What is your BATNA (Best Alternative To a Negotiated Agreement)? In other words, what options can you fall back on if the negotiation fails? That will be your baseline from which to advocate for yourself.
What is your conflict management style—accommodating, avoidant, compromising, competing, or collaborating? How is your style likely to impact the negotiation? How can you guard against the drawbacks of your style?

Expand your thinking beyond binary choices. Where are you willing to compromise? How can you broaden the negotiation beyond your ask (e.g., I am willing to take a new course prep on in the fall, but I really need the course release in the spring to finish my book)?

Highlight what you are willing to give up or what you have already given up (e.g., this opportunity is so exciting to me that I am willing to give up tenure for this untenured administrative position, but if I am to move to the Bay Area, the salary needs to be right).

Cultivate empathy. Put yourself in the shoes of your negotiation counterpart. Who are they? What are their values? What are their goals? What is their conflict style? What constraints are they under? What arguments do they respond to (e.g., stories, data/tables, profits, benchmarking to peers, appeal to fairness and equity, potential for reputational gains, impact on student success, etc.)? What's the best way to frame your ask in terms they can resonate with?

Build flexibility. You will not likely get everything you want, but research has shown that flexibility is important in negotiation. How can you build flexibility in your ask without negotiating with yourself?

Summon your ethicality. If you have a long-standing relationship with your counterpart, hopefully you have established yourself as trustworthy, competent, credible, and altruistic. How can you bring those dimensions into your ask? If this is a new relationship, how can you quickly bring elements of those dimensions into the negotiation?

Ask with assertiveness. Using all the elements above, and anything else that is pertinent, script yourself an assertive, empathetic ask as preparation for the in-person conversation.

Practice reframing. To be prepared for all outcomes, script yourself a response to a negative outcome that leaves the door open for a future conversation ("what I am hearing is that the timing of my request is not right. The need is not likely to go away, so I will bring this back up when the context is more favorable.").

References

Babcock, L., & Leschever, S. (2007) *Women don't ask: The high cost of avoiding negotiation—and positive strategies for change.* Bantam.

Belcher, L. (2019) *Writing your journal article in twelve weeks: A guide to academic publishing* (2nd ed.). University of Chicago Press.

Cameron, J. (2016) *The artist's way: A spiritual path to higher creativity* (25th anniversary edition). TarcherPerigee.

Carnegie, D. (2021) *How to win friends and influence people.* Fingerprint! Publishing. Originally published in 1936.

Ganote, C., Cheung, F., & Souza, T. (2016) *Responding to microaggressions with microresistance: A framework for consideration.* English Language and Literature: Faculty Publications, Smith College, Northampton, MA.

Grenny, J., Patterson, K., McMillan, R., Switzler, A., & Gregory, E. (2021) *Crucial conversations: Tools for talking when stakes are high* (3rd ed.). McGraw-Hill.

Huston, T. (2009) *Teaching what you don't know.* Harvard University Press.

Huston, T. (2016) *How women decide: What's true, what's not, and what strategies spark the best choices.* Houghton Mifflin Harcourt.

Huston, T. (2021) *Let's talk: Make effective feedback your superpower.* Portfolio.

Kaufman, S. B. (2020) *Transcend: The new science of self-actualization.* TarcherPerigee.

Kilmann, R., & Thomas, K. (1977) Developing a forced-choice measure of conflict-handling behavior: The "MODE" instrument. *Educational and Psychological Measurement, 37,* 309–325.

Lyotard, J. (1984) *The postmodern condition: A report on knowledge.* University of Minnesota Press.

Maslow, A. H. (1954). *Motivation and personality.* Harper & Row.

McQueen, A., & Klein, W. (2006) Experimental manipulations of self-affirmation: A systematic review. *Self and Identity, 5,* 289–354.

Schneider, A., & Kupfer, D. (2017) *Smart & savvy: Negotiation strategies in academia.* Meadows Communication.

Stephens, G., Silbert, J., & Hasson, U. (2010) Speaker–listener neural coupling underlies successful communication. *Proceedings of the National Academy of Sciences of the United States of America, 107*(32), 14425–14430.

Tannen, D. (2005). *Conversational style: Analyzing talk among friends* (revised ed.). Oxford University Press.

6
HOW DO WE BUILD A FULFILLING VISION?

The third-eye chakra

A self-defined option

I always knew I wanted to teach, and I let it be known to everybody. I left the corporate world, working as an actuary, to go to grad school in statistics because I wanted to become a professor and teach at the college level. I informed the department from the very beginning that I was interested in education, and they were supportive. My university had a self-defined option, so after getting in I petitioned to do a PhD in statistics education. It felt great to know the department was behind me as I did all the legwork to create a curriculum for myself and demonstrate to the university that it was just as rigorous as the regular PhD in statistics. I also had to take the qualifying exam and pass it at the PhD level before they allowed me on the self-defined path, and I did. It was a turning point for me to realize that I could get other people on board with my plans, that I was so determined in my vision that it had no choice but to eventually happen. This was a lesson that would come back handy in my life as an anchor to hold on to.

After graduating, I wanted to stay true to my interest in teaching, so I jumped around a few universities in the Midwest, mostly in positions off the tenure track with emphasis on teaching. Having moved through the world as a butch lesbian, I was used to being "other," and this position was another way in which I definitely felt "other." On the plus side, I was doing good work and making a name for myself in the statistics education community. I experimented with a new teaching format, the HyFlex model, collected data on its impact, and published about it. HyFlex teaching exploded during the pandemic, but I had been at the forefront of that movement for ten years already. I am proud of that work, but I never felt it was particularly valued by my university. Instead, the bureaucracy has a million little ways of making you feel "other" when you are not on the tenure track.

Midway through my career, I realized I was "other" in yet another way: I realized I was trans. This wasn't a struck-by-lightning instantaneous flash of insight for me. It was a process that unfolded. I knew the labels I had been using didn't fit anymore, but I had to elaborate something that fit, first to myself and then to everybody else. If I'm not a she, am I a he? A they? At the end of this process, my self-identification is as nonbinary transmasculine. It became clear that gender-affirming surgery was part of my journey. But when I looked into it, the healthcare benefits the university offered to somebody in my role did not cover surgery. The surgery was too expensive for me without the insurance covering it. I tried to navigate the system to make something happen, to no avail.

I eventually was recruited by another R1 state university in the Midwest, again for a lecturer position not on the tenure track. I did my homework, and discovered the health benefits would cover my transition. I never looked back. My future self was calling me forth. This too had no choice but to happen. I was delighted! Within a year of being at the new university I had arranged everything and scheduled my top surgery. I had anxiety about the operation, so to take my mind off it I registered for a statistics education workshop at a university in California. I am so glad I went! The workshop was transformative and energizing. I was able to network with a community of passionate, like-minded educators, with whom I remained connected, which sustained me through the years. And I met my future spouse there!

Unfortunately, after the honeymoon period, the same old politics surfaced at my new university. The divide between tenure track and non-tenure track faculty is so entrenched that I found it hard to even chit chat with people across that barrier. It really does feel like a barrier. And then there are the rules. After almost ten years of service at this university, I still have little control over my teaching assignments, and I feel overtaxed rather than recognized for my work. For instance, when I teach a course with an enrollment of 400–500 students, it counts as one section, but when a tenured professor teaches the same course, it counts as two sections for them. That is unjust and unsustainable, and it makes me feel like a second-class citizen. In my worldview, teaching contributions should be as valuable as research ones to the university, with tangible, tenurable rewards. It is so unsustainable that, when a tenure-track position with a teaching emphasis was posted at an R1 university in California, I immediately applied—and I got the job, and because of my years of experience they will be hiring me already with tenure. Once again, my future self is calling me forth, and I am packing my bags.

—Lucien, nonbinary transmasculine, teaching faculty in statistics and statistics education, multiple institutions

The wrong order

My path is not the usual path. I spent the beginning of my career in survival mode, as a single, divorced mother with a toddler diagnosed with developmental delays. I have a BA in anthropology and Japanese studies, but one of my undergraduate professors invited me to apply to graduate school in statistics in 1997. I didn't know if that was a good fit for me, but I was so broke that it was either flipping coins with binomial probabilities or flipping burgers at McDonald's. I did fine in school, but I was attracted more to the service aspect of the profession than the numbers and the theory. I got involved in the American Statistical Association with the caucus for women in statistics, and in a few years, I became program chair of the government statistics sessions. I also started doing fieldwork in human rights statistics, interviewing refugees, and dealing with the statistical problems involved in collecting messy data from traumatized people with gaps and distortions in their memories. I am proud that some of my works was used in the trial of Milošević for his crimes against humanity in Kosovo.

As fulfilling as the months of fieldwork were, they distracted me from graduate school. Meanwhile, I was getting remarried and moving to a different city with my husband. I proposed my dissertation pregnant with my daughter. My advisor, Eli, was steadfast and kept pushing me, but there were issues with the data collection, delays, all kinds of things. I started working. I did a bit of adjuncting too. I volunteered at my daughter's school. I'm sure my depression and attention-deficit/hyperactivity disorder (ADHD) all helped push me off track. Years later, I got the news that Eli was dying of cancer. On October 16, 2016, I went back to the university for a daylong celebration of life. It was so touching. All his other students were there or sent video tributes. He told me once again to finish my thesis. I felt something compelling. I had to finish the thesis now. And I could actually see myself finishing it. I worked so hard to get it done. I came back once again in November and spent Thanksgiving with Eli and his wife Nessa. Eli was so thin by then. I realized he would not make it to the end of the year. They were so generous. They let me stay with them. Eli gave me feedback, I worked all day making edits, and Nessa would cook delicious meals. Finally, I got the manuscript to the point Eli was comfortable approving it. It was actually the last document he signed. I defended on December 13, and he died the next day.

I had become close with Nessa, so we kept in touch when I went back home. I was certainly proud of finally finishing my doctorate after almost 20 years. But at the same time, I was stuck. My son graduated from college. My career was in a rut. I didn't know who I was anymore. On October 27, 2018, I saw on TV the horrific news of the massacre at the Tree of Life synagogue, the deadliest attack on the Jewish community on the United States soil, and shortly after I was devastated by the news that Nessa was one of the 11 people murdered. This poor family. As I rode the train back to her funeral, I had an epiphany. Eli and Nessa believed in me, and I need to honor them by living out my fullest self. And who I am is a statistics professor.

I always felt guilt at the way I did statistics. I did it all in the wrong order. I got involved in service first. I actually made Fellow at American Statistical Association (ASA) before even finishing my PhD. I taught, albeit as an adjunct. Some of my work in human rights and sexual violence has been published in prestigious journals. Then what was this guilt? I walked an unconventional path, but I hit all the stops on it. And through all these experiences, I could see the red thread—service. I spent the two weeks after the funeral filling out applications. I got interviews at big and famous research universities, but I privileged schools with an emphasis on teaching. I am a legacy to Eli and Nessa, and I want to pay it forward to future students. I accepted a tenure-track job at a university that emphasizes experiential learning and community-engaged practices so I could develop service-learning experiences for students to use their statistical knowledge to serve the community. I also co-founded and serve on the board of a non-profit organization dedicated to spreading interfaith understanding, formed to honor Nessa's memory.

—Aida, White bisexual disabled Jewish single mother, tenure-track associate professor of statistics in a medium size rural state college

Black people can do math!

If anybody would have told me I would become a statistician, I would have laughed at them. I played trumpet—music was my thing—I thought I would be a musician. Then, in eighth grade, I took ninth grade algebra and did well. That showed me I had skills. Later, I took precalculus in my junior year of high school with a very nonconventional professor. He wore a leather jacket and rode a motorcycle, a real rebel-without-a-cause character. He was a disciplinarian, but he saw something in me and encouraged me to take AP calculus and develop my quantitative skills for a career. Usually, people make assumption about Black men and their math ability, so, as a young Black man, the mentoring of this old White teacher meant a lot to me.

I was a double major in college, music and math, but decided to focus on math for grad school. I was admitted as a PhD student to a very theoretical math department. I did fine with the coursework, but I started second guessing my choice. It was boring—and lonely. I decided I needed a reset, so I took an internship in statistics in Washington, DC. That's where I learned about data science, and where I was able to do math in teams. Now *that* I enjoyed, using my quantitative skills to make sense of data from real-world problems. Unfortunately, I came back from my internship with an HIV diagnosis. It tore through me and wrecked my next year. I was getting Cs in some classes. I was depressed, gutted. I made an appointment with my department chair to explain my poor performance and private details of my life. I had no idea what would happen, but he was understanding. The department gave me an extra year to patch up my work, let me leave with a masters, and arranged for me to transfer to statistics. I had to retake some undergraduate classes, but I didn't mind, because I realized that I could use my quantitative skills to have an impact in the world. I studied HIV risk in women who were seeking treatment for drug use disorders. At the facility where we gathered the data, I had conversations with those women and the people who cared for them made me realize that I could not only be accomplished but make a difference.

My first job after my PhD was as an educator. I stepped into the classroom to all these Black students who thought they couldn't do math, and it was amazing. I could not believe the impact I was having on them, taking them places where they thought they couldn't go! It was a transcendent moment that changed the trajectory of my career. I had planned on an industry job, but I only got one call back. I slid into academia reluctantly, as a backup, but it has been a key shift. I now identify as a statistician and as an educator.

Now that I am an assistant professor of statistics, I carry those moments with me, and I know where I want to go with them. I want to be a leader in academia, either as a statistician or as an administrator. Ideally, I want to be the chair of a statistics department at an Historically Black College or University (HBCU)—a founding chair, in fact, because most HBCUs do not have one. I can see myself also being a university president eventually. I am laying the foundation for that goal by making sure I am a solid, respected scientist. And I am networking. It's not an obsession with power. I want to move science forward with my expert quantitative skills applied to public health projects. For instance, I am trying to model the relationship between stress and heart disease. We could lengthen people's life and make it more fulfilling! But beyond my own personal accomplishments, I want to show the world that Black people can do math! I want to be a leader to bring up generations of Black students in statistics!

I am still figuring it out. For instance, I haven't perfected politicking in academia. I express my opinions, but I want to make sure that happens in a productive way. And I am still part of the LGBTQ+ community and its subcultures, and that identity is important to me, but I don't know if it will affect my goal of becoming a leader. Can I become the first Leatherman university president? Or are they mutually exclusive? I don't know. But I try to be okay with not knowing and still work toward my dream.

—Kendrick, Black gay man research assistant professor of statistics at a private research university

What is going on in these stories?

Besides the fact that all three stories involve statisticians (what are the odds?), they revolve around vision. Lucien can't help but follow their compelling vision across multiple institutions as it evolves and transforms their whole identity. It is a coherent vision that ties together, personal, professional, and even ethical dimensions and serves as a guiding light for action. Aida almost stumbles into statistics, a decision driven by necessity and opportunity more than passion at first. Even though she does good, valuable work, she gets sidetracked in various directions and struggles for years to finish her degree. Later still, her career is in a rut, and it takes a moment of shocking grief to bring clarity. Like many others, she struggles to see her unconventional path as valid, even after attaining a level of national recognition (ASA Fellow) most statisticians will never reach in their lifetime. But when that dissonance is resolved, her vision guides her through important choices, such as deciding between prestigious research institutions and teaching- and service-oriented ones where she can carry out her mentor's legacy.

Kendrick thought he had a vision. He would be a musician. But a new vision began to compel him when he realized there were areas of mathematics where complexity is not the path to higher and higher levels of abstractions but to solving problems in the real world in collaborative fashion. This insight, coupled with his quantitative skills, created the possibility of fulfillment on multiple fronts—from possibly life-extending contributions in public health and medicine to social vindication for Black men. That idea, in turn, led to the formulation of an even grander vision, that of becoming a (founding) chair of a statistics department at an HBCU or a university president, so that he could positively influence a generation of Black statisticians. There is a possible snag in that plan though, his commitment to other parts of his identity. Out and proud LGBTQ+ gay university presidents are becoming more common, but nonnormative identities (such as Leatherman) are still not openly discussed at those leadership levels. While most of us do not wrestle with that dilemma, we might be familiar with having multiple competing visions, and the tension of navigating them all or having to abandon some. If we persevere in the dogged pursuit of seemingly incompatible visions, what is at the end of that road? A trailblazing success or an abject failure punctuated by many I-told-you-so?

These stories help surface some of the issues related to our professional vision. How do we articulate a fulfilling professional vision? To what degree should our vision integrate the personal and the professional? How do we pursue it in the face of the obstacles in our path? How do we reconcile competing visions? We will explore these themes in the remainder of the chapter, but we need to add relevant chakra theory first.

What does chakra theory say?

So far, we have worked on finding ground, nurturing our desires, building our power, finding love, connection, and balance at work, and growing our voice to express our truth. As we ascend further up along the sushumna, we are now completely in the head, the academic's province. The sixth chakra is Ājnā, meaning command, or perceive, or beyond wisdom. This chakra corresponds to the third eye, located in the space between the eyebrows, and is therefore dedicated to the concept of seeing, and ruled by the element of light. Ajna is represented as a lotus flower with two petals, containing a downward-pointing triangle with the Om symbol inscribed at its center. While the petals in the lotus flowers have been growing in number in every chakra so far, here we see a contraction, down to only two petals. They represent the two nadis, Ida and Pingala. In fact, after winding their way around the lower chakras, the two energetic currents of Ida and Pingala reconnect from each nostril into the third eye, where they reunite with each other and with the sushumna and proceed to the crown chakra as one. Symbolically, that means that the dualities of our life come together in this chakra. A full activation of the third eye requires the integration of masculine and feminine, of active and passive, of giving and receiving, and so on. Whatever chasm is still lingering in our life, it needs to be bridged for good to reap the full benefits of the third eye. In traditional imagery, this chakra is associated with the deity *Ardhanārīśhvara* (अर्धनारीश्वर), the half-Shiva/half-Shakti figure, symbolizing the balance of masculine and feminine qualities.

What function does a third eye add beyond the two physical eyes? With our eyes we see the world as it appears to our senses. In Hinduism, the physical world is called māyā (माया), or illusion. The next chakra will unpack this concept more, but, for the purposes of this chapter, suffice it to say that, with a healthy third eye, we can see the world for what it really is. In her piece "Pedagogy of Buddhism," Eve Sedgwick (2003) gives the example of her cat. When she points at a mess the cat made to scold him, the cat keeps staring at her finger. In the third-eye chakra we have the intelligence of signs, and we can follow the signifier, the finger, all the way to the signified, the mess, and make sense of our reality. In this scenario, the cat would be deficient in the third-eye chakra because it is unable to see that the finger has a meaning beyond the digit itself. Developing the intelligence of signs means becoming attuned to pattern recognition. One of my faculty was remarking about the clumsy machinations of a scheming colleague, and she laughed them off: "They don't bother me, because I see them coming." That kind of seeing is what a well-developed third-eye chakra can do for us. In fact, some cognitive psychologists have conceptualized cognition and expertise as a set of if-then statements. If A happens, then B usually follows. If X happens, then Y is the best strategy. With a large enough set of these "production rules" (Anderson, 1990, 1993), derived from experience, we are ready for contingencies, not surprised by them.

With the third eye, we go beyond the words on the page, and we can read between the lines, or see the writing on the wall. We can also see things that haven't happened yet—insight, discovery, or vision for new projects or new paths. Therefore, a main function of this chakra is imagination. In previous chapters, we have discussed healing our chakras from traumas. Bullying can be destabilizing to the first chakra, sexual harassment at work can destabilize the second chakra, and so on. Working with the third-eye chakra, we don't necessarily encounter trauma. More likely, our imagination has not been encouraged, and this chakra is a bit atrophied. The work related to this chakra is to develop it more. For instance, Aida could not conceive that her career accomplishments amounted to a faculty trajectory because she didn't do them in the sequence other people traverse. In addition, Aida could not finish her dissertation until she could "see" herself finishing it. The third eye is where this seeing happens. Therefore, it is also the chakra of dreams (either sleeping or waking), such as Kendrick dreaming of becoming a founding department chair or university president. Building on the purifying work of the previous chakras we are nurturing a new consciousness that can imagine possibilities for a more fulfilling professional and personal life. When Lucien feels called forth by their best/future self, that too is a third eye visualization.

A fully expressed and balanced third-eye chakra displays strong intuition, insight, creative imagination, pattern recognition, and good memory. Excessive characteristics might include difficulty concentrating, persistent daydreaming and fantasizing, as well as obsessions. Deficient characteristics, on the other hand, might include lack of imagination, difficulty visualizing, undue skepticism, and inability to imagine alternative options and solutions. The right associated with this chakra is the right to see, and the demon of this chakra is illusions, visions that instead of clarifying reality distort it.

Faculty insights: Vision

What does it mean to cultivate a vision? One of my favorite dictionary definitions is "the ability to plan the future with imagination and wisdom" (Google Dictionary Box, n.d.). The imagination of this chakra is grounded by the values of the root chakra, fueled by the desire of the pelvic chakra, and expressed by the creativity of the throat chakra. When that ascending current meets the descending current of the wisdom of the crown chakra (see next chapter), the result is a fulfilling vision.

Wisdom and imagination are apparent in Donna's case. She perfected her vision with the help of a professional coach: "To be a steadfast advocate for justice, cultivating community, conjuring conspiratorial creativity, and

> **BOX 6.1 VISON CHAKRA CHART**
>
> Sanskrit name: Ājnā
> Meaning: To perceive or to command
> Element: Light
> Function: Imagination
> Color: Indigo
> Identity: Archetypal
> Right: To see
> Demon: Illusions

welcoming wonder." It is both concise and broad, and it has guided her in her research, her leadership when she became department chair, her activism, and especially at her crossroads moments, such as deciding whether to stay in academia or pursue public policy work in Washington. And that is the power of a vision informed by both currents—to be able to light the way.

Even if they had not polished a statement with a coach, most of the faculty answered without hesitation when I asked them what their vision was. By far, the prevalent vision for most is to make a difference in their students' lives, using the tools of their discipline to nurture their sense of wonder, develop their expertise and confidence, contribute to their upward mobility, prepare them as citizens, and generally equip them for life's challenges. Clara, the adjunct professor of psychology, exemplifies this perspective:

> I can feel the weight of the world very heavily, but I can't let it crush me. My vision is literally a visualization of me and the million students I've taught and the million people whose lives they are going to touch. If I keep doing what I'm doing, and doing it well, it will impact thousands if not hundreds of thousands of lives. My students will become teachers, counselors, therapists, and if I can affect their thinking and stretch their minds, this can't help but have a ripple effect in the world. It gives me hope.

That's right, a vision can literally be a visual image impressed on the third eye. The words—from the throat chakra—are simply an articulation of the visualization.

If the most common vision was about making a difference with one's students, the next common category centers on scholarship. Felix expresses it so: "My vision has to do with reaching people with my ideas. I want them to read my work, digest it, and have a sense of illumination. It is essentially my research agenda."

A third group of visions clustered around service and leadership. Like Kendrick, people in this group see themselves improving their institution through their service, influencing it through a formal leadership position, or maybe being the leaders they wished they had early in their careers.

Others did not funnel their visions through the areas of faculty performance. Rather, they went broader. Olivia has a succinct vision: "I am creating a community of people who all work for the betterment of society." This vision is always at play, in the community she creates in her courses, with the graduate students she mentors, with her colleagues in her department, and beyond. Pondering the questions "how can I enrich this community further?" defines her next endeavor. For instance, she is currently organizing an interdisciplinary symposium to bring together people who study her same issues from a variety of fields to all learn from each other and to explore the idea of what an issue-focused community could be.

Dennis, the lecturer we left doing splits to disco music with his students during class, simply says: "My vision is to make things a bit weirder." Some visions create a path to follow. If Kendrick wants to rise through the academic ranks to become president of a university, he will likely have to become provost first, dean before that, and chair to jumpstart that process. On the other hand, when I discussed vision with Bridget, the English professor who took her three children to the National Endowment for the Humanities institute and mounted a vote of no confidence against her president, she simply described a commitment to nurture her desire chakra:

> I'm curious, in a greedy way. I am passionate about learning, developing expertise in things I don't know, and I love traveling, going to places I've never been. My university had made international education a priority, so I got involved in study abroad. I did it for ten years, and I realized it was a different kind of learning experience from the learning that happens in a classroom. I got curious about that and started exploring embodied cognition, which eventually led to my most important scholarly project, and to a book.

While the full tapestry only becomes apparent after the accumulation of experiences over the years, this is a strategic vision. Bridget devised a way to attach her passions to the strategic plan of the institution, and she expertly worked in that intersection for a decade.

Lachlan, the English professor who left his tenured position to move to California, is candid in his strategy:

> Part of my vision is recognizing opportunities and figuring out how what is good for me can also be good for the institution. As an example, we had a

large lecture poetry class that was a service course but also an opportunity for graduate students to gain teaching experience. I was asked to take it over, and the department chair nonchalantly suggested I reinvent the model for the course. I took him up on that challenge. I thought about what graduate students would need and decided they need autonomy and control, with strong mentoring. So rather than creating a master syllabus, I structured it so they were responsible for selecting texts and shaping their section to a degree, working with me to ensure standards across sections. It was a success. Next thing you know, I was asked to revamp the fiction large lecture course too, which I did according to the same principles. On the heels of those two successes, I volunteered to create a non-fiction large lecture course with the same structure. So now I have all these courses, and I mentor graduate students year-round on their teaching. I proposed a pedagogy course so that all the work I put into mentoring them could be counted as part of my load. The department loved the idea because having a strong future-faculty program helps them recruit high-caliber graduate students. I even got a new title as Pedagogy Coordinator! At this point, most of my teaching load is filled by these large lecture courses and by mentoring graduate students—all things I love and am really good at. I saw a need and made it into an opportunity, where my creativity and expertise could be brought to bear to strengthen the department. Everybody wins!

Everybody wins is right. On the rainbow bridge, an "everybody wins" vision activates all the chakras. Lachlan's vision taps into what his department values, which gives it that root chakra stability and sustainability. It builds around one of his passions—mentoring graduate students—so that his second chakra desires are nurtured. It rewards the mentoring he was already doing in his own time and structures it into his performance agreement, which increases his power. It builds on the empathy from the heart chakra, walking a mile in the graduate student's shoes to understand what they really need from the experience, so they too win. And it strengthens his voice, so that after being asked to take over the first two courses, he can credibly ask for the remaining pieces of his vision.

What should the timeframe for a vision be? There is no singular answer to that question. Kendrick will likely spend his whole career striving to achieve his vision. By contrast, Aida is already living out her vision just by being a professor. And Lucien's vision kept refining itself as they expanded their personal and professional identities, pulling them toward the next goal at every major transition. If your vision already calls for a specific timeline, then you can simply follow that. But many of those I interviewed gave examples of medium-term visions. Rahul, who we encountered in the ground chakra as his efforts to survive the pandemic were being frustrated by an unresponsive HR department, reminds us that envisioning our future self can also connect to a first chakra function, survival:

> After my transplant, I made it a point to periodically imagine my future self, because studies show that life expectancy after a liver transplant is only five years for about 25% of patients. It was important to me to paint a rich visual of what my next years could be like, so that I could live life to the fullest.

Research indeed confirms that people with a strong sense of purpose tend to live longer (Shiba et al., 2022), so the benefits of having a motivating vision can stretch all the way down to the first chakra.

Simon, who we left in the last chakra taking risks with using his voice, explains:

> My postdoc mentor asked me, where do you want to be in five years? And I found it a very useful question. So now I plan in five-year increments. Five years is a nice set of time. You can't accomplish all your career goals but it's enough to make some moves, get some things off the ground. The guiding question of the current five-year chunk is: How do I create a space for students and postdocs to come together and support each other in doing research in queer health? Of course, the COVID pandemic derailed that, but it still is an energizing question.

Organizations routinely create strategic plans on a five-year horizon. As long as the plans are flexible enough to allow for contingencies (such as the pandemic), they can be quite beneficial. Simon's postdoc mentor was onto something. Starting at the end of the five-year period allows us to work backward and plan the intermediate steps that will get us there. For instance, Gabby worked backward seven years after:

> I have rejected academic norms of publication. I see this as my strategy. For instance, in 2011 I realized we were seven years away from an important centenary in my field. The realization was captivating to me, so I spent seven years planning how to celebrate this anniversary. I ended up co-curating an art exhibit with a professor in the arts, among other things, but it was a whole year and a half of events. We had 6,000 people attending throughout. The exhibit has a catalog, which has been reviewed in many places, and my department allowed me to count that as a publication toward full professor. It started as a whimsy of an idea, but I got professional credit for it. It didn't just happen though: I had to make an argument for it. Many celebrations happened in academia, but I made mine stand out by finding a unique angle for the exhibit.

Seven years for a whimsy might sound too much, but again we see the alignment along the chakras. Planning this celebration fostered Gabby's intellectual interest, forced her to get creative and come up with a novel approach, brought an aesthetic value, and nurtured an interdisciplinary relationship with a colleague, and, because it was well planned, it could count toward her career advancement.

Some of the faculty I interviewed didn't center their vision on academia at all, like Conrad:

> I'm a writer. I didn't get my PhD because I wanted to be an academic. I only wanted it to give legitimacy to my writing, so I could write about queer topics in pop culture with authority. And so, my vision is to use the academy without letting it use me.

While Conrad's language is pointed, he was one of several who deemphasized academia in their vision. In this category, I also found visions that cast the professoriate simply as a job and the source of financial support, while emphasizing family as the source of fulfillment. Those visions helped these faculty set firm boundaries at work to protect their time with families, staving off the guilt demon.

Finally, some faculty shrugged at my question. They said they are not following a grand vision. Most of the people in this camp were older women looking back on a storied career that saw them rise through the professorial ranks and into leadership positions as chair, director, dean, or university administrator. Desiree explains:

> I don't have very many ultimate dreams and goals that I am trying to get to. I always do the next thing, work with this person I want to work with. I am relationship-oriented, and then a relationship leads to a project, or another relationship.

The language of "doing the next thing" was common in this group. One could characterize this approach as a vision to honor one's passions as they arise, the way Bridget did above, but they chose to say they did not follow a long-range vision. While this is satisfying to them for personal purposes, it might not be enough for advancement. This book is proof that I too favor a vision that follows my unconventional passions as they arise, but a senior administrator at a prestigious university commented during a job interview that my résumé looked "opportunistic." I clearly failed to tell my story in a way that made sense to both of us. Desiree elaborates: "On the other hand, I am an outlier in my department. Especially for promotion purposes, I need to paint a vision of myself and my work for them, so they can see me." Others were quick to add that while this approach might have worked for them, they would advise young academics to develop and cultivate a vision for success in today's university.

Is a vision just a gimmick then? Pierce, a gay scientist off the tenure track at a midsized research university, certainly sees the downside to many corporate-sounding vision statements:

> I could have benefitted from this advice, but nobody told me early on. And maybe it didn't matter as much back then, but there seems to have been a shift, and now everybody asks about vision—and not only vision, but brand. What do you do that's a little bit different from other people? It came to me as an understanding, nobody told me. Seems especially useful and important for promotion purposes. I don't like the idea of branding myself. Feels very business-like. It's all about the pitch. And that's too bad, because I actually do have a vision. I want to infuse my personal interests in my professional life. Right now, I want to create a course on the science of fitness, since that's a big part of my identity. And I want to connect with LGBTQ+ organizations on and off campus and see how I can be and be helpful to my community from that angle.

Like Pierce, many of us have seen fungible vision statements that merely regurgitate corporate buzzwords without expressing anything real. In the third-eye chakra, to create a fulfilling vision for ourselves, the downward current from our higher consciousness (see the next chapter) needs to meet the upward current, energized by our values, passions, will, and heart. A naïve assumption of some early-career faculty is that "If I just do good work, everyone will notice" (Ambrose, Huston, and Norman 2005, p. 816). But others see us filtered through their values, assumptions, prejudices, misconceptions, etc. Our scholarship is often measured against their idea of what a serious scholar ought to be working on, and how. We need to communicate this vision to others, not only to achieve it, but to be seen, as Desiree astutely reminds us. That communication inherits the qualities of the fifth chakra, our voice, and will only be our truth (and not a gimmick) if the two currents work in harmony with each other.

Faculty insights: Archetypes

We have been highlighting how each chakra corresponds to one of our identities. The further up in the chakras we get, the more we connect with expansive pieces of our self beyond our physical identity. In the third eye, we connect with our archetypal identity. Archetypes, popularized by Jung (1991), are innate patterns inherited from the collective unconscious that express themselves in our life, shaping how we think of ourselves (e.g., the sage, the leader, the alchemist). As we work with archetypes, we recast our individual story as an instantiation of a universal template. When we speak an inconvenient truth in a faculty meeting and our colleagues are upset at us, we are reliving Cassandra's myth, and we can depersonalize the matter because we remember it is human nature to shoot the messenger.

Jung described a few archetypes in detail but posited that their number was infinite. Mark and Pearson (2002) have structured Jung's theory into 12 archetypes based on four major drives of the human condition—to leave a mark, to connect with others, to provide structure, and to transcend one's reality. Each of these drives can express itself in three dynamics, originating the 12 archetypes presented in Table 6.1. Archetypes have been criticized for reifying oppressive gender roles, pushing women into nurturing categories and men into assertive ones. I am highlighting a gender-neutral version here, with the hope that they could help free, not constrict, humans of any/no gender.

The shadow, which we met in Chapter 2, is one of the archetypes Jung identifies. Caroline Myss (2013) pushes that concept forward by remarking that each archetype can succumb to its shadow side. The Ruler can be seduced by the throne and become the Tyrant. The innocent Ingenue can easily slide into the Damsel in distress needing to be rescued, and so on. Some of my faculty gained insights by recognizing the archetypes they embody. Many of us will gravitate to the Sage. After all, we have invested years in building our expertise. But other archetypes can be meaningful too. Speaking of archetypes outside of traditional gender roles, Calliope, the adjunct professor of English whose story we met in the throat chakra, offers this one:

> Back in the 80s, I caught a lecture by Joseph Campbell on TV. It changed my life. I started incorporating mythology in my teaching. My favorite archetype is Lilith. She refused the gender roles imposed on her. She is my portal into the feminine divine.

We can see ourselves in a combination of multiple archetypes too. Desiree explains:

> What is my archetype then? I would say a combination of Artist, Sage, and Explorer. The explorer is the one I was least clear on, until I realized I have been seeking freedom for myself in my career. I have taken many disparate positions inside and outside academia, none of them the traditional tenure track position. And in all of them I was seeking a way to be freer.

Grace elaborates on how her archetype shines light on her work:

> I want to leave this world better than I found it and I don't know how much time I have. I often ask myself what seed do I want to plant in the world and how can I alleviate more of people's pain? Is Healer my archetype? I don't

TABLE 6.1 Archetypes identified by Mark and Pearson

Drive	Leave a mark			Connect with others		
Current	Liberation	Power	Mastery	Intimacy	Pleasure	Belonging
Archetype	**Outlaw**	**Magician**	**Hero**	**Lover**	**Jester**	**Regular Person**
Drive	Provide structure			Transcend one's reality		
Current	Service	Control	Innovation	Safety	Knowledge	Freedom
Archetype	**Caregiver**	**Ruler**	**Artist**	**Innocent**	**Sage**	**Explorer**

dare to say yes because it is a privilege to be that, but it is an aspiration and a work in progress for me. It's hard to heal others when we are traumatized ourselves. But the classroom does present beautiful opportunities for healing, and I want that to be a healing space. The classroom is a sanctuary, I say. And teaching, and my students, have brought me enormous healing.

Grace brings up a great point. There is an aspirational quality to archetypes. Every day, we might fall short of the ideal, but they represent our true north.

Sheila, whose story we will encounter fully in the next chapter, reminds us that the system also forces archetypes, particularly on minoritized faculty:

I am not surprised when I experience racism at work. The United States has a 400-year history of understanding Black women bodies as sources of extraction only, wet nurse, mammy, etcetera. Being in the teaching profession as a woman, it's built on the archetype that you care deeply. And so you are going to give and give and give, and that's part of the extraction. And if you don't give that means you must not care.

Archetypes are no consolation for systemic racism, but they can allow us to articulate our experiences with power.

Chakra right: To see

Unsurprisingly, the right associated with the third-eye chakra is the right to see. When I asked my faculty whether this right was supported or challenged in their experience, the answers were layered. The right to see is generally supported in research. We are literally paid to see. Research labs are equipped with powerful microscopes and telescopes to look in new places and in new ways. But when I asked faculty what they struggle to see, some mentioned that academia is not transparent, and they can't see through it. Some of the stories in this book certainly speak to that opacity.

As a follow-up, I asked what they see now that they did not see before. Common answers were that they see the dysfunction, the personal agendas, the deception, the lip service, the racism, and other isms. Those who were able to see the various forms of oppressions also reported seeing their own intersectional privilege, particularly as full-time faculty on the tenure track compared to faculty who teach part-time and faculty on other tracks. Relatedly, Dennis, the professor of gender studies, remarked that, as a visiting lecturer, it is hard to "see" a future for himself in the academy. On the positive side, some faculty learned to see higher education as a complex system, with many interlocking and moving parts beyond the thin slice they see every day in their job. Some have an appreciation for this complexity, which moved them away from demanding simplistic solutions of their leadership, and others wonder if it is even possible to change academia for the better, due to its intricacy. Some faculty also reported learning to see the students in a new way over time, specifically as full persons, with hopes, dreams, histories, identities—and being better educators for it.

Chakra demon: Illusion

An illusion is an image we see that is not actually there, or a distortion of what is there, like a mirage. Illusions are the demon of the third-eye chakra because they diminish our ability to see the world for what it is. Honorine highlights a dangerous illusion:

> I labored under the illusion that if I work harder the institution will recognize my work and reward me. It doesn't work that way. It's not reciprocal but transactional. When I saw it for what it is, I could decide what the terms of the transaction were going to be for me.

Certainly, many faculty work hard and are rewarded for their hard work. But the system is far from perfect, and many fall through the cracks, especially those whose work exposes the flaws of the system. When you shake the illusion off, you can approach the situation in more realistic terms and make informed choices.

Aida wrestled with the concept of expertise as illusion:

> We are credentialed as experts, but we all have so much to learn still. I read a lot about R. A. Fisher, the father of inferential statistics. That's the area of statistics concerned with the generalizations we can make from the sample data we have and the evidence necessary to do so. He was so influential that the American Statistical Association established the Fisher lecture as one of its highest awards. But when Fisher's work in eugenics was publicized, the ASA retired the lecture. Here is one of the most brilliant minds of his time

doing bad in the world by getting entangled in the arguments that justified the Holocaust. The irony is that his statistical contributions rest on the principle that our assumptions must be verified before we use any model, and yet his own unchecked assumptions were his downfall. I'm less worried about being seen as the expert and more worried about doing good in the world and minimizing the harmful consequences of my actions. Expertise can be an illusion.

Donna elaborates on the fear that change in the academy might not be possible:

I worry about illusions a lot. Is the whole project of trying to change engineering—a field so wedded to capitalism that has embraced sexism, racism, colonialism, and more—delusional? Most days I'm fine but some days I wonder.

This brings up an important point. How do we know if something is an illusion or not? Is it an illusion as a part-time faculty to go above and beyond the terms of the contract hoping the department will realize your commitment and eventually create a full-time position for you? Is it an illusion as a tenure track faculty to take on an exacting service load in an understaffed department hoping they will remember during tenure reviews how much value you brought the department even if your scholarship suffered a bit? My faculty overwhelmingly seem to think the latter is definitely an illusion, given that the committee must apply the standards equally to all faculty. As for the first one, there are not enough full-time positions to create for all faculty in part-time appointments. Will you be the lucky one? It is important to walk into these situations with all three eyes wide open.

Prompts for reflection

- What dualities have you balanced and integrated in your life? Which ones are you still struggling with (think masculine/feminine, active/passive, giving/receiving, teaching/research, professional/personal, working within the system/subverting the system, and so on)?
- What are your archetypes and how do they empower you? What archetypes are others trying to push you into and how do they limit you? What's your aspirational archetype? What is one step you can take to realize it?
- What do you see now that you didn't see years ago? What patterns and signs have you learned to recognize, in yourself or in the outside world?
- How is your right to see supported in your context? How is it threatened? What can you do to protect it?
- What illusions have deceived you? What lessons have you gained from this demon?

Tools, strategies, and possibilities

This section will present some strategies. As usual, we start with strategies related to the activation of the third-eye chakra and then contextualize the strategies toward academia.

Keep a dream journal. I don't regard dreams as premonitions or messages from the beyond, but as elaborations of our unconscious through our imagination. As such, they are in the third-eye chakra domain. Keeping a dream journal allows us to track recurring themes and reflect on connections between the dreamscape and our waking life. This can be especially helpful for those who feel stuck and are trying to pinpoint causes and solutions. If you don't remember your dreams, try setting an intention (another sixth chakra function) to remember your dreams right before going to bed. Do your journal when you wake up, before you forget your dreams.

Surround yourself with colors and beauty. Colors are simply refracted light, so they fall in the domain of this chakra. So do patterns and beauty (read: fashion). Surrounding ourselves with unusual colors, shapes, and patterns can exert a subtle shift on our routine and make us see things in new ways. When I was started writing this book and felt stuck, I followed the advice of Helen Sword (2017) on writing with joy. She suggests surrounding oneself with whatever brings one joy. I used colored pens and patterned notebooks, made origami and put them on my desk, placed a kaleidoscope near my laptop and peered at the shifting patterns every day. Soon, the joy of sitting down at my desk replaced the dread of staring at the blank page. In general, do more of anything that grows your imagination and sparks joy.

Use storytelling to sketch your vision. This exercise was created by my colleagues Linda Stewart and Este Jordan (2020). We have used it at our new faculty orientation with great success. To start, call to mind your story, the story that brought you here to this very moment. Visualize the key moments that stand out. Jot down some notes about moments in these four categories: a Discovery you made, something you have Created, something you have Overcome, and a Gratitude you hold in your heart. Use these notes, and whatever else comes to mind, to write down your story. Give it a headline, as if it was a story in a newspaper. Ideally, do this exercise in groups so that you can share your story with others (in two to three minutes) and listen to theirs. Next, and using the same categories as before, write the story you want to be able to tell about yourself in one year, or in five years, or whatever time frame makes sense to you. This might be a first draft of your vision.

Create a vision board. Like Clara, you can use imagery. You can draw, if you feel inclined, or you can use other artistic techniques. A popular one is collage. Sift through a bunch of magazines and cut out the images that speak to you. Arrange them in ways that make sense to you, maybe using Venn diagrams or arrows/flowcharts. Alternatively, create a Padlet of images from an internet search. The composite image might show a holistic visual of your future.

Develop a systematic teaching philosophy. We have all seen those professors teaching on autopilot from ten-year-old slides. For our teaching practice to be energizing, it must be intentional and guided by a coherent set of principles. You will need such a statement for job interviews, tenure and promotion portfolios, awards applications, at least, so you might as well invest in it. Make it a key piece of your professional vision rather than a chore. Seldin, Miller, and Seldin (2010) and Schonwetter et al. (2002) provide comprehensive guides to writing teaching philosophies, and a simple Google search will return many more suggestions, but as a starting point to a fulfilling vision for your teaching, you can start by answering these questions:

- Why do you teach the way you do?
- What are you trying to accomplish in your courses?
- What critical incidents in your past, good or bad, shaped your beliefs about teaching and learning?
- What values guide your practice?
- When you feel energized and at your best in your teaching, what is happening?
- Are there gaps between your ideal teaching practice and your current situation?
- What steps could you take to bridge them?

Establish a coherent and compelling research agenda. We engage in research because we are passionate about what we are researching, but without a strong vision to keep us focused on the value and purpose of our work, the structures and requirements of research at many universities have a way of eroding the pleasure of the second chakra and replacing it with drudgery. A research statement can be a tool to keep focusing on the big picture and might be especially helpful for job searches and portfolio reviews. This document describes the current state of your research and the future directions you wish to investigate. Many universities have produced guides to this document for their graduate students, and you can find them with a simple internet search. You can also consider these questions to jump-start your thought process:

- What problems in your field fascinate you and why?
- Why are you the person to carry out this work? How has your work so far prepared you?

- In particular for early career academics, how is your approach innovative and different from your dissertation advisor and other key researchers?
- Conversely, how does your work fit in with the state of the field and create avenues for collaboration with others?
- What is the significance of your work so far? How does it move the field forward?
- What are some promising future directions for your work?
- What will keep your research thriving (space, equipment, personnel, and other needs)?

Develop a leadership philosophy. If your vision involves pursuing a leadership position, you might benefit for clarifying your leadership philosophy—to others as well as to yourself. You might want to read widely on leadership, especially on academic leadership, to develop a language to describe the kind of leader you are. Kouzes and Posner (2023) and Buller (2013, 2014) are excellent starting points. Current leadership development models emphasize starting from one's values, so you can build on the value clarification work we did in the ground chakra (see Chapter 1). You can also start reflecting on these questions:

- Which leaders do you admire and why? Conversely, whose approach to leadership would you actively avoid?
- What critical incidents in your life have shaped how you think of leadership, and what lessons did you take from them?
- What is your archetype for a leader (ruler, servant, magician, maverick, etc.) and why?
- How would your values shape your actions as a leader?
- How would you motivate others and bring out their best selves?
- How do you handle conflict and ensure a fair decision-making process?
- How would you lead in times of turbulent change?

Write a diversity statement. Diversity statements have been used for a number of years in job searches as they can help the search committee understand how candidates approach matters of diversity, inclusion, equity, and justice. Unfortunately, they have recently been targeted for criticism and, in some cases, completely forbidden during the application process at a number of public universities. Nevertheless, writing a diversity statement for yourself can also clarify for you the role this dimension plays in your life and can help you assess whether opportunities that come your way would be a good fit for you and your values. I again recommend reading widely on this topic to develop a language, map the terrain of the interconnected issues, and reflect on your personal stance on them and your vision for a more just world. Saad (2020) is a great starting point with lots of journaling prompts for self-examination.

As usual, scour the internet for advice on how to draft such a statement, or start by responding to these questions:

- How have your intersectional identities given you insight into issues of privilege and oppression?
- How do your values inform how you approach this work?
- What have you learned about the issues faced by groups whose identities you do not embody?
- How do (or would) you make the courses you teach, your research lab, the committees you serve on inclusive?
- How do (or would) you take an asset-based approach rather than a deficit-based approach to diversity?
- How do (or would) you go beyond the personal aspect of this work to identify and address systemic issues in your sphere of influence?
- How do you hold yourself accountable on this work?

Be strategic about your service. Sometimes, research and teaching are so time consuming that we squeeze our service in the leftover interstitial spaces. What would happen if we were intentional about the kind of service we want to do? Looking for ways to tie our service into our vision, even inventing ways as Lachlan did, can be a great way to make our service more fulfilling. Think about where you can make the most difference in terms of the things that matter to you. Olivia, whose vision was to create community, could achieve that by sitting on a variety of committees. Think about the impact you could have if you stepped up to chair a committee rather than simply serving on it.

Explore roles at your institution. If you are still looking to crystallize a vision, consider opportunities beyond your department. For instance, many institutions now utilize faculty fellows in a variety of ways. Faculty fellows join a unit for a time-limited fellowship, one to two years usually, at half time release from their departmental duties. At my university, faculty fellows have been funded by the Center for Excellence in Teaching and Learning, the Distance Learning Center, the Office of Research, and several academic colleges, on a range of topics. Fellows usually have some latitude in their role and can explore within the fellowship topic. Many former fellows have continued in other institutional roles or have used the fellowship as a launching pad outside of the institution. They are limited in time, one to two years usually. Therefore, if you realize that role is not fulfilling, you can easily return to your department.

Reflect on the integration of your performance areas. Integration can make life more fulfilling, if you manage to weave your passions and commitments into all areas of your workload. Aida and Kendrick, for instance, have integrated their commitments (in service and in public health, respectively) into multiple facets of their professional life. At some institutions, some degree of integration among all performance areas is one of the criteria for certain awards as well.

Ensure alignment between your vision and the university's vision. Advancement through the ranks often rests in being able to prove that our work is advancing the university vision, that is, we are helping the university go where it wants to. This is often fairly easy to establish. For instance, every university is invested in the success of their students, so be sure to emphasize this aspect when talking about your own vision. In this case, this strategy is more about the communication chakra than the vision chakra as it is all in the framing. But there are cases where our vision and the university's vision might diverge. For instance, a school might set as its goal that of moving up through the rankings, achieve national or international reputation, or advance to a different Carnegie classification. In all those cases, this will involve changing expectations for the kind of work it requires of its faculty (e.g., more publications and more research grants). In those cases, think about what parts of your vision still fit with the university's vision. Maybe those parts will be enough to make your work and career fulfilling. Maybe you will be able to contain work and find fulfillment outside of work. Or maybe you might want to look at other jobs more in alignment with your vision and values.

Slash careers. All through graduate school, we are socialized to see academia as the logical next step in our journey, certainly the purer if not the only possible one. This vision might be sufficient for some people, but might be inadequate for others—for you, maybe. There is absolutely no shame in admitting that not all your professional desires are satisfied or your basic needs met by the university. Some of us are not fulfilled because no one career can embrace all that it takes to fulfill us, and so they embrace multiple careers. Beyond those that do because their passion won't allow them to make ends meet (think actor/waiter), there are those that find it energizing. Is it you? Marci Alboher has made a successful career for herself by promoting the concept of "slash careers." Her book *One Person/Multiple Careers: The Original Guide to the Slash Career* (2012) promotes the concept of professional pathways that allow for multiple interests to be satisfied and disparate skills to be put to good use in a congenial domain.

A famous *slasher* whose work most academics have heard of or read is Jorge Cham, whose comic strip PHD Comics has brought levity to many of us in graduate school. From 2003 to 2005, Cham churned out those comics while being an instructor and research associate at the California Institute of Technology. Not all slashers will have careers as disparate as academic and cartoonist. Many slash careers will be complementary and, for some, even necessary to our work in higher education. For instance, you will recall Damian, from Chapter 1, professor of psychology with a specialization in clinical work. A part of his story is that, when he was an assistant professor, early in his first semester, his chair took him out to lunch. During their casual conversation, the chair dropped a nugget. "Just so you know, Damian, the clinical professors that went through the tenure process successfully at our school, they all had a private practice." As general advice, pay attention to those just-so-you-know comments camouflaged within a casual lunch. They are word to the wise and indeed, in this particular case, likely the main reason why the chair called the lunch in the first place. Damian listened and established a private practice. When his tenure case was threatened, it was reassuring to know he had a fallback option, but even before that moment, the fulfillment he derived from helping his patients with their mental health was a significant part of his professional satisfaction.

I too identify as a slasher, a university administrator/public speaker. I am not suggesting to simply put more on your plate. Rather, I am referring to the possibilities that open up in the in-between spaces. As an administrator, I have no research expectations. I am not required to write books. But I meet a lot of people and hear a lot of stories through my speaking engagements at other universities, and if I simply have an IRB ready, presto! Those conversations double up, with permission, as stories for this book! Look for the piggy-backing, the double duty, the synergy, always work within the policies of your institution (e.g., IRB, conflict of interests, intellectual property, and consulting), and don't be afraid to follow your vision!

Consider taking advantage of professional coaching. You will recall that Donna worked with a coach to craft her vision. Universities (and state university systems) have started offering coaching as one of their professional development services for faculty. I have employed several coaches, and they were one of the highest rated services we offered. Faculty appreciated the environment of confidential positive regard coaching creates and the agency it reclaims. The agenda for coaching is completely set by the faculty member. Coaches are process rather than content experts, and they help clarify goals, create action plans, marshal resources, and troubleshoot. They also hold their clients accountable so that their project advances. I have seen faculty use coaching to conceptualize a research project, manage conflict with a colleague or a chair, and of course create a professional vision that aligns with their values.

Explore professional development programs. If you are dissatisfied with your current situation, try to buy yourself time to create a new vision. Many schools have a sabbatical program. Even in states that do not allow sabbaticals, some schools have reassignment programs where faculty members can have their workload reassigned to a research project for a whole semester. An archeological dig in India or a fall scouring the Cambridge archives is a great reset toward a new vision, on top of a definite boost to one's research agenda. If you are being bullied, a change of scenery could do wonders. At those institutions that raised research expectations, a semester in Silicon Valley learning new technologies, equipment, and methodologies can reawaken passions set aside. Maybe, like Bridget, study abroad is the cable jump you need for a new direction. Consider options beyond your institution. A Fulbright adventure or a voyage with Semester at Sea might bring just the inspiration you need.

Explore leadership development programs. If your vision involves a leadership position, take advantage of opportunities to develop your leadership skills. Many universities offer executive leadership programs. Such programs will help you develop your leadership skills, give you options for pathways to leadership, connect you with a cohort of individuals with similar goals, and put you on the radar of university leadership as a potential candidate for future leadership positions.

WORKSHEET 6.1 COALESCE YOUR VISION

Bring forward the values you clarified from Chapter 1. How do you see them contributing to your vision?
Now recall your passions from Chapter 2. What will you need to do to pursue them?
Now recall your goals from Chapter 3. As you put values, passions, and goals in alignment, what coalesces?
Now recall those you declared yourself accountable to in Chapter 4. How does your vision honor them?
What skills do you add to this equation?
Now recall the archetypes you reflected on earlier in this chapter. How do your archetypes inform your vision?
How do others see you? Do they mirror your values, passions, goals, and skills to you? Do they see you in the way you see yourself? If not, how?

Copyright material from Michele DiPietro (2026), *The Faculty Guide to a Balanced and Harmonious Career*, Routledge

How does your vision bring value to the world?
What time frame do you need to realize your vision?
How does your vision square with your current situation? What changes would you need to make to fulfill it?
Is your vision geography-neutral or do you need to be in a particular place to realize it or to feel empowered?
Is your vision viable and sustainable? Can you make a living from it? If not, what steps can you take to make it viable or to at least realize parts of it?
Let's put all these pieces together! Take a first stab at your vision statement! Remember, your first draft doesn't have to be perfect.

References

Alboher, M. (2012) *One person/multiple careers: The original guide to the slash career.* Business Plus.

Ambrose, S., Huston, T., & Norman, M. (2005). A qualitative method for assessing faculty satisfaction. *Research in Higher Education, 46*(7), 803–830.

Anderson, J. R. (1990) *The adaptive character of thought.* Lawrence Erlbaum Associates. ISBN 0-8058-0419-6.

Anderson, J. R. (1993) *Rules of the mind.* Lawrence Erlbaum Associates. ISBN 0-8058-1199-0.

Buller, J. (2014) *Change leadership in higher education: A practical guide to academic transformation.* Jossey-Bass.

Buller, J. (2013) *Positive academic leadership: How to stop putting out fires and start making a difference.* Jossey-Bass.

Google Dictionary Box (n.d.). Burnout. Retrieved March 6, 2025 from www.google.com/search?q=vision+definition

Jung, C. G. (1991). *The archetypes and the collective unconscious* (R. F. C. Hull, Trans.; 2nd ed.). Routledge. First published in 1959.

Kouzes, J., & Posner, B. (2023) *The leadership challenge: How to make extraordinary things happen in organizations* (7th ed.). Jossey-Bass.

Mark, M., & Pearson, C. (2002) *The hero and the outlaw: Building extraordinary brands through the power of archetypes.* McGraw-Hill.

Myss, C. (2013) *Archetypes: A beginner's guide to your inner-net.* Hay House.

Saad, L. (2020) *Me and white supremacy: How to recognize your privilege, combat racism, and change the world.* Sourcebooks.

Schönwetter, D., Sokal, L., Friesen, M., & Taylor, K. L. (2002) Teaching philosophies reconsidered: A conceptual model for the development and evaluation of teaching philosophy statements. *The International Journal for Academic Development, 7*(1), 83–97.

Sedgwick, E. S. (2003) *Touching feeling: Affect, pedagogy, performativity.* Duke University Press.

Seldin, P., Miller, E., & Seldin, C. (2010) *The teaching portfolio: A practical guide to improved performance and promotion/tenure decisions* (4th ed.). Jossey-Bass.

Shiba, K., Kubzansky, L., Williams, D., VanderWeele, T., & Kim, E. (2022) Purpose in life and 8-year mortality by gender and race/ethnicity among older adults in the U.S. *Preventative Medicine, 164,* 107310.

Stewart, L., & Jordan, E. (2020) Narrative interventions: Power-sharing and boundary-crossing in action. Plenary presentation at the 47th conference of the POD Network in Higher Education, online.

Sword, H. (2017) *Air & light & time & space: How successful academics write.* Harvard University Press.

7
WHAT KIND OF CONSCIOUSNESS WILL BEST GUIDE US?

The crown chakra

Brainwashed and cultified

Six months before #MeToo exploded in the national conversation, I was sexually harassed by a high-level administrator at my university. It's still hard to put how it felt into words. The shock, the revulsion, the horror, the need to escape, the paralysis, the uncontainable rage, the urge to contain it anyway, because women can never be emotional at work, the disbelief that this could be happening to me, the disillusion that a religious institution with a social justice mission was not immune, did I mention the shock?

As any faculty member who's been at an institution a number of years, I have had to report other things in the past, albeit not of a sexual nature, and I was always told by my chair and dean to go through the proper channels. I knew that was even more important this time, because the guy was on the president's good side. So I brought all the big guns, HR, Title IX, the bias incident response team. I knew I could not live with letting this person do the same to another woman faculty.

It was immediately clear to me that the investigator assigned to the case knew nothing about sexual harassment. He read my statement to the guy and asked him if it was true. When he denied (duh!), the investigator said it was a "he said/she said" situation and found him not guilty. He also said that nobody had ever reported him. So I told them, "Now you're on notice. You said there is nothing in his file, well now there is." From my contacts at the Women's Center, I found out there was a whisper network of women faculty, administrators, and students alike, who all knew about him. Conversely, all the men I interacted with during the incident denied any wrongdoing. I am a sociologist. I teach about these

DOI: 10.4324/9781003487371-8

topics, and this was a textbook case. That alone should have been foreboding because I know what happens in all the textbook cases. But I thought I could make a difference with my authority as a tenured associate professor.

There was one thing that really bothered me. This man organizes community engagement initiatives and conveniently drives students to the various community events. I didn't want any more female students alone with him in his car for up to an hour each way ever again. So I asked that at least one outcome be to not let him drive undergraduate women in his car. The school said they couldn't do that. The only consequence for him was that they told him to "watch his language."

Me, on the other hand—they told me all the things I had done wrong this time. They told me what to say and what to do next time, as if the fight/flight/freeze response wasn't a thing. They clearly knew nothing of this. Ten years in, tenure, multiple teaching awards and they are talking to me like I am an idiot. I had done everything by the book throughout my career and in this investigation, gone through the proper channels as they always said, and I realized nobody would protect me, or even the undergraduate students, from this predator.

It left me so broken. I was so distraught that I wasn't able to be productive at work. I simply could not focus. I had to take a leave of absence. No pay, no insurance. Once again, it is the victim who is quite literally paying the consequences. I moved back in with my parents. I had to get on Medicaid. I borrowed money from my mother. I dealt with anxiety, depression, a sick stomach that felt like I couldn't eat anything. I had to force myself to put food down for six months. Sometimes I couldn't get out of bed in the morning. I felt frail. I had terror dreams and night sweats.

Most of all, I could not unlearn what I now know. He was valuable to the university. His initiatives brought millions into the coffers. I'm replaceable, there are a million other sociology PhDs who could teach my courses. My supposedly progressive colleagues did not stand with me. Such a topsy-turvy world. I gave my blood, sweat, and tears to my institution, but I learned what I was worth to the system.

A number of well-meaning colleagues told me, If you leave you'll never get another academic job, especially if you speak out. Instead, their advice was: Why don't you come back and just be smaller? I was so lost. I didn't know who I was anymore. I extended my leave to buy time to rebuild myself. A friend found me a part-time gig locally. I taught one class. Then another. With the help of family and support system, I started getting better.

It took two years for me to make a decision that wasn't just out of pain and brokenness. I could not come back and find a place in a system that was fine with my mistreatment and was only trying to extract more labor from me. I teach women not to be small! How could that be an acceptable solution? It's completely against my values, my identity, and integrity. But it took me so long because I had to unhook my identity from being a tenured professor. I was crying to my mom, "I don't know who I am if I am not a tenured faculty member." She said, "Do you think dad or I care one bit if you are tenured? What you have to give to the world has nothing to do with that." I was so brainwashed and cultified by academia that I didn't know my worth outside of that.

Now I know I am a teacher writ large and a creator, heart and soul. There are a million things I can do and create in the world. I am thinking of leaving academia altogether. There is no institution that needs to be stamped beside my name on a business card. I don't need rank, title, or institutional affiliation. I have incredible public speaking skills. I am deserving and worthy of love just because I exist. I had to remove the hooks sunk into me by the system. But I now know I am a warrior woman.

—Matilda, White female associate professor of sociology at a small religious liberal arts college on the West Coast

Joy is my North Star

My grandmother used to say, "When people show you who they are, act accordingly. Otherwise you only have yourself to blame." When I first started my tenure track job, there was a colleague who visited harm upon women in the department. He did not like working with women and even said that outright to students in the program. He called women faculty princesses if we asked questions. He called me specifically a child once. I compared notes with other female-identifying faculty in the department, and they all felt undermined by him but unsafe to speak up about it. They coped by contorting themselves around the issue and hoping the abuse wouldn't escalate, which reinforced all his bad behaviors. So I acted accordingly and filed a title IX suit. They interviewed other women. Full professors confirmed all my allegations, but justified themselves by saying they never wanted to rock the boat. So the harm got passed down to new generations of untenured women.

His reaction? He would trap people in their offices, yelling and screaming at them if he knew they were testifying. The Title IX officer told him he couldn't do that. It was amazing that he only got a verbal warning for harassing women—at the same time that he was being investigated exactly for harassing women! There are lots of books out there celebrating resilience and grit in higher education, but the way I see it is that this is only telling Black women to endure even more harm.

He carried a gun! And it was clear my institution would not protect me. This happened in a state where campus carry is allowed, so they said they could legally do nothing until he actually did something to me, *then* they would protect me. No preventative measures were even considered. I found solace in a group of Black, Indigenous, and People of Color (BIPOC) women. We came together because we all felt beat down and harmed by the institution. We were all from different departments, but we all shared experiences of extraction. They want us here but all they understand to do is to extract from us once we're here without protecting us. I was working twice as hard to meet all my performance targets while navigating the challenges of the investigation, not to mention the emotional labor my colleagues felt entitled to from me. Notwithstanding the fact that I had become a "troublemaker" for sounding the alarm about this person, I had a general reputation of being a warm, empathetic person. Many faculty members cried in my office about this or that issue, with some expectation that I would console them. Yet, they never asked me how I was doing, not even when graffiti with the N-word showed up at work one day.

I knew I had to act according to how I was treated, so I followed my joy. Joy is my North Star, and exactly what White supremacy does not want for me. So I know I always have to embody it, as a matter of self-preservation. And my joy is in my connection to spirit. This is foundational for me. I practice this connection every day. I pray and meditate before I get out of bed. I do a series of stretches. I get in alignment with myself and with something larger than myself. I don't have a name for it because I feel names limit it, and I know it's limitless. I turn over the day to my higher power, from the stage to the classroom. This connection to something greater than myself is also where I got the strength to resign. Oh yes, I left, and moved to a saner state without campus carry. For the where are they now category: that guy continued harassing women even after the verbal warning, so they eventually let him go. Me? I won an Emmy and completed two book projects, among other things.

—Sheila, Black queer female associate professor of contemporary and musical theater at a large conservatory

The spirit of the law

Half of my research is about the rights of people who are not physically alive anymore. There is a way in which it is important to talk about it in academic terms, and I use philosophy and the law as a container, but there is certainly a part of me that is doing it because I believe that some dimensions of people who are not physically alive anymore continue to live on. At a minimum, they are alive in people's memories. Their legacies are still alive, which is something people in life spend a lot of time thinking about, what they want to leave behind. And if there was discrimination against them while they were alive, their ability to leave a legacy was affected. I have to read about lynchings and such things, remember that those were human beings, and the accounts of what happened not only in the lynchings, but after the lynching, are absolutely horrifying. I cry when I read these sources, and I often need to step away for a moment, but it is important that I do not stop writing about this, and also that I talk about it with other academics.

You could say that I write about spirit because I write about the dimensions of people's existence beyond the body. The body is a useful vessel to help us appreciate the metaphysical qualities, such as dignity, which is why bodies get disrespected in and after death—at least for people belonging to groups that are the face of dehumanization and inequality. Things like memory, will, dignity, and reputation are much less tangible, connected but not directly contained by the body.

The other half of my research consists of writing about people who are suing the government. These areas are conceptually distinct in law, but I see a thread connecting them, the dignity of the people involved. For instance, in December 2014, I was in St. Louis County, Missouri, during the unrest in Ferguson following the killing of Michael Brown by the police. I was staying with another civil rights attorney who was representing a group of young people who got stopped by the police every time they were protesting. It was a small group of as few as four or five of them, at every protest the police would surround them, and say "This is an unlawful assembly, you need to disperse," but the police would encircle them, so there was nowhere to disperse and they were given no time to disperse. Then the police would tear gas them for failing to comply, young adults in their late teens or early 20s. They were clearly victimized by the police.

So there was a lawsuit and the next day there was a hearing, and I got to help prep the lawyer for the hearing. The piece that moved me was watching these individuals who had not spent a lot of time in federal court. There were people who testified they would protest despite the tear gas and others who testified they were scared of protesting because of the tear gas. The judge was a Reagan appointee, a former prosecutor, and she was visibly horrified. She seemed old enough to remember the civil rights movement, she was probably a teenager back then. She found for the plaintiffs and issued a court order. Rather than taking the hint, the police fell back on some of their tried-and-true tactics. They would give people tickets and arrest them. The fees were arbitrary, the number of days detained was arbitrary, they were told that they would be jailed but not for how many days. Just that until they paid the amount, they would have to stay imprisoned. Often, people could not pay the fees, especially since they were in jail and unable to work. People missed loved ones' funerals, or were fired because they missed jobs, all over a traffic ticket. Some lost their home and had to move in with family. We had to meet one person in a barbershop because he did not have a home. Watching the devastating exploitation was formative for me in terms of how I write and think about federal courts and the best ways to vindicate people's rights.

I said I write about spirit. I feel very connected to the ancestral realm. That's where I draw my inspiration to advocate for the interests of people who are or were not in a position of power. Vindicating those interests is spiritual to me.

I want to make these issues more salient. I want people in the law world to think more about that. I write about it from a mass inequality perspective. If we accept that there are parts of the human dimension that go beyond the physical and the body, then it follows we can still be doing violence to their body, their will, their reputation, and so on. But that also opens the possibility that we can do some remediation work. That possibility animates me.

—Tim, Black queer endowed chair professor of law at a private research institution in the Southeast

What's going on with these stories?

On the surface, the struggles are what ties these stories together. Mathilda endures sexual harassment, and the heartbreak of not being believed or protected by her institution. Similarly, Sheila endures misogynoir—the combination of anti-Black racism and misogyny—compounded by red tape that also results in no protection from the institution. And Tim relives the deadliest expressions of racism, such as lynchings or police brutality, admittedly vicariously, but at a level so deep that it regularly moves him to tears. Yet that is only the first level. At a deeper level, the stories are joined by a shared disillusionment. Tenure will not protect Matilda; the institution will not protect Sheila; the law will not protect Black citizens. It would be depressing if pessimism and cynicism were the end of the story.

But, and this is the most powerful common thread, all three protagonists go through a crucible experience, where they are able to emerge stronger with a deeper consciousness about themselves and their worth. Mathilda realizes that she is a warrior woman and does not need degrees, titles, or institutional affiliation to validate her. Sheila stands tall in her connection to spirit and joy. Tim situates himself in the ancestral realm that allows him to see events playing out as reiterations of universal stories, which allow the possibility of hope. For all their tribulations, all three faculty maintain or recover a positive, empowered, and agentic outlook on life.

Acquiring a full consciousness immediately raises attendant topics. How do we access our higher self? In these stories, the protagonists arrive at a higher consciousness through spirituality, community, or ancestry. The paths might be many, but they all involve seeing oneself as part of something greater, and drawing a sense of purpose from that connection. We are talking about experiences of transcendence, which also bring up the issue of legacy, as Tim suggests. Guided by this purpose drawn from a higher consciousness, what are we leaving behind in the world? How do we want the world or our institutions, or our students, to be different, and better, because of our efforts? To engage these questions, we need to bring in the last chakra, the crown.

What does chakra theory say?

We are now at the end of our journey. Shakti energy has traveled all the way up through each chakra, opening them up and reestablishing balance and alignment, and reunites with her consort Shiva in the crown chakra. The Sanskrit name of the crown chakra is Sahasrāra, meaning thousand-petaled. This chakra is described as a lotus with 1,000 petals, depicted as 20 layers with 50 petals each. The full moon is at the center of this lotus, and a luminous upward-pointing triangle inside it. Remember the petals of the lotus flowers increased through the chakras, then contracted down to two petals in the third eye, and now explode out in the final step. The number 1,000 is a stand-in for infinity. That, and the fact that the main deity of the crown is Shiva, personifying the transcendent aspect of divinity, signal that this chakra is about realizing our own divine nature, further symbolized by the fact that in some texts it is represented above the head, symbolizing a stepping out of ourselves and a reunification with the universe.

Some yoga circles teach that the greeting *namaste* (नमस्ते) means "The divine light in me honors the divine light in you." While this translation is spurious, and namaste is simply a greeting, the ascribed meaning reflects this awareness. Because of the transcendental nature of this chakra, no elements are associated with it, although some say the "element" of this chakra is thought. The petals are represented in shades of different colors traditionally, but in the modern description, the crown chakra is purple, thus completing the rainbow. The seed sound to meditate on this lotus is Om.

The guiding principle of this chakra is consciousness. Our capacity to think, remember, predict, and interpret is the one thing about ourselves that is least tethered to the physical limitations of life in our bodies—and as academics we are well acquainted with this capacity. So what is the work of this chakra for us? Well, chakras are about energies, and an excess of energy in the crown means less energy in other areas. Those with excessive crown energy tend to overintellectualize and overanalyze matters and get stuck in their head. The stereotype of the absent-minded professor, with genius smarts but unable to function in the real world, captures this dynamic. Conversely, a crown chakra with energy blockages might show up as apathetic, or cynical. But when the crown is fully expressing, in alignment with the other chakras, it channels wisdom, full presence in the moment, openness to other perspectives, and a sense of purpose.

The function of this chakra is understanding, making sense of the world, organizing it, finding patterns, so that order emerges from chaos. This meaning-making gives purpose to our life and gets digested into a set of guiding beliefs. This is a dynamic activity, in that beliefs arise from processing our experience, but the way we process our experiences is also informed by our beliefs. Some beliefs can hold us back, as we saw in the case of Matilda, who had over time sedimented a belief that she needed to be a tenured professor for her life to be meaningful. Therefore, it is essential that the meaning-making start with the self. In fact, one of the Niyama practices is *svādhyāya* (स्वध्याय), or self-study.

As we study our self, the identity we cultivate in this chakra is our universal identity. We started from our individual, physical identity in the ground chakra, and we added to it gradually. The upper chakras are about self-actualization, expressing what we have inside (whether it's our next book, or a truth we need to speak to power), or envisioning possibilities for our career. But in the crown, we go beyond self-actualization to the next level, self-transcendence, feeling part of something greater that gives us purpose. Sheila claims a connection to spirit. Tim draws meaning from his connection to the ancestors.

To illustrate this universal interconnection, recall Eve Sedgwick's cat (2003), introduced in the third eye chakra. In the vision chakra, the cat is the fool, unable to realize the finger pointing to the mess the cat made is not the mess itself. But here in the crown chakra, we enter the paradox of realizing we were the fool all along, believing that the finger, the mess, the cat, and ourselves were distinct things, when we are really all interconnected and emanating from the same universal source. That's why this philosophy refers to the physical world as māyā, illusion (the demon of the vision chakra), because it supports the fraudulent notion of separateness.

Another aspect of feeling part of something greater is the idea of legacy. What is the mark we want to leave in academia, in our field or in our institution, that will persist even when we are gone? A healthy crown chakra will orient us to this issue, making sure the legacy we work toward is in line with our values, passion, truth, purpose, and so on.

Within this context, it makes perfect sense that the right associated with the crown chakra is the right to know, and that the demon is attachment. When we are trying to transcend to a higher consciousness of ourselves, attachments to things like money, prestige, title, and tenure status are the ballast that weighs us down, as Matilda discovered. That's why one of the Yama restraints is *aparigraha* (अपरिग्रह), or non-attachment. As usual, the next sections will expand on all these issues, and then we will offer some strategies.

Faculty insights: Consciousness and purpose

If a principal function of this chakra is to nurture a higher consciousness, what would that look like for faculty? Through her suffering and healing, Matilda acquired the consciousness of being a warrior woman and a creator. From her connection to spirit, Sheila draws her joy and her internal barometer that tells her she deserves much better than how she is being treated. Through the connection

> **BOX 7.1 CROWN CHAKRA CHART**
>
> Sanskrit name: Sahasrāra
> Meaning: Thousand-petal lotus
> Element: Beyond elements
> Function: Consciousness
> Color: Purple
> Identity: Universal
> Right: To Know
> Demon: Attachment

to the ancestors, Tim is connected to the sense of dignity for all human beings, particularly oppressed ones, which animates his research. Others through their own unique journey arrived at other compelling insights. Let's start with Lachlan's musings:

> I believe my work matters. I know living a life of the mind gives you a better life, and if my students are paying attention, they will be enriched. I'm not here to save their soul, but I am here to enrich their lives. I'm not evangelical, but I know this to be true. I am not talking about the specificity of the content per se, but of a certain approach to life—caring, being curious about other people through their writing, being empathetic. Gratitude is a big part of that approach. When I had a sabbatical, I titled the last section of my report "Overwhelmed with gratitude." The provost said that, in all her years, no faculty had included gratitude in a sabbatical report. I can't imagine not including gratitude in a report about having a full paid semester to myself to pursue my own intellectual dream.

Lachlan knows that approaching life with empathy, curiosity, and gratitude matters, and that's what he tries to communicate to his students. Here's how Emmett understands himself at his best:

> I think of my life as constant incremental growth. It's a basic but revolutionary idea, for me at least. When I realized that, it reframed how I approach life in an astronomical way. Who do I want to be the rest of my life? My identity is not fixed. I'm not tied to my abusive parents anymore, or to the mistakes of the past. I can step forward and be better. I would love if people thought of me as the idea of growth itself. Whatever happened, I know that I can be better at the end of each day than I was at the start.

In describing her experience, Charlene, the professor of French we met in the throat chakra, refers back to Dr. Maya Angelou's quote: "I come as one but stand as ten thousand." This consciousness rests on a felt sense of one's history, the strength they draw from the love and support of those who stand with them.

All these facets echo the work of Donna Hicks, the author of *Dignity* (2011) and *Leading with Dignity* (2018). She describes dignity as a state of "inherent value and worth" bestowed on every human being. Dignity is vulnerable and can be violated, but our dignity cannot be taken from us without our consent. She arrived at this conclusion talking with Archbishop Desmond Tutu and reading Nelson Mandela's autobiography after he had been incarcerated for 27 years. Mandela realized at the beginning of his incarceration that the guards would do everything they could to rob him of his dignity and that his job was to hold on to it. This did not free him of the guards' abuse, but it allowed him to look at it in a way that did not break his spirit. Hicks was so struck by his approach that she dubbed this higher consciousness "Mandela consciousness." Most of us will never face the circumstances Mandela faced, but that attitude is precisely what Matilda had to develop over the two years of her leave.

In the previous chapters, as we ascended the liberating current, we have often invoked the energy descending from the crown that would meet the energy rising from the ground and express at different chakras. This consciousness is that energy. When we are fully present to our inherent value and worth, this consciousness generates a purpose in the crown chakra. It's that purpose that we can take down and express as a professional vision in the third eye, or express as will in service of our plan in the power chakra, and so on. So what do faculty say is their purpose? By far, most faculty declare without hesitation that their purpose is to make a difference with their students. For instance, Petra states:

> I love this Maya Angelou quote: People may forget what you said, but they will never forget how you made them feel. I want to make my students feel that I believe in them, in their potential to succeed.

The attribution to Maya Angelou is erroneous, but the sentiment is powerful. Bridget's purpose develops this idea further:

> I want to lift up teaching and learning as intellectually complex endeavors but full of joy. I love the idea of education being about the delight of learning things. It can be healing to pursue your curiosity. I would like for my students to find meaning, purpose, and fulfillment, because I know firsthand that being the beneficiary of information changes people's lives.

Cyrus expresses an additional dimension that other professors in his same situation also echoed:

> I wanted children, but that path did not open up for me. I have transferred some of my sense of purpose onto my students. I want to create a better world for them, academically and beyond. I love it when they text me years after I had them to let me know they are engaged or to share other life updates.

Beyond their students, faculty have an array of purposes, some related to their area of scholarship or expertise. Dennis gives a vivid illustration of how his purpose flows from his self-consciousness: "I think of myself as a chaos Muppet, so I just want to make things a bit weirder. For instance, I know I want to weave queer content into the fabric of the program."

Felix, who does research on people's beliefs, describes his purpose as follows:

> I go back to the Delphic oracle maxim—know thyself. I see myself as developing intellectual tools that will allow people to understand themselves better. One of the most important things one can do, morally, is to not be alienated from oneself. This mission of authenticity is my signature.

Brody, who expressed he was "all about relationships" in the heart chakra, expands on that idea:

> Since I was a child, the people that have poured the most into my life have been Black men, Black families. So my purpose in life is to do whatever possible to create better race relations. I also have a gay son, so I have become a champion for the LGBTQ+ community. It's more challenging for people to give kindness to others who are not just like them. So that's where I want to make a difference and have an impact.

On a related note, Simon states: "What I am really interested in is centering Black queer work."

And finally, for this section, we close with Alfred and his purpose:

> I don't take the fact that I teach in a med school lightly. The goal of med schools is that their graduates come out full functioning practicing physicians or research scientists, because the medical advances of our society are depending on their shoulders. My particular goal is that we create physicians who understand all the different pieces that patients bring with them. It's not just their disease, but their histories, their families, their addictions, everything. I want to create holistic physicians who are caring and empathetic. You are all incredibly bright, I tell my students. You will not be tripped up

by medical knowledge. But what will trip you is your ability to connect with other humans. I am lucky that my own physician is a former student, and I see how he treats me and things he does as direct consequences of activities I taught in class.

When faculty are clear about who they are and the value they bring to the world, the purposes that flow from that awareness are compelling and powerful. In the next section we will explore how our consciousness and purpose are related to us feeling part of something greater than ourselves, and the legacy we want to leave behind.

Faculty insights: Transcendence and legacy

Let's revisit Alfred's narrative from the previous section. We can see that his story contains an awareness that he is able to manifest his purpose, judging from what his former student physician mirrors back at him. This idea also expands on the concept of transcendence. The crown chakra is about realizing we are part of something greater than us, which predates us and will continue after us. How do we find our place in this current? How do we realize our transcendence? And what will we leave behind to bear witness to how we contributed? Faculty had a lot to say about these concepts.

The most common answer to the transcendence question was teaching. It is very evident to faculty that teaching the next generation is an act that is bigger than any of them individually, sacred even. For instance, Angel explains: "The mission of higher education for underserved communities can change the world. The message that these lives have meaning and value, that they can affect change, is so important. That is how I feel part of something greater." Carly focuses on helping students reframe their beliefs:

> I have worked with some students who felt that the world would preclude certain paths to them because of their gender or race, but then gradually they could imagine themselves in those paths. If I can make that shift happen for them, that's when I feel part of something greater.

Colin highlights prison education as another context ripe for insights:

> I do not expect people to remember any single topic I've taught them, but I hope I manage to change their perspective in some ways. For instance, once a month I take my students to a maximum-security prison. The experience is so powerful. One cosmic truth we all learn is that you can't sum people up by the worst thing they have ever done. I know this experience will have a lasting impact on my students, and to be a part of that is very rewarding.

Serena understands transcendence in terms of energy, which is a very similar perspective to the chakra approach:

> Ripples. That is a great way of transcending. It all plays on a high energy level in the universe. When you put out that kind of energy, you are also able to receive it, and then you are able to give even more.

Lachlan adds an important reminder:

> In terms of my teaching, I've been influenced by teachers since first grade, but I know some of my teachers never got to see the fruits of the seeds they planted with me. By the same token, I also know that I don't get to see all the ripples from my own teaching. But I trust the impact will resonate wherever it's useful.

As part of this great universal flow, we leave behind a trace, our legacy. When the conversation turned specifically to legacy, most faculty immediately turned to their scholarship. Books, articles, discoveries, and insights are things that endure, certainly because of digital records but also hopefully because our ideas resonate with others. Immediately after their scholarship, faculty declared their students their legacy, as well as anybody else they mentored (i.e., postdocs and colleagues). Sheila is very conscious of how being part of the universal flow and leaving a legacy are connected:

> My legacy is in my mentorship. Not only do I love and enjoy doing it, but I also know it is super important because I always am "the first"—first queer, first Black, first tenured. So it is crucial to open that door, widen it. When we talk about "predominantly White institutions," the truth is it takes a lot of work to stay predominantly White year after year. So I counter that by widening open the door for others, so that others after me might have an easier time, just like I have had an easier time than those who came before me. I don't know the stealth work they had to do for me to enter. Maybe they were cleaning the room, so I can teach in the room today.

Gail already left multiple legacies and is able to compare across them:

> I am very fortunate. I started a program that has taken hold at multiple universities and now has numerous chapters across the nation. They also named a national advising award after me. But most prominent in my mind are the students. One of my student said: I know I'm gonna be okay in my life because I'm Gail-taught. And that became a cute hashtag amongst some of my former students, #Gail-taught.

For others, like Sasha, the realization that their legacy is in their students was precipitated by institutional events:

> For many years I thought the institutional programs I created and grew to national prominence would be my legacy long after I retired. But administrations come and go. Eventually, the university moved on. None of my programs exist anymore. So, recently, I've come to appreciate that, if I have any legacy, it is the students I've taught. The beauty of social media is that I'm in touch with students from 30 years ago! I'll see an accomplishment they post, I congratulate them, and they say: You are the one who taught me to do X!

Similarly, Olivia had a moment of visual clarity at a conference:

> I was asked to be a discussant for a panel. When they sent me the names of the panelist and their papers, I realized all the panelists were former graduate students of mine! What a joy it was to be on that panel and watch them shine and push the field forward!

When asked how they wanted to be remembered, faculty gave answers ranging from profoundly articulate to disarmingly simple. Here's Donna's answer: "I want to be remembered as a steadfast advocate for justice, as someone who changed engineering in a direction that made it more just." Justin, the philosopher of education who transitioned into administration, puts his values at the center of his legacy:

> My first impulse is to say I want to be remembered as somebody who pushed for honesty over hypocrisy; transparency over hiding behind corporate-speak; and being okay with our non-model self over pretending to be perfect.

Calliope, the adjunct professor who identifies with the Lilith archetype, puts that at the center of her legacy too:

> I want to be remembered by my students as that crazy woman who promoted mythology in every class she taught. A student who took classes with me and switched her major to English is now the chair of English at a high school, and she too uses mythology the way I have used it, so I have successfully passed it on.

Vivian answered concisely: "I want to be remembered as a friend."

Faculty also offered caveats through this process. Some opened up the possibility that our legacy might not be (primarily) in academia. This was true of those who were thinking of leaving but also of some who were not actively trying to leave. Some saw their legacy in their family. As a practicing psychologist, Damian saw his legacy more in the patients he helped than the papers and books he wrote. Audre was more pointed in her analysis:

> Once upon a time I thought institutions would be part of building my legacy. But the truth is, you can love your institution, but institutions do not love you back. They have no capacity for love. So I don't depend on an institution to solidify my legacy. I only look for it in the human connections.

Others, such as Wendy, highlight the ephemeral aspects of legacy: "There is a quick amnesia when people retire. Only a few people endure with their research as a legacy over centuries. So I think about being and working in the moment."

Ernest unpacks the same dynamic for teaching:

> My legacy is only in my students, in the sense that I have no children. My family line is coming to an end. That's a limited legacy. It will be gone in a generation. But it's enough for me. I'm writing about some indigenous people whose tradition was to never say the name of their dead parents. When they died, they were no longer remembered, and their name reentered the available name pool. This clears the worries of [asking] was my book good enough, was my course good enough? I find it freeing.

While Ernest finds freedom in this idea, most of the faculty in my sample found comfort and fulfillment in being remembered fondly. Ezra, a professor of theater arts and chair of his department at a research university on the West coast, plainly stated: "I would like people to say of me that I contributed to things that matter." I end this section with Ezra's quote because his wish connects people's desire for legacy to developmental theory. In Erikson and Erikson's (1998) theory of human development, the last identity crisis as faculty near retirement and look back over their career is the tension between ego integrity versus despair, heralded by the question, "Is it okay to have been me?" I have consulted with faculty one year away from retirement who were suddenly worried about their legacy. At that point, the legacy is already established. Others will remember you the way they will remember you. If that question is salient to you, it is important to think about the legacy early on and be intentional about building it. The chakra approach will help us build our legacy by ensuring our actions are aligned with our values from the ground chakra, our passions from the pelvic chakra, our vision from the third eye chakra, and so on.

Chakra right: To know

Academia is founded on the right to know. Universities are about the universality of knowledge and the investigation of topics from multiple perspectives with a variety of disciplinary and interdisciplinary tools and approaches. Academic freedom is one of its guiding principles, and the institution of tenure is there to guarantee free and independent inquiry. Universities supports this right with numerous resources, research labs, libraries, museums, software licenses, research assistants, and support for sponsored research. They also regulate this right through institutional review boards and ethical research trainings to ensure the pursuit of knowledge is not at the expenses of human subjects' health and well-being. And, importantly, they reward faculty based on the standards of quality and significance of the knowledge created. Faculty generally agreed on these points.

We already mentioned some exceptions to this general idea, brought up by the faculty whose tenure and promotion process was derailed for reasons unrelated to their scholarship. As a follow-up, some highlighted some of the challenges to the right to know. One of these areas is the university itself, as Xander points out: "Transparency is a top concern of faculty, but academia is far from transparent. We don't get to know how money flows, who is put up for awards, all these processes are nebulous."

In addition, Amy, the professor of neuroscience and administrator who we met in the heart chakra, laments another challenge to the right to know: "The right to know is threatened when legislators write bills to decide what professors can and cannot teach and what students can and cannot learn." Indeed, in recent years we have witnessed a series of concerning events across the nation, including the dumping and even outright burning of books. Legislatures have challenged what topics can be taught in schools and universities, have issued academic gag orders, and mandated content or perspectives. All of which have eroded the pursuit of knowledge for its own sake as the right of universities (Kamola, 2024). These bills actually have maintained that teaching about structural racism, gender identity, or unvarnished accounts of American history actually harm students. As aspects of the right to know get increasingly threatened, it is good to consider Rahul's stance:

> Out of all the chakra rights, the one I never felt [was] threatened is the right to know. Try as they may, nobody can take my hard-earned knowledge from me. I know what I know, and even if they limit my speech or actions, I still know.

Chakra demon: Attachment

After addressing fear, guilt, shame, grief, lies, and illusions, we are now at the last demon, attachment. The fact that it shows up last underscores that even after all the work done on the other demons, we will remain anchored at a lower consciousness level if we can't conquer it. What are faculty attached to? This is the second most mentioned demon, after fear. In my interviews, faculty brought up several attachments related to status: title, salary, rank, and so on. As we already discussed in the context of the shame demon (see Chapter 3), on their worst moments, part-time faculty wish they were employed full-time, full-time lecturers wish they were on the tenure track, faculty with an EdD feel it is the "wrong" degree and wish they had a PhD, faculty with a PhD in a medical school wish they had an MD; full professors feel they should be center directors by now; center directors feel they should be department chair by now; and so on, in a never-ending perverse chain. They all mentioned they know better, and they all realize these things don't really matter in the end. And still, they feel the seductive pull of a higher salary, a better-sounding title. And underneath it all, the inner critic whispers that if they were *really* good, the salary and the title would have already found them. So what insights can come from facing the demon of attachment? Felix orients us toward the first insight:

> Attachment draws you away from what got you to be a scholar in the first place. If all you care about is success and getting published, you end up going through the motions instead of really saying the things that matter to you. It pulls you toward superficial accomplishments and playing the game.

The pull is real. Publish or perish is real. The system is set up in ways that encourage us to do whatever it takes to meet institutional metrics. A healthy attitude should balance survival in the system (a ground chakra concern) with the actions aligned with our higher purpose.

Sheila confirms the pull and shares her own hard-earned lesson:

> I was so attached to the brass ring of tenure that I endured racism, sexism, and bullying. I felt I truly learned that lesson when I was able to tell myself "A crown, if it hurts us, is not worth wearing," and walked from that unacceptable situation.

Sheila is quoting a famous maxim by Tony-award-winner actor, singer, and author Pearl Bailey. If we can lucidly assess the cost of our attachments, we start the process of letting go of them.

Beyond attachments to title and rank, Steffen, a White gay male instructor of computer science at a community college on the West Coast, shares a rarely articulated kind of attachment: "My perspective on teaching is tied to how I was taught, so my ideas might be a little old school. Old school might be valuable, but maybe I'm not realizing the value and affordances of new ways." In educational development circles, this is an open secret. Without pedagogical training in graduate school, many faculty fall back on the way they were taught

(Schroeder, 2022), leaning heavily on lectures and slow to adopt more impactful forms of pedagogy such as high impact practices or other forms of learning-centered teaching, and they unknowingly pass their approach on to the next generation of faculty.

A related kind of attachment is that described by Emmeline:

> I can't retire, because I'm too attached to what I do. But then I wonder—am I growing by still being in the classroom, or am I refusing to grow by staying there and not moving on to the next thing?

Audre wrestled with similar issues at certain points in her career:

> I'm a person of a certain age, the last of the boomers. We were raised that you get a job, and you stay there. That comes up for me occasionally, but I have conquered it. You have to know when to stay, know when to leave, and know how to leave. The old adage says to not burn bridges. That's why my resignation letters (and I have left a few jobs in my days, when I realized they were trapping me) always include a recap of all the good I've been able to do there. Those letters are also part of my personnel record at that institution, so I always set it straight.

All these instances are an attachment to the way things used to be. This affection for the familiar ways and difficulty to embrace change is wired into us like antibodies protecting us from the unknown, as Robert Kegan and Lisa Lahey remark in their book *Immunity to Change* (2009). And yet, change we must. Higher education is cycling through some rapid changes, technological, demographic, and financial, which all translate to changes in policies and procedures. Justin astutely reflects on this attachment:

> I like the status quo, because I have figured out how to work it. So this is really an attachment to my perfection image, my legitimacy, my being impressive. I have this Zen quote on my fridge, because I need the reminder often: Opening fully to the unwanted is the key to awakening.

While people in many professions can experience these attachments, Eden mentions one attachment that is particularly relevant for academics:

> Something I have to guard against is being attached to my research, my results and discoveries. If I become protective of them to the point of foreclosing inquiry, I am actually holding back the field I am so passionate about. I remind myself that science (including the science I do) is not the truth. It is the process of arriving at the truth. What I think I have discovered might be

disproved by other psychologists. It might even be my students who go on to disprove me! That's how science works. The best I can do is help that process of refinement along.

We end this session with Vivian's attachment and her realization:

I'm attached to people liking me. The pull is to do the things that keep me in their good graces. If there is a lesson for me there, and I know this is a cliché, it is to trust my instincts and do the things that I want to do. At my best, I chose being happy over being liked, and I have every right to be happy in my work!

Praise, recognition, legitimacy, and status are all attachments of the ego. If we want to access a deeper consciousness, we need to learn to relinquish them.

Prompts for reflection

- How do you understand your highest self?
- How would you describe your professional purpose that stems from your highest self?
- What big things are you grateful for in your life? What little ones?
- What do you know now (about yourself, academia, your field) that you didn't know when you started your career? What patterns have you noticed?
- An open crown chakra doesn't let disillusionments turn to cynicism or nihilism. Instead it manages to hold onto the positive. How have you navigated your professional disillusionments?
- How do you feel part of something greater?
- How is your right to know supported in your context? How is it threatened? What can you do to protect it?
- What are you attached to? What lessons have you learned from your attachments?

Tools, strategies, and possibilities

We have summoned important, lofty issues in this chapter, and it is time to build some strategies to cultivate them. As usual, we will introduce some general strategies to activate the crown chakra, and then some other strategies specific to academia. Even if the issues of transcendence and consciousness place us in a philosophical, even spiritual, realm, we should remember that restoring a sense of purpose is one of the four vectors of burnout recovery, according to Pope-Ruark (2022), so that as we work on the crown chakra we also restore our foundation and well-being in the ground chakra.

Cultivate silence. We can think of purpose as received wisdom. Michelangelo famously said his sculptures were already in the marble and he was simply freeing them. Jazz musicians speak of the music coursing through them. If we think of ourselves as conduits—and this is where feeling part of something greater than ourselves comes into play—then we need to listen and receive, for which silence is essential. Silent walks in nature can be precious moments of emptying out the mental clutter and allow new insights to emerge.

Meditate. We already brought up meditation as a strategy in the first chakra for its grounding benefits. But truly, the fruits of meditation can be reaped across all chakras. In particular, meditation is about emptying the mind, going past the fluctuating, reactive thoughts, and this facilitates the process of opening up to greater truths and perspectives.

Practice mindfulness. In the power chakra we discussed attention thieves because they derail our will and our plans and promote procrastination. But they are relevant in the crown chakra as well because they take us away from the present moment, from ourselves, and from our purpose. Conversely, there are a myriad mindfulness practices just a Google search away. A lighthearted one is learning to notice because it puts us back in the here and now. Rob Walker's book, *The Art of Noticing* (2019), contains several playful tools and exercises to train ourselves to notice the world around us and the world within.

Practice gratitude. In addition to the reflection prompt, consider keeping a gratitude journal. The point is to go beyond stating our gratitude for the glaring big things. A daily practice will surface those easily in the first few days and then will force our gaze on the non-obvious little things. It will stimulate an attitude of presence and paying attention and foster an outlook of appreciation on the world.

Reframe limiting beliefs. The crown chakra interprets our experience to find meaning, and crystallizes that meaning in a set of beliefs, which filters further experiences, in a dynamic feedback loop. This process starts early in life, which means some of our sedimented beliefs are unconscious. Some might be no longer helpful, or factually incorrect. The worksheet at the end of this chapter will shine light on the beliefs we hold that impact our professional life and offer a process to reframe them.

Invoke the sacred. Sociologist of higher education call attention to a function of the university as secular temple in modern society, as the guarantor of knowledge (Stevens et al., 2008). The accruing transactional aspects of our job can make us lose sight of the higher purpose behind our teaching and our research or creative activity, so it's important to keep that fire burning. Olivia shares one of the ways she stays mindful:

> I take time to get quiet and say a prayer before class, and the prayer is: let me be fully present with my students. Statistics can be dry, but I never teach class the same way, because I ride the wave of where students are.

Olivia's way works for her, but we can all reflect on ways to stay mindful of the sacredness of our work.

Learn something new. This is the chakra of knowledge, so there is no better way to energize it than to keep learning. Pick up a new skill, or sport, or craft, or topic to explore in detail and have fun with it. It might spill over into a research question or connect us to a new community. And it will keep a learner's perspective fresh, which will help us counter the expert blind spot that makes us lose touch from the student experience in our courses (Lovett et al., 2023).

Teach with the purpose of learning. Some professors choose to periodically include a new course in their teaching rotation. They do it intentionally in order to stretch themselves to learn in a new area. Some find that teaching what they don't know helps them keep their teaching purposeful rather than on autopilot (Huston, 2009). A new course preparation is more time consuming, but if you can dedicate the time, it is another way to keep this chakra open.

Ponder a question. Certain questions can help us focus and catalyze our thought, especially when we make a habit of returning to them. They become a kind of meditation, but they shape how we experience the world. As an example, while I was writing this book, my enduring question was "what is the title of my book?" While the final title was ultimately suggested by the publisher, reworking that question in my mind for months helped me clarify my audience, my message, and my strategy. Some of the faculty shared that they too have guiding questions they return to. For instance, Honorine's question is: How do you operate from a space of excellence?

Teach wonder. A sense of wonder is at the root of so much of human exploration, but formal schooling has a way of eclipsing it, for instance, by making physics about math equations rather than about understanding natural phenomena. To counter this, a professor makes his students keep a "wonder journal," where they are asked to record entries that begin with "I wonder…". This gets students oriented toward a sense of awe about the mysteries of the world. The math equations come later, as tools to unravel those mysteries.

Articulate your purpose. Faculty are accountable in several ways—annual reviews, program reviews, accreditation, pre-tenure, tenure, post-tenure, promotion reviews, and likely more—to the point that all the box-checking can lead us away from our purpose. Bending our work to these processes ensures our survival in the system (a ground chakra concern) but does not guarantee our fulfillment. Therefore, it is important to articulate our purpose to ourselves. This is especially true for those who are feeling stuck in their career. Think about what makes you come alive. Think about what frustrates you, such as societal challenges you would like to have a hand in addressing. Think about the accomplishments you already have, and the ones you are particularly proud of. Think about possible contributions you could make, and how valuable each is to you as a way to prioritize among them. Then articulate your professional purpose in 25 words or less.

Refine your purpose. If you are struggling to realize your purpose, your purpose might be at a too-low level. While I hope that everybody reading this book gets tenure and has a fulfilling job, getting tenure and finding a new job that doesn't stink are low-level purposes. Why should the university give us tenure? Or why should a different university hire us and allow us to leave our bad job behind? Similarly, our dream of funding a new research center is still lacking a core. Why is this center needed? What problems would it tackle and solve? Why should we be the person in charge of those efforts? The first two examples are instances of "having" purposes, while the second two are "doing" purposes. "Being" purposes connect us with our higher self, and show both the value of our purpose and open up possible paths for its realization. Brody's purpose of being an ally to marginalized groups, Alfred's purpose of embodying a holistic approach to medicine, and Petra's purpose of being in the students' corner are all examples of being purposes. Of course, being purposes detail down to doing and having, but those are not the starting point.

Talk to others about your purpose. Activate the throat chakra in service of your purpose. Talk about it with supportive friends and colleagues (but avoid the naysayers). This will help you speak the purpose into existence; articulate it into a plan; enlist their emotional support and practical help; and even troubleshoot some of the possible roadblocks.

Anticipate the obstacles. Speaking of roadblocks, every purpose will meet theirs. When others achieve their goals, it's not because they did not meet challenges, but because they solved them. Brainstorm possible challenges, be they institutional or personal, and plan how to address them. In fact, the chakra framework can be a helpful tool for this brainstorming. Are your ideas and visions fully formed? Are they well-articulated? Are the right people on board for your project? Are your plans actionable? Will you be able to stick to them and not procrastinate? Have you enlisted your passion fully to continue the momentum when the challenges hit? Do you have the right subroutines established? And so on.

Ensure alignment between your purpose and the university's mission. Study your institutional identity documents. While the vision is where the university wants to go, the mission of a university is its purpose. Is your purpose congruent with the university's, independent from it, or at odds? For instance, if your purpose in teaching is to maintain the rigor and select only the best students for advancement, you might be at odds with institutions with a broader student success mission. If your philosophy is knowledge for knowledge's sake but your institution emphasizes workforce development above all other concerns, you might be at odds. Can you cut out for yourself pockets of professional life where you can work according to your purpose? Conversely, have you tried to understand the purpose of the university on its terms? For instance, the institution that emphasizes workforce development might find itself as the economic engine of its region, and its students' best chance at upward mobility. If you cannot reconcile the two purposes, it will be much harder to find fulfillment.

Study your attachment. Beyond the reflection prompt, try taking a deep dive into an attachment you hold. If the demons are our teachers, the following questions might open the door to some lessons. What purpose does your attachment serve? Or, maybe, used to serve? What emotions are connected to this attachment? Do other demons activate in conjunction (e.g., fear, guilt, and shame)? Is there a hurt that the attachment is masking? How does the attachment show up in your professional life? What are the costs of holding it? These questions might open up further questions.

Plan your legacy. As we pointed out earlier, if we care about our legacy, we need to be intentional and build it early on, while we can still shape it. It should come as no surprise that this intentionality would align all the chakras, making sure your legacy is in line with your vision, your values, your passion, and so on. The final worksheet of this chapter will sketch a process to plan a satisfying legacy.

WORKSHEET 7.1 UNCOVER AND REFRAME YOUR LIMITING BELIEFS

As we interpret our experiences, we derive our beliefs as part of our meaning-making process. Our beliefs help us further filter our experiences in a self-sustaining loop. Because this process starts early, many of our beliefs operate at an unconscious level, including those that no longer serve us. Making them explicit is part of intentionally choosing beliefs that support our fulfillment. For each of the following concepts, describe what you believe about them using I statements: I believe that _____ is/are …. Watch for the emotions that come up as you describe your beliefs.

- My career
- Teaching
- My students
- Research
- My field
- My scholarship
- Tenure
- My health
- My family
- Higher education

- My department
- My colleagues
- My chair
- Institutional politics
- My abilities
- My power
- My time
- My prospects
- My legacy
- My worth

Are there items that are missing from this list that seem important to include? Add them here.

Next, focus on the beliefs that have the most negative emotional charge for you. List them here. For each one reflect on the following questions:
1. How does this belief operate in your life? What advantages has it given you? How has it held you back?
2. When did you acquire it? Was it a conscious process?
3. Who would you be if you did not have this belief? What would your life and career look like?

Copyright material from Michele DiPietro (2026), *The Faculty Guide to a Balanced and Harmonious Career*, Routledge

Next, flip those negative beliefs. Turn a negative into a positive, then elevate it. For instance, flip "I am an impostor" to "I am a competent," then maximize it to "My skill set allows me to make a unique contribution to my field." (What is it? Articulate it.)

Negative Belief #1:

Negative Belief #2:

Negative Belief #3:

Alternatively, backward-design your beliefs based on the emotional charge you are inviting.

What feeling is associated with your current belief? Example: when I think of my upcoming career options in academia, I feel dread. What feeling would you like to feel instead? If the answer is hopeful and excited, what belief would create that feeling? For instance, I bring many strengths to the table and many institutions would be excited to have me.

Negative Belief #1:

Negative Belief #2:

Negative Belief #3:

Copyright material from Michele DiPietro (2026), *The Faculty Guide to a Balanced and Harmonious Career*, Routledge

Beliefs are tenacious, they don't go away after one worksheet exercise. But it is helpful to have counter beliefs to short-circuit your thought processes when you realize you are falling back into old patterns. Reinforce your new, more accurate, albeit more tenuous, beliefs to strengthen them. Put them on a sticky note, memorize them and repeat them, laminate them and put them in your wallet, repeat them here even:

WORKSHEET 7.2 PLAN YOUR LEGACY

What is the legacy you want to leave behind? How do you want to be remembered? How do you want your institution or your field to be different because of you?

Recall your values, your passions, and your goals from the lower chakras, as well as your vision and purpose from the upper ones. How do they flow into your legacy?

Work backward. How many years do you have to establish your legacy?

What significant contributions would you need to make in this time? If you think of your time in chunks of three to five years, each can be dedicated to a significant goal.

Keep working backward. What are the long-, medium-, and short-term milestones you need to reach?

What actions do these milestones point to that you can take today? (For example, if you want to leave a legacy in your discipline, you might want to join committees in your professional associations and look for opportunities there; if you are hoping for a big research breakthrough, you might want to work with your office of research to develop your grant-writing skills.)

Make a plan. How will you keep this process going year after year? Enlist institutional processes as appropriate (e.g., your plan might be to revisit your legacy plan during every annual review).

References

Erikson, E., & Erikson, J. (1998) *The life cycle completed.* W.W. Norton & Company.

Hicks, D. (2011) *Dignity: The essential role it plays in resolving conflict.* Yale University Press.

Hicks. D. (2018) *Leading with dignity: How to create a culture that brings out the best in people.* Yale University Press.

Huston, T. (2009) *Teaching what you don't know.* Harvard University Press.

Kamola, I. (2024) *Manufacturing backlash: Right-sing think tanks and legislative attacks on higher education, 2021–2023.* American Association of University Professors.

Kegan, R., & Lahey, L. (2009) *Immunity to change: How to overcome it and unlock the potential in yourself and your organization.* Harvard Business Review Press.

Lovett, M., Bridges, M., DiPietro, M., Ambrose, S., & Norman, M. (2023) *How learning works: Eight research-based principles for smart teaching* (2nd ed.). Wiley.

Pope-Ruark, R. (2022) *Unraveling faculty burnout: Pathways to reckoning and renewal.* Johns Hopkins University Press.

Schroeder, R. (2022*)* Faculty teaching the way they were taught*. Inside Higher Ed*, October 4. Accessed online at www.insidehighered.com/digital-learning/blogs/online-trending-now/faculty-teaching-way-they-were-taught

Sedgwick, E. S. (2003) *Touching feeling: Affect, pedagogy, performativity*. Duke University Press.

Stevens, M., Armstrong, E., & Arum, R. (2008) Sieve, incubator, temple, hub: Empirical theoretical advances in the sociology of higher education. *Annual Review of Sociology*, *34,* 127–151.

Walker, R. (2019) *The art of noticing: Rediscover what really matters to you.* Ebury Press.

CONCLUSION

We have arrived at the (temporary) end of our journey. We started in the ground chakra, guided by safety concerns. We compassionately examined our own burnout, and our feelings of depletion and instability. We began to counter that by building a solid foundation, examining our values, grounding ourselves, and establishing our subroutines. We nurtured our body and our physical identity so that it could support our higher-level aspirations. We faced our fears and nurtured our right to exist and take up space.

We then moved up to the pelvic chakra. There, we pondered the idea of duality and how we encounter the variety we see in the world. We owned the gamut of emotions the world elicits in us, the dualities and polarities it establishes, the movement it creates toward the things that attract us and away from the things that repel us. In other words, we embraced our passions. We considered ways to protect the passions and the time necessary to advance them, generating safe ways to say no to other requests in the face of the guilt we sometimes feel when we try to make space for ourselves. Looking at the parts of ourselves we set aside in an effort to do what is socially accepted, we discovered our shadow. We nurtured the right to feel in academia, a space that was built to exclude emotions in pursuit of objective knowledge. In other words, we grew our emotional identity.

We progressed to the solar plexus chakra, the chakra of transformation, where we discovered our power, our capacity to act in the world. We enlisted the will in service of the goals activated by our passions and our values. We faced our perfectionism, the impostor within and the inner critic, and the shame they bring. We considered the destructive aspects of our power when we lead with anger, and nurtured our ego identity, our interface between our base emotions and desires and the professional, established ways to act in the world to obtain the results we want. We flipped to the positive side, owning our superpowers and activating our right to act.

Having passed the lower chakras and the D-realm, we rested midway through our journey, at the heart chakra. We considered what it means to sustain connections in our context which primarily praises individual accomplishments, growing our social identity, what it means to center the heart in a place that privileges the mind, and what it means to love in the academy. In fact, we reinforced our right to love, starting with our whole self and our shadow, in the face of the various professional griefs we encounter in the university context. Observing that the heart is the midpoint between the gut and the head propelled us into the idea of balance, harmonizing the polarities we encountered in the lower chakras, in particular, the balance between professional and personal life.

We then entered the upper chakras, starting with the throat, the nexus between the head and the body, which ushered in issues of communication. We worked on growing our voice to speak our truth, as a harmony between the consciousness energy coming down from the crown and the grounded energy coming up from our values and passions. We reflected on the importance of self-expression, speaking things into existence, and supported our creative identity, including through purification practices. We reflected on the enduring and emerging challenges to our right to speak, especially in the face of lies, both the ones we are told in academia and the lies we tell ourselves.

We advanced to the third eye chakra, with its function of seeing through things. We fed our imagination and generated a fulfilling professional vision. We connected with universal truths by nurturing our archetypal identity. In preparation for the last chakra, we integrated our dualities. We meditated on our right to see and worked on the demon of illusions.

We finally arrived at the crown chakra, the chakra of infinity, and embraced our transcendence and higher consciousness. Shiva and Shakti, masculine and feminine, transcendence and immanence, finally reunited. We examined the beliefs our consciousness constructs as it tries to make sense of the world, including those beliefs that hold us back. From our higher self, we developed an animating professional purpose. We experienced ourselves as part of something greater, that is to say, we embrace our universal identity. Embedded within that universal flow, we reflected on our legacy and made plans for it. We reaffirmed our right to know and to create knowledge as academics, and we faced the last demon, the attachments that threaten our ascent to our higher consciousness. Recall that Table 0.1 summarizes the purposes, identities, rights, and demons of each chakra.

Along the way, we also encountered, the Yama, or restraints, practices of containment, and the Niyama, or observances, practices of cultivation. They are summarized in Table C.1, along with the chakra where we encountered them.

TABLE C.1 Summary of Yama and Niyama

Yama			Niyama		
Name	Meaning	Chakra	Name	Meaning	Chakra
1. Ahimsa	Nonviolence	Ground	1. Saucha	Purity	Throat
2. Satya	Truthfulness	Throat	2. Santosha	Contentment	Heart
3. Asteya	Non-stealing	Ground	3. Tapas	Discipline	Solar Plexus
4. Brahmacharya	Moderation	Pelvis	4. Svadhyaya	Self-study	Crown
5. Aparigraha	Non-attachment	Crown	5. Ishvara Pranidana	Surrender	Solar Plexus

What would this theory mean to faculty who feel stuck in their position? What would it mean to Conrad, as he faced several dilemmas in the introduction? As it happens, I had the opportunity to catch up with Conrad and do a follow-up interview. This is what he had to say a couple of years later:

> I did apply for that position, and I was offered it. I guess the years away, and the published book, made a difference. Now that I have been in the position for a while, I don't feel like I am sliding backwards, nor do I feel like I am seen as little more than a graduate student by the colleagues who voiced those objections back then. I am back to a place I call home, close to friends and family. But I am familiar with the chakras from my therapy, and I knew I had to do a number of things to make this situation work for me.
>
> First, the appointment matters. I am a lecturer. I am not on the tenure track, and I am not expected to do research. There will never be those dreaded conversations about whether I am producing enough articles, and whether they are of the "right" kind. I write what I want to write when I want to write it. Of course, salary is commensurate with the expectations and lower than if I was on the tenure track, but I am okay with that.
>
> I also had to set boundaries with my time. I asked for what I want, a schedule on two days of the week, which for a lecturer is a challenging teaching load. And I asked for multiple sessions of the same course instead of multiple courses, so I don't spend energies switching back and forth. Monday and Wednesday are my teaching days. Tuesday is still in that teaching mindset, so I use it for grading, writing letters of recommendation, course prep, and so on. But on Thursday I switch, and I devote long weekends to my writing. My next book is well under way now. I make sure to do enough from a service standpoint, so when I say no I do not worry about my good standing in the department. I definitely think of myself as a slash academic, professor/essayist. In that sense, I am living my dream of being a public scholar. The good thing is that my field lends itself to that, because feminists

and critical race theorists have been challenging the traditional ways of knowledge production. There is a strong tradition, and I follow proudly in its footsteps. Speaking of being proud, I love that I am in a discipline that has been shown in empirical studies to increase empathy in its students more than other disciplines do. That is a foundational value of mine.

All in all, I am a survivor. The professional adversities have grown my determination and my capacity to face the challenges. In fact, I just got promoted to Senior Lecturer. In retrospect, I am glad I did not get the job the first time around. It forced me into the uncomfortable, and that made me grow, pedagogically and academically. It also taught me to not put all my validation eggs in one basket. I no longer look to the academy for validation. I know the value of my writing even when others don't value it. I resonate with Prometheus stealing fire from the gods. So, steal. Find somebody who has done a version of what you want to do. And watch them closely. I study those who have developed community in academe, since that is a challenge for me, and copy the strategies that make sense to me. I also paid close attention to how my mentor in grad school structured her life and molded my vision on her model.

Recently, an episode happened in one of my courses that brought a lot of these issues into focus. I still love teaching, and I love my students. They are amazing. This is a graduate course, and I have gotten to the point where I feel I can be the queer feminist mentor to them that I wish I had. One day, we were reading a book that is a scathing critique of a sociologist being complicit in studying African American communities as deviant and as other. So the students started grieving their own experiences with racism in class, because they felt safe doing so in our environment. One older White female student asked me: "Is this normal? Is this part of grad school? Are we supposed to have this identity crisis at this point of the curriculum, or does this go beyond that?" What a question! It took me back to my own disillusionment with sociology. I chose to reply honestly, telling them how graduate school destroyed my expectations that sociologists were noble. I had to say to her, "Yes, this is normal—we study these issues, and we want to fix them, and we invoke feminism and anti-racist and queer solidarity, but we fall short." It broke my heart all over again to tell the truth, but I could also say that, despite all that, there is still value in trying to understand the world and trying to better it.

Conrad has certainly walked his own path along the liberating current. He solidified his foundation and clarified his values, paying attention that the job he took did not actively counter them. He continued to cultivate his passions, negotiating with his chair a teaching schedule that would protect his writing time. He used his time away to grow his power and confidence. He privileged a job that would allow him to nurture connections with his friends. He spoke his truth to his students but without allowing his grief and disillusionment to drag him into cynicism and nihilism. He reconciled masculine and feminine energies and embraced a feminist identity and an ethics of care. He nurtured his archetypal identity, identifying with Prometheus, stealing fire from the gods and stealing strategies from people he admires. He freed himself from the attachment to salary and title, drilling down to what really mattered to him, his own non-academic writing. Through his challenges he came into the higher consciousness of being a survivor, freeing himself from the anxiety of what happens next. Whatever happens, he knows he will be able to navigate his circumstances.

This journey will look different for each person, but what broad ideas can we abstract from the whole framework? If there is one principle that stands out, it is that of alignment. When I wear my educational developer hat, alignment is key in that world. That is how we create powerful learning experiences for our students, by aligning all the components of our courses. Align the learning objectives of the course with the broader program goals. Align the assessments with the learning objectives. Align the instructional activities with the assessments. Align what we do in class with what our teaching assistant does in recitation. The more aspects of our courses are aligned and marching in the same direction, the more effective our pedagogy will be. The same is true of our career. The power of the chakra system is that it shows how all those energies relate to each other. As we build our professional life, the more energies we align, the more fulfilling our career will be. Align our purpose with our values. Align our vision with our emotions. Align our words with our actions. Align our will with our heart. Make sure this alignment is reflected in our teaching, the way we approach our relationship with the students and with the content. Make sure this alignment is reflected in our research, from the topics we choose to investigate to the way we run our lab, fundraise, and disseminate our results, to how we treat our human subjects, if that's a part of our research. And make sure this alignment is reflected in our service and leadership, the way we relate to our colleagues, the way we participate in committees and task forces, the way we engage in shared governance and our relationship to senior leadership, the way we contribute to our disciplinary associations and our field.

A few other principles round out this idea. One is the principle of balance. Chakras regulate the flow of energy within the self and the exchange of energy between the self and the world. If there are blockages in any of them, we need to clear them. Blocks not removed create areas of imbalance, either energy deficit or its excess. When certain chakras are blocked, the energies are pushed into other chakras and create imbalances that threaten the alignment. One common configuration for academics who have dedicated themselves to the life of the mind is to have the upper chakras very well attended to, and to neglect their grounding or their emotions. Other configurations are also possible.

It is possible to do all this work—activating, expressing, balancing, aligning—and still not find fulfillment in our careers. In fact, sometimes the more we cultivate our chakras, the more areas of frustration and mismatch with our work will appear. In some of the featured stories, faculty dared to stand in their values, say no, speak truth to power, and were met with bullying and other ugliness. When those profoundly ungrounding experiences happen, rare as they may be, they push us back to square one in the ground chakra, our safety and even our survival. It is crucial at that point to work to reestablish safety. In extreme cases, that might mean radical changes. That is why I felt it important to feature faculty who gave up tenure and shifted to a different track to harmonize their professional and personal life, faculty who changed institutions, and professionals who left academia altogether. Those are all valid career strategies.

A final thought. The liberation current we traversed together is not the end of the journey. Starting from the most embodied, physical features and ascending up to abstract, universal concepts is certainly a valid path of personal and spiritual inquiry, and it is related to our traditional understanding of Eastern philosophy, as an ascetic path of renunciation to arrive at enlightenment. But yoga and the chakra framework derive from *Tantra* (तन्त्र) philosophy, which emphasizes both the high path and the low path to arrive at transcendence (Wallis, 2012). The opposite current, bhukti, meaning enjoyment, is just as important. This is where we descend the chakras, taking the higher consciousness we arrived at and bringing it down to the ground, one chakra at a time, creating new physical realities informed by that higher consciousness. Once this cycle is complete, the tantric wheel spins again to begin a new cycle, in an ever-expanding spiral of fulfillment. The descending current is beyond the scope of this book, but my wish for all my readers is that they use the insights from chakra theory and from the faculty experiences to find both liberation and enjoyment in their career.

Reference

Wallis, C. (2012) *Tantra illuminated: The philosophy, history and practice of a timeless tradition.* Mattamayūra Press.

INDEX

Note: Tables are indicated by **bold**.

accountability 34, 96, 112, 114, 122, 123
agency 31, 74–101, 110, 177, 187
ahimsa 19, 135, **213**
Aida 31, 157–8, 159, 161, 164, 170, 176
air 8, 92, 107–9, 113, 122
Ājñā 9, 160, 162
Alfred 113, 146, 148, 192–3, 203
alignment 9, 18, 26, 53–6, 78, 80, 87, 92, 120, 131, 135, 166, 176, 179, 185, 188, 204, 215
American Association of Colleges and Universities 34
American Association of University Professors 26
American Psychological Association 112
amplify voices 13, 135, 138, 144, 146
amrita 136
Amy 120, 197
Anāhata 8, 107, 109
Angel 66, 90, 110, 117, 146, 193
Angelou, M. 191
anger 1, 60, 80, 87–8, 93, 105, 121, 141, 211
annual review 59, 66, 203, 209
aparigraha 189, **213**
archetypes 6, 9, 97, 162, 167–8, **169**, 171, 174, 179–80, 195, 212, 215
Aretha 26, 140
assumptions 61, 167, 171

asteya 20, **213**
attachment **6**, 10, 189–90, 197–200, 204, 212, **213**, 215
attention thieves 96, 201
Audre 93, 97, 111–12, 137, 196, 199
authentic assessments 65

Babcock, L. 138
backward design 95, 165, 206, 208–9
Bailey, P. 198
balance 4–10, 20, 22, 31, 35, 37, 41, 52–3, 79, 94, 106, 108–9, 122, 123–4, 135–6, 160–1, 171, 188, 198, 212–13, 215; work-life balance 115–20, 122, 126–7
beholding 107
beliefs 24, 89–91, 104, 124, 135, 173, 188–9, 192–3, 201, 205–9, 212
believing game 85
Berg, M. 31, 125
bhukti 5, 216
blockages 5, 18, 38, 52, 107, 144, 188, 215
boundaries 7, 22, 51–3, 55, 58–9, 69, 87–8, 116–17, 120, 123, 125, 166, 213
Brahmacharya 52, **213**
breath 37, 94, 106–7, 122–3
Bridget 32, 36, 75–6, 77, 82–3, 118, 139, 163, 166, 178, 191
Brody 59, 111, 137, 192, 203

Brookfield, S. 61
Brown, B. 42, 58, 60, 69
bullying 1, 35, 97, 161, 198, 215
burnout 29–31, 35, 37–9, 84, 94, 98, 122, 200, 211

calendarization 95
Calliope 131–3, 135, 138, 146–7, 168, 195
Cameron, J. 38, 64, 144
capitalism 61, 119, 171
Carly 25–6, 67, 112, 138, 193
Carnegie, D. 141
change 6–7, 14, 17–19, 24, 26–7, 34, 36–7, 39, 41–2, 47, 49, 51, 56, 79, 83–4, 87, 92–3, 110, 117, 133, 146, 158, 168, 170–1, 174, 178–80, 191, 193, 195, 199
charge 5, 7, 24, 40, 52, 79, 125, 139, 143, 205; discharge 19, 22, 29; recharge 37, 125; right charge 94
Charlene 36, 137, 191
circuit analogy 19, 22, 52, 79
Clara 32, 55, 57, 58, 64, 121–2, 162, 172
coaching 161–2, 177
code switching 140, 145
Colin 12–13, 17, 19–20, 39, 88, 119–20, 139, 143, 193
communication styles 1, 49, 145
community-accountable scholar 112
conflict 7, 9, 41, 94, 97, 133, 140, 143, 147–52, 174, 178; conflict management style 147; conflict of interest 177; inner conflict 25–6, 56, 69
connected knowing 64
connection 8, 35–6, 38, 67, 86, 104, 106, 108, 111, 113–14, 122, 124–5, 144, 147, 160, 196, 212, 215; to ancestor 189; to the earth 22, 124; to ourselves 26, 124; to spirit 185, 187, 189; between topics 55, 112, 172
Conrad 1–4, 6–10, 20, 22, 60–1, 166, 213–214
consciousness 9–10, 87, 125, 135, 139, 161, 167, 182–209, 212, 215–16
contemplative pedagogies 124
contrasting statements 148
coping strategies 17, 35
core, internal 87, 111
Covey, S. 67, 95
creativity 9, 36, 38, 56, 125, 134–5, 144, 161, 164

crown 2–3, 5, **6**, 10, 30–1, 57, 86–7, 124, 139, 160–1, 182–209, **213**
current 4–5, 9–10, 18, 31, 60, 81, 107–8, 135, 139, 160–3, 167, **169**, 191, 193, 214, 216
Cyrus 87, 111, 192

Damian 24–5, 58–9, 68–9, 113–14, 138, 145–6, 177, 196
dance 58, 63
Deirdre 61, 121, 142
demon 5, **6**, 11, 20, 33, 79, 100, 107, 204, 212; *see also* each individual demon
Dennis 58, 83, 163, 170, 192
depression 76–9, 116, 121, 156, 183
desire 5, **6**, 7, 49–72, 78–9, 85, 98, 106, 109, 115, 119, 136, 145, 160–1, 163–4, 176, 196, 212
Desiree 56–7, 86, 91, 139–40, 145, 166–8
Devlin 25, 54–6, 68, 88, 141
development: faculty and educational 11, 56, 82, 106, 145, 198; leadership 174, 178; organizational 84; personal and identity 2, 28–9, 115, 120, 196; professional 41, 65, 77, 177; workforce 204
dharma 137
dignity 186, 189, 191
discomfort *vs.* resentment 69
disillusionment 1, 3, 10, 70–2, 182, 187, 200, 214–15
diversity statement 174–5
doing the next thing 166, 199
Donna 15–17, 20, 32–3, 39, 88, 112, 139, 141, 143, 161–2, 171, 177, 195
doubting game 85
dream journal 172
duality 7, 51, 52, 57–8, 61, 63, 69, 122, 160, 171, 211–12; *see also* polarity

earth 4, 6–7, 18–22, 36
eat the frog 96
eating, healthy 21, 37, 76
Eden 26–7, 33, 69, 112, 118, 137, 199
Emmeline 82, 110–11, 124, 136, 199
Emmett 62, 90, 115, 142, 190
emotions 2, 6–7, 9, 28, 30, 35, 49, 51–4, 59–60, 62, 78, 87–8, 92–3, 100–1, 105, 107, 110, 112, 114, 118, 125, 134, 137, 148, 182, 204–5, 211, 215; emotional intelligence 7, 52, 60; emotional labor

60, 94, 185; recovery 53, 70; emotional support 17, 203
energy 4–9, 18–19, 22, 30, 52, 78–9, 81, 94, 108, 111, 118, 120, 135, 188, 191, 194, 212, 215; excessive 5–10, 19, 34, 79, 108, 134, 161, 188; deficient 5–10, 52, 108, 134, 160
Ernest 21, 38, 65, 75–7, 82, 87, 120, 144–5, 196
ether 134
exercise 42, 94, 111, 172, 201, 207; physical exercise 21, 36, 37, 76
existing while Black 85
expectations 32, 38, 40, 66, 89, 113, 116, 121, 176, 185, 213–14; accruing 30, 33, 61; gender 57; meeting 7, 29; research 177–8
experiential learning 55, 64, 157
Ezra 196

failure 21, 79, 92, 98, 121–2, 126
fear 5, **6**, 9, 17–18, 20, 24, 33–5, 41, 76, 80, 87–91, 100–1, 105, 107, 118, 142–3, 171, 197–8, 204, 211
feedback 1, 49–50, 91, 137, 145–7, 156, 201
feeling part of something greater 10, 86, 189, 193, 201, 200–1, 212
Felix 67, 84, 114, 120, 139, 162, 192, 198
Felten, P. 41, 54, 110, 124
fight/flight response 6, 19, 27, 183
fire 7, 79–81, 122, 214–15
forgiveness 38, 108, 123
foundation 3, 6, 12, 17–19, 21, 23–4, 34, 36, 51, 74, 78, 107, 118–19, 123, 131, 134, 149, 158, 185, 200, 211, 214

Gabby 34, 62, 94, 141, 165–6
Gail 49–51, 53, 60, 136, 142–3, 194
Ganesha 18
giving 4, 29, 122–3, 126, 160, 171
goals 7, 14, 36–7, 42, 60, 66, 69, 74, 79, 96–7, 134, 147, 150–2, 165–6, 177–80, 208–9, 211, 215
Grace 41, 60, 62, 68, 87, 106–7, 109, 118, 121, 168–9
granthi 5
gratitude 37, 172, 190, 201
grief **6**, 8, 105–6, 109, 121–2, 159, 197, 212, 215
ground 4–5, **6**, 12–43, 53, 55, 60, 63, 67–8, 83, 94–5, 97, 119–20, 122–4, 134, 139, 149, 160–1, 164, 174, 179, 191, 196, 198, 200–1, 203, 211–12, **213**, 214–16; ungrounding 3, 14, 17, 19, 22, 24, 33, 35, 38, 40, 83, 92, 216
guilt **6**, 7, 30, 50, 53, 60–3, 66, 80, 83, 87, 90, 100–1, 107, 123, 143, 157, 166, 197, 204, 211

habits/habit loop 19, 21, 23–4, 37, 40, 63, 94, 98, 110, 202
Hanuman 108
heart **6**, 8, 25, 28, 31, 38, 41, 54, 62–3, 67, 86, 103–27, 131, 139, 141, 158, 164, 167, 172, 184, 192, 197, 212, **213**, 214–15
High Impact Practices 55, 65, 98, 199
highest self 200
hobby 38, 63
Honorine 29–32, 40, 80, 118, 120, 131, 133, 135, 143, 170, 202
Huston, T. 29, 147, 149, 167, 202

Iḍā 4, 52, 160
identity 5, **6**, 9, 14, 18, 24–5, 27, 29, 35, 53, 84, 108, 117, 120, 131–2, 135, 144, 149, 158–9, 167, 183, 190, 196–197, 214–15; archetypal **6**, 9, 162, 167, 212, 215; creative **6**, 134–5, 212; ego **6**, 7, 79, 81, 211; emotional **6**, 53–4, 59, 211; physical 5, **6**, 20, 167, 189, 211; social **6**, 8, 107, 109, 115, 212; universal **6**, 10, 189–90, 212
identity crisis 29, 120, 196, 214
illusions **6**, 9, 143, 160–2, 170–1, 182, 189, 197, 212
imagination 6, 9–10, 25, 35, 53, 75, 94, 107, 114, 118, 130, 134, 142, 161–2, 165, 172, 190, 193, 212
immersion 111
impostor 3, 8, 14, 75–6, 78–9, 90–1, 93, 97–8, 206, 211
integration 107, 118, 122, 160, 175–176
invalidators 97
Īśvarapraṇidhāna 90, **213**

journaling 11, 21, 38, 76, 145, 172, 174, 201–2
joy 7, 15, 25, 30, 50, 53, 55, 62, 64, 106, 117, 121, 172, 184–5, 187, 189, 191, 195
Jung, C. 53, 167–8
Justin 67, 195, 199

kanda 52
Kaufman, S. B. 80, 134
keep track of time 59, 68–9
Kendrick 89–90, 157–9, 161, 163–4, 176
kosha 4
Kundalinī 5, 18

Lachlan 23, 47–8, 50, 52, 79, 110, 119–20, 163–4, 175, 190
leadership 9, 27, 29, 56, 62, 69, 94, 98, 109, 111, 131, 140, 159, 162–3, 166, 170, 174, 178, 215; leadership philosophy 174
learning 15, 20, 41, 53, 67–8, 88, 98, 105, 110, 113, 123–5, 170, 173, 175, 178, 191, 199, 201–2; embodied 106; the learning process 37; student learning 19, 22, 55, 64–5, 104, 124, 157, 163, 215; *see also* Scholarship of Teaching and Learning
leaving 1, 6, 20, 29, 39, 47, 81, 84, 93, 97, 107, 121, 130–1, 148, 158, 168–9, 183–5, 187, 189, 191, 193–4, 196, 199, 203, 208–9
legacy 5, **6**, 10, 157, 159, 185, 187, 189, 183–96, 204–5, 208, 212
liberation 5, 18, 90, **169**, 216
lies **6**, 9, 105, 133, 135–6, 141–4, 146, 197, 212
listening 9, 41, 87, 106, 124–5, 130, 134–5, 137–8, 141–2, 145, 172, 177, 201
lotus 5, 10, 18, 51, 80, 108, 123, 134, 160, 188, 190
love 2–3, 5–6, 8, 21, 28–9, 47, 49–50, 53, 55–7, 64, 76, 88, 96, 103–27, 131–2, 134, 160, 163–4, 169, 184, 190–2, 194, 196, 212, 214
Lucien 139, 154–5, 159, 161, 164

Makara 51–3
Mandela consciousness 191
Manipūra 7, 78, 82, 136
Maslach Burnout Inventory 39
Maslow, A. 80, 134
Matilda 182–4, 187, 189, 191
māyā 160, 189
meditation 20, 37, 79, 94, 110, 123–4, 185, 188, 201–2, 212
mentoring 1–3, 27, 29, 32, 40–1, 47, 54, 56, 62, 65, 75, 77, 82, 85–7, 103, 123, 129–30, 132, 136, 145, 157–8, 159, 163–5, 194, 214; mentor map 40–1; mutual mentoring 32, 145
microaggressions 146–7
mindfulness 11, 37, 201
moksha 5
mothering 75, 116, 156–7
motivation 7, 79, 86, 96, 129, 147, 165, 174
movement 5, **6**, 7, 22, 52, 63, 80, 124; social 27, 83, 92, 99, 154, 186
Mūlhādāra 5, 18, 20
multicultural organizational development 84

nāda 135
nādī 4, 52, 160
namaste 188
nano conferences 124–5
nature 35–6, 113, 118, 124, 201, human nature 47, 148, 168, 182, 188
negotiation 9, 40, 47–8, 66, 132–3, 141, 143, 148–51, 214; negotiation strategies 66, 148–52
Newton's second law 80
Nīlakaṇṭha 91
Niyama 79, 90, 119, 136, 189, 212–13
No Committee 69
nothing, doing 119, 125

obstacles 18, 159, 203
Olivia 49–52, 85–6, 89, 113, 117, 120, 163, 175, 195, 202
Om 134, 160, 188
Open The Front Door process 146–7

Palmer, P. 99, 110
Pareto principle 67, 118
Parker, P. 108
passion 3, 7, 11, 47–72, 78–9, 86, 96–7, 100, 107, 113, 120, 133–5, 139, 155, 159, 163–4, 166–7, 173, 175–6, 178–9, 189, 196, 199, 204, 208, 211–12, 214
perfectionism 42, 67, 75, 91, 118, 143, 199, 211
petals 18, 51, 80, 108, 123, 134, 160, 188
Petra 22–3, 55–6, 64–5, 116, 120, 139, 191, 203
Pierce 167
Pingala 4, 52, 160
pleasure 7, 52–3, 55, 58–60, 62–5, 78–9, **169**, 173

polarity 7, 51–2, 69, 107, 109, 126, 136, 211–12
Pope-Ruark, R. 30, 122
power 1, 3, 5, **6**, 7–10, 13, 15, 21–3, 30, 36, 57–8, 74–99, 107–9, 111, 114–15, 116–20, 133–6, 139–40, 142–44, 146–7, 158, 160, 162, 164, **169**, 171, 180, 185–6, 187, 191, 201, 211, 215; disciplinary 21
prana 4, 19, 107–8
pranayama *see* breathing
productivity 21, 24, 29, 30, 38, 53, 61, 66, 114, 116, 119, 144
production rules 160–1
professional development 41, 56, 65, 77, 177
psychological contract 89
psychological safety inventory 29, 39
purification 9, 108, 134, 136, 144, 161, 212–13
purpose 3, 10–11, 31, 35, 54, 60, 67, 105–6, 112, 118, 124, 134–5, 137, 148, 160, 173, 187–90, 198, 200–4, 208, 212, 215

question, developmental 28–9, 120–1, 196

Rahul 14–15, 17, 19–20, 32, 39, 80, 142–3, 164, 197
realm: B-realm 134; D-Realm 80, 134, 212
receiving 4, 122–3, 126, 160, 171
reflection 11, 18, 34, 35, 38–9, 42, 51, 62–3, 93, 98, 122, 126, 141, 143, 149, 171, 199–204, 204
rejected selves 53, 60, 63, 107
research 8–9, 25, 31, 40–1, 55, 61–2, 65–7, 70, 82, 86, 98, 109–10, 125, 129, 145, 163, 169, 173–4, 177–8, 196–7, 199, 201–2, 205, 208, 215; research agenda 50, 55, 103, 162, 173, 177–8
right 4–5, **6**, 11, 212–13; to be **6**, 19–20, 31–2, 35, 80, 119, 211; to feel **6**, 7, 53–4, 59–60, 63, 211; to act **6**, 79, 81, 87–8, 93, 119, 212; to know **6**, 10, 189–90, 197, 200, 212; to love **6**, 109, 120–21, 212; to speak **6**, 9, 135–6, 141–2, 144, 212; to see **6**, 9, 161–2, 169–71, 212
root 5–6, 18–21, 23–4, 31, 33–7, 52, 79, 87, 139, 161, 164
Rudra 80

sacred 193, 201–2
Sadāshiva 134
safety 3, 6, 17, 27–9, 31, 39–40, 60, 81, 88, 94, 104, 106, 114, 116, 123, 133, 135, 142, 144, **169**, 211, 214, 216
Saffron 56
Sahasrāra 10, 188, 190
sailboat metaphor 80, 100, 134
Samādhi 90
santosha 119, **213**
Sasha 28, 80, 81, 105–6, 108, 116, 125, 195
ṣaṭkoṇa 104
satya 135, **213**
saucha 136, **213**
say no 67–9, 78, 116, 123, 123, 211, 213, 216
Scholarship of Teaching and Learning 92, 145
Sedgwick, E. 160, 189
Seeber, B. 31, 125
seed mantra 18, 51, 80, 108, 134, 188
seeing 7–10, 26, 32, 47–53, 58, 72, 80, 82, 83–4, 99, 111, 114, 118, 137, 141–42, 156–7, 166–71, 176, 180, 186–7, 211–12
Serena 33, 118, 146, 147, 194
service 19, 56, 59, 62, 65–6, 68, 70, 80, 89, 109, 124, 141, 145, 163–4, **169**, 170, 175, 211, 215; lip 84, 170; service archetype 167–9; service-learning 65, 157
shadow 53, 63, 107, 168, 211–12
Shakti 18, 91, 160, 188, 212
shame **6**, 8, 30, 39, 78–81, 87, 90–3, 100, 107, 119, 123, 143, 176, 197–8, 204
Sheila 169, 185, 187, 189, 194, 198
Shiva 18, 91, 134, 160, 188, 212
signs 9, 25, 31, 99, 160, 171
silence 82, 124, 137, 201
Simon 55–6, 115–16, 130–1, 133, 135, 165, 192
six-pointed star *see* ṣaṭkoṇa
slash career 176–7, 213
slowing down 21, 31, 54, 94, 106, 116, 118, 125
sleep 37, 119, 126, 161
stability 6, 18, 21, 33–4, 51, 164, 211
STATE your path process 148
Steffen 198
stereotype (threat) 92
Stockdale paradox 39

story 9–10, 16, 28, 35, 39, 50, 85, 96–7, 120, 124–5, 134, 148, 167, 172, 187; the helpless story 97; the victim story 96–7; the villain story 96–7
storytelling 94, 124–5, 172
stress 19, 24, 29–30, 36–8, 62, 77, 83, 91, 116, 119, 125, 158
subroutines 6, 19–24, 34, 40, 119, 204, 211
superpower 86, 147, 211–12
survival 6, 15, 19–20, 31–2, 39, 40, 60, 62, 80, 156, 164–5, 214–16; academic 17–18, 27, 29, 34, 199–200, 206
sushumna 4–5, 18, 160
Svādhiṣṭhāna 7, 51, 52
svadhyaya 189, **213**
Sword, H. 65, 172

talking 9, 75–7, 83–4, 89, 99, 103, 108–10, 111, 118, 120, 122, 125, 130, 132, 134, 139, 145, 147–9, 183, 185, 203
tantra 216
Tapas 79, **213**
Tatum, B. D. 36, 115
teaching 8–9, 19, 40, 52–5, 61–6, 70, 82–3, 88, 91, 98, 105–5, 109–11, 117, 119, 121–2, 124–5, 128, 145, 154–5, 157, 168–9, 171, 188, 191–2, 196–8, 201–2, 213–14; teaching philosophy 173–4
tenure and promotion 6, 12–15, 17, 19, 21, 25, 29–30, 33, 38–9, 47–8, 50, 52, 62, 74–5, 91, 114–18, 121, 129–30, 147, 154–5, 171, 173, 177, 183–4, 203, 213
third eye 4, **6**, 9, 31, 89, 97, 139, 154–80, 188–9, 191, 196, 212
throat **6**, 8–9, 55, 91, 129–49, 161–2, 168, 191, 203, 212, **213**
Tim 57, 85, 138, 140, 187–90
transcendence 5, **6**, 10, 18, 108, 158, 168, **169**, 187–9, 193–6, 200, 212, 216
transformation 5, **6**, 7, 78–9, 81–2, 94–5, 155, 211
trickster *see* demon
trust 2, 50–1, 60, 69, 115, 118, 129–30, 143, 146, 194, 200; distrust 26; trustworthiness 143, 146

truth 5–6, 9–10, 24, 36, 59, 88, 94, 109–10, 132–7, 139, 141–4, 146, 160, 167–8, 189, 193–6, 196, 199, 201, 212, **213**, 214–16

Urgent-Important matrix 95–6

Vahni 80
Valerie 53–4, 68, 76, 78–80, 90, 110, 124, 139
Varuna 51–2
Vāyu 105
vibration 134–5, 139, 143
Vishuddha 8–9, 134, 136
vision 3, 5–6, 9–11, 82–3, 97, 124, 150, 154–78, 189, 191, 196, 203–4, 208, 212, 214–15; Vision board 172–3
visual representation 94–5
Vivian 28, 31, 82, 92, 114, 116, 125, 195–6, 200
voice 3, 5–6, 9, 13, 18, 30, 36, 60–1, 91–2, 110, 129–49, 160, 164–5, 167, 212–13

water 7, 52, 54
Wendy 61, 83–4, 88, 104–5, 107–8, 117, 124, 138, 196
will 7–8, 77–80, 95, 98, 105, 119–20, 151–2, 170, 186–7, 187, 204, 211, 215, 216
wisdom 4, 9–10, 80, 87, 107, 136, 139, 160–1, 188, 201
wonder 161–2, 202–3
worth, knowing one's 107–8, 119, 123, 143, 183–4, 191, 198, 205
writer's block 21, 78, 144
writing 1, 7, 10, 40, 65, 82, 95–6, 110, 114, 130, 139, 141, 145, 166, 172–74, 185, 190, 196, 202, 208, 213–15; accountability groups 130, 145; freewriting 38; with joy and pleasure 55, 64, 172; writing your values 149

Xander 27, 59, 147, 197

Yama 20, 52, 79, 135, 136, 189, 212, **213**
yoga 18–20, 37, 79, 90, 119, 122–24, 135–6, 144, 188, 216

For Product Safety Concerns and Information please contact our EU representative GPSR@taylorandfrancis.com
Taylor & Francis Verlag GmbH, Kaufingerstraße 24, 80331 München, Germany